Soldiers of the Mists
Minutemen of the Alaska Frontier

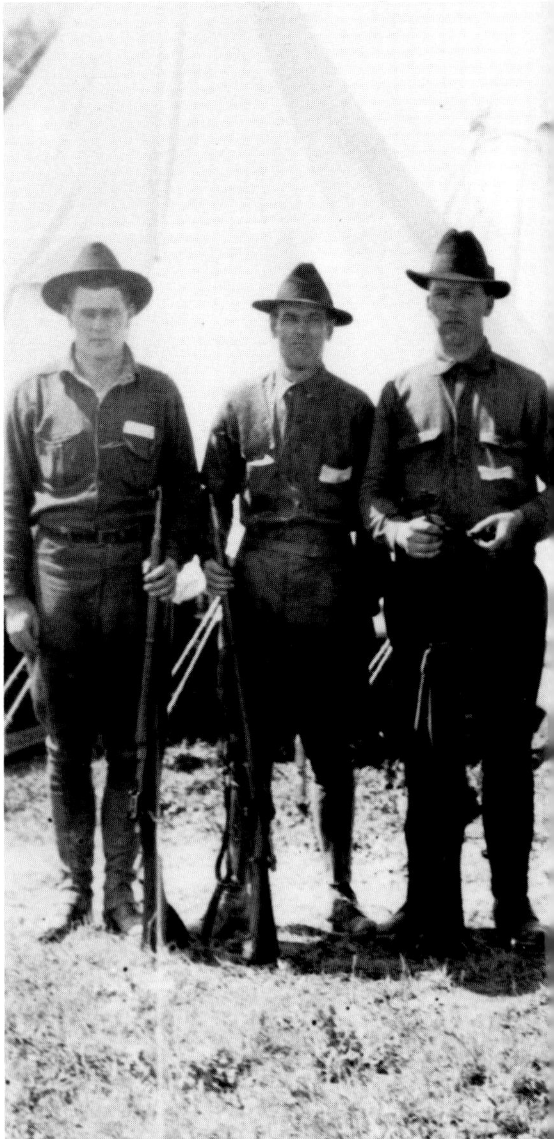

National Rifle Matches, Camp Perry, Ohio, circa 1918–20. The Alaskans could be Home Guard Militia. They were never issued uniforms and many joined gun clubs after World War One. A few Ohio Guardsmen posed with the Alaskans.
ALASKA STATE LIBRARY, JUNEAU

Soldiers of the Mists

Minutemen of the Alaska Frontier

by
C.A.SALISBURY

PICTORIAL HISTORIES PUBLISHING COMPANY, INC.
MISSOULA, MONTANA

LIBRARY OF CONGRESS
CATALOG CARD NO. 92-80007

ISBN 0-929521-37-4

First Printing: March 1992

Typography: Arrow Graphics
Layout: Stan Cohen
Cover Artist: Steve Hillyer

*Partial proceeds from the sale of this book will
be used by a special fund to be administered by the
Adjutant General of Alaska.*

PICTORIAL HISTORIES PUBLISHING CO., INC.
713 South Third West
Missoula, Montana 59801

PREFACE

THE GREAT LAND was covered by mists from the beginning of time which took many forms and served many purposes. The rain laden mists of Southeastern Alaska hid a land so enchanting it created legends of a great Northwest Passage across the continent which would elude man for hundreds of years.

In the Aleutians, blankets of moist fog dominated a chain of beauty known to few but sought by the major powers of earth. The arctic coastal areas of Alaska hid behind curtains of snow fronts and beyond that, fire and steam masked the birthplace of great mountain ranges which ran a dozen directions across the face of the land.

Collectively, the ice fogs, the arctic whiteouts and the dull rain-filled clouds protected the land from human encroachment for thousands of years. Later, when man migrated from Asia, he learned to love what had been created for him and the need for defense became a reality.

As the mists of antiquity swirl back through time over the Great Land, only an occasional glimpse reveals the presence of human beings. Whence came the Soldiers of the Mists? They have been here for thousands of years in one form or another to defend the rugged terrain of their chosen homeland. The vast distances in time and space dominated their very existence in the beginning as it still does today in that magnificent far corner we call Alaska. The Soldiers of the Mists had one thing in common, though this brotherhood in arms varied in time, function and area. The spirit of dedication to defend what they loved—tribe, clan, family or nation— almost magically coursed the veins and touched the soul generation after generation.

What makes a warrior patriotic—willing to take up arms to defend to the death if need be? It is a phenomenon behavioral scientists have been unable to fully explain. The Soldiers of the Mists had it in the early remote villages of ancient Alaskan history. It worked through the agony of defending a way of life from Imperial Russian traders advancing an imposed form of slavery across the Aleutian Islands. It surfaced briefly in flairs of resistance towards an inept American government in the late 1800s, yet rallied around the red, white and blue banner at the turn of the century.

The Minuteman concept caught up with the Alaskan frontier at the time of the Great War of 1914–1918 in the form of the Home Guard Militia units scattered across an almost forgotten portion of America. The militia nearly disappeared along with the international crisis in 1918, but the dream of an organized National Guard did not go away during the inter-war years. For a time, the Minutemen were obscured by the political mists that whirled around the efforts of a few dedicated territorial governors but they reappeared in force to join the 297th Infantry when the Guard became a reality in the early 1940s.

Swept up in the tide of World War Two and scattered over the globe, the early Guardsmen left a void which needed to be filled. The Territory of Alaska needed defensive soldiers that could supplement the offensive minded regular military forces assigned to Alaska. The Great Land once again called upon the Soldiers of the Mists who appeared in the form of an unpaid volunteer militia—the Alaska Territorial Guard. They were organized through the vision and wisdom of the giants of the land—Ernest Gruening, Otto Geist, Jay Williams, Carl Scheibner and Marvin "Muktuk" Marston.

When the war was finished, the regulars, for the most part, went home and the Territory once more sought a National Guard. A reluctant Federal Government in the face of a potent Soviet Russia only a few miles to the west of an ice curtain finally changed its mind. In 1949, the 297th Infantry of the Alaska National Guard came home to become an established part of Alaskan life.

The Soldiers of the Mists are the home grown Minutemen of Alaska. Their great adventure runs thousands of years from pre-written history to the present-day Army and Air National Guard of Alaska. They range from the ancient hunter and defender of the village to the men and women who operate the sophisticated complex weapons systems of a modern day Army and Air Force. Although uncountable numbers of people have served as Northern Minutemen, their history is not a familiar one. They have always been a factor in the shaping of Alaska history and in one form or another they have always been ready to defend the Great Land. This then, is their story.

INTRODUCTION

THIS IS THE STORY of my people—all of my people who ever served as Soldiers of the Mists. Some of them lived thousands of years ago while many continue to serve the State and Nation today as members of the Alaska National Guard. The Guard has been a part of my life from boyhood on and I have been honored beyond words to serve as its Commanding General.

When Cliff Salisbury approached me about writing a history of the Guard and Militia, I realized it was important for the present and future generations to understand the sacrifices our Minutemen and Women have always made for Alaskans. Upon reflection, I also realized that this would have to be much more than just another soldier story. It would be a tale of the Alaskan natives, Russians, traders, merchants, politicians and ordinary citizens who were all artisans, to some degree, in molding Alaska's history.

My first contact with soldiers came during World War Two. As a young boy, I watched my father, relatives and family friends in Kotzebue drill and shoot as members of the Alaska Territorial Guard. I remember Major Marvin "Muktuk" Marston visiting our village and my father's house. I dreamed of being an Eskimo Scout in the Tundra Army and the warrior spirit which had been passed down from generation to generation of my people called me to join those Soldiers of the Mists at an early age.

This book will be an important contribution to the understanding of one aspect of Alaskan life that has been largely overlooked. It is my fervent hope that all who read this will gain a new appreciation for all the Alaskan warriors who have always stood guard over the Great Land.

Sergeant, you have assembled the troops. Now, Alaskans whom they have served well can sit back and watch them Pass in Review.

—Major General John W. Schaeffer
The Adjutant General of Alaska
1986–1991.

Acknowledgments

THE NEED FOR A VOLUME telling the story of the citizen soldier in Alaska has long been recognized. Many attempts have been made through the years to gather the material needed for such an undertaking. The late Major General William S. Elmore commissioned a study during his term of service as Adjutant General of Alaska during the early 1970s. Lieutenant James R. Richardson wrote a history that has served as a major source of information for many subsequent short histories. Brigadier General Charles Casper likewise wrote a fine short history and shared much insight with the author during an interview in 1989.

This project became a reality when Major General John W. Schaeffer assumed office as Adjutant General of Alaska in 1986. General Schaeffer, a long-time Guardsman with an appreciation for the lessons history can teach, saw a need in preserving the story of all the minutemen in Alaska's history. He said, "We natives of Alaska had our own version of the militia in the early days to defend our territory. We raided, fought and waged war among ourselves and against others long before the white men came to Alaska. You should research the native warrior spirit." His comment expanded the concept of the story from its original narrow idea of a purely military style history limited to facts, figures, heroes and soldiers to a broadly based popular history that would more likely appeal to the general reading public.

This led the author on a fascinating journey through the literature on Alaska's native peoples and put him in contact with talented natives who remember their history. The author learned that Alaska's "Beautiful People" are not to be found in the metropolitan areas or on University campuses, but among the ordinary Alaskans in the smaller cities and towns and among the native peoples living out their lives in the small villages of the Great Land.

The author recognizes the futility in attempting a complete history of the Guard and Militia in Alaska. Too many personalities have served in too many capacities throughout the years. This story is an attempt to present Alaskans as soldiers across a broad range of years and circumstances. I apologize for the limits of the work with the full knowledge that to have pursued another route might have resulted in a Gibbon-sized product with a corresponding reader interest rate. This book differs from an official history in that selected personalities and events were chosen to tell the story. It is only a starting point. Any one chapter could be expanded to stand on its own as a historical study. One of the objectives of this work is to encourage a new generation of historians to explore this possibility.

This project could not have been completed without the support of many people. Much of the Alaska National Guard's history would have been lost had Captain Mike Haller not insisted that a history program is important. Lieutenant Colonel Jack Bozarth, a history major in college, made it possible for the project to continue and the author is eternally grateful for his support and encouragement. Major General Larry Lars Johnson, the Alaska National Guard's first Adjutant General, is a great Alaskan and a good friend. His help was invaluable. Brigadier General Lee Lucas, born and raised in Juneau, is a gold mine of information on early Guard history. Gordon Homme of Anchorage made major contributions to this project.

A series of taped interviews were made with Major General Conrad F. Necrason, Brigadier Generals Robert Steele, Fred Reger, John V. Hoyt, Charles Casper and members of the family of the late Brigadier General John R. Noyes. Colonel Roger Schnell, Col. Dean Stringer, Lt. Col. Gerald McLaughlin, Lt. Col. Myron Christy, Lt. Col. Micky Jelsma, CWO Stan Beadle and the late CWO Guido Vial were taped as well. This information made the book possible.

I would personally like to thank the following individuals and organizations: Major General Edward Pagano, Colonel John Spaulding, Colonel Tom Carroll, Lt. Col. David Mock, Lt. Col. Charles Tatsuda, Major Carl Heinmiller, Mrs. William Egan, Dean Williams, Captain Max Lewis, Sergeant Pat Hagiwara, Sergeant Jimmy Tatsuda, all the World War Two 297th veterans, Gretchen Lake, Marge Naylor, India Spartz, Tommy Thompson, the staff at the University of Alaska Fairbanks Archives, the Alaska State Archives staff, the Alaska State Library staff, the U.S. Archives in Anchorage and the Sheldon Jackson College Library staff in Sitka.

A special thanks goes to Chris Beaty, a patient computer teacher, Karen Sims and Michele Hobbs, cheerful workers always willing to help, Major Del Wiegele who found me a home and Staff Sgt. Ray Calver, a professional NCO who deserves two more stripes than he wears—all of Camp Carroll, Alaska.

This book is primarily about the Army National Guard and soldiers. The Alaska Air National Guard plays an important part in the development of the National Guard as well. It has its own unique story which warrants the writing of a separate book. That interesting project is under consideration at the present time.

Scholars will no doubt note the absence of formal footnotes. The book was written for the enjoyment of the general public and was never intended to be what publisher Stan Cohen sometimes irreverently refers to as an "academic dust gatherer." Much of the research was conducted at the University of Alaska Fairbanks, the State Archives and the State Library in Juneau, the U.S. Archives in Anchorage and at public libraries in Juneau, Haines, Skagway, Palmer, Nome and at the Loussac Library in Anchorage. A selected bibliography is included for those readers interested in additional reading on the subject.

The author's reward is in having had the privilege of meeting and interviewing hundreds of men and women from all walks of life. Mechanical and logic errors are those of the author, not by those who gave of their time and knowledge so freely. This book is dedicated to all the Minutemen and Women of Alaska who ever served and to those future Soldiers of the Mists who will add to an already interesting history.

Finally, the book is also dedicated to one who endured the mood swings, the lost weekends and the late night writing binges—my very best friend, Marjorie, who is also my wife.

C.A. Salisbury
Marcliff Haus
Palmer, Alaska

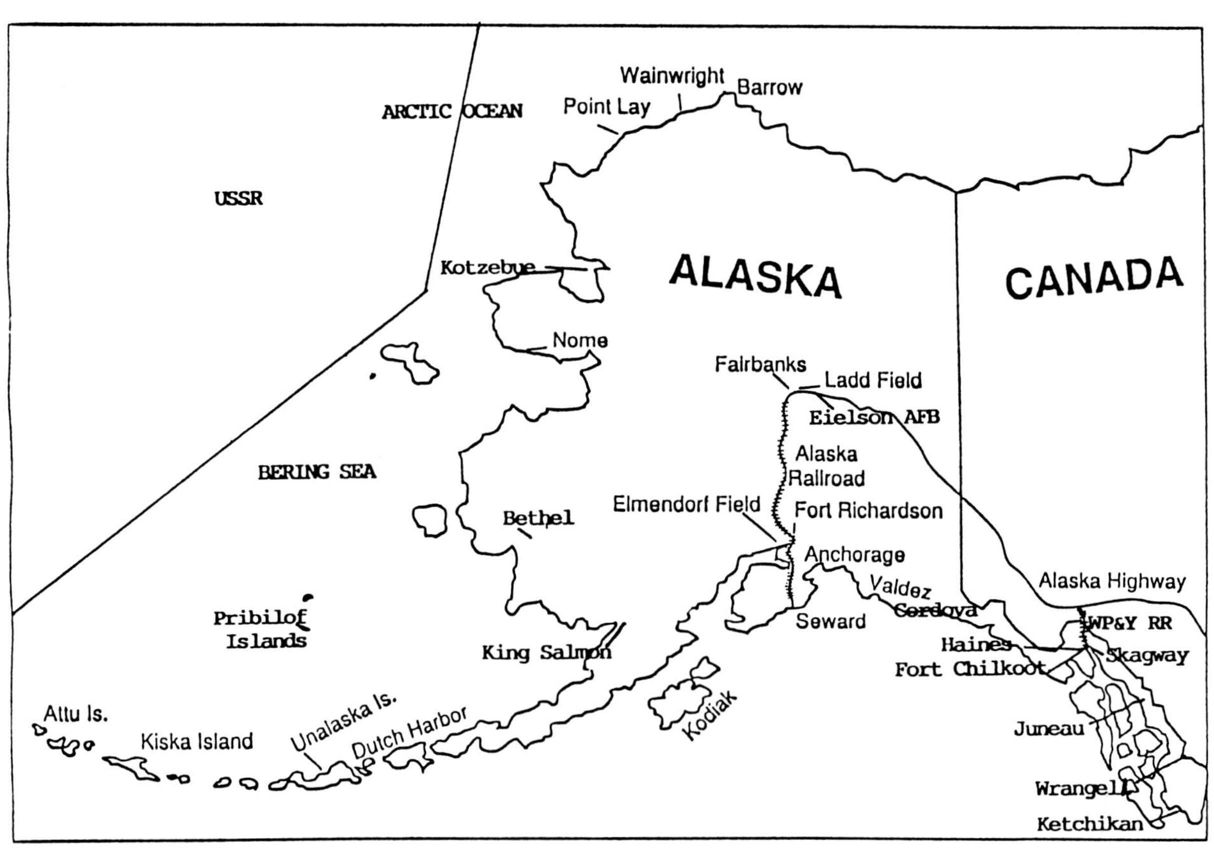

TABLE OF CONTENTS

Let's All BACK THE ATTACK!
4TH WAR LOAN

THE HERITAGE

IN THE FARTHEST northwest distance of America lay an area of mists and darkness where land, sky and sea seemed to merge into one great mystery. Ice Age followed Ice Age leaving a history open to interpretation only by trained scientists. The land behind the hiding mists over the Bering Land Bridge may have appeared bleak and featureless to those first hunters following migrating animals into Alaska. But from the beginning, that same magical magnet which would draw mankind to Alaska for the next thousands of years seemed to be a part of the original recipe which formed the land.

A force seemed to whisper the same message that has come down to the present generation of true Alaskans. "This is the place—there is no other like it on earth and this shall be home." The winds of time sang a song which said, "I am beautiful, I can be cruel, but I am worth fighting for." Those first people recognized value and formed a great heritage for the unnumbered generations to follow who would be pleased to call themselves Alaskans.

The first people brought the original methodology of history with them. The spoken history of Alaska was retold from primary source to secondary source—generation to generation—for at least 15,000 years, maybe more. Those stout sons of survival, descending down through the generations, would pass on stories of courage, loyalty and mighty warrior feats. Was it the ancient tradition of defending the family unit that produced the fierce pride and deep patriotism found in today's native Alaskan Guardsmen and Women?

Alaska was shaped by fire, ice, water and wind. The elements tempered manhood into steel and produced Alaska's first warriors. The very nature of this rugged land produced a need for Minutemen and thus was born a warrior spirit which would remain forever within Alaska's first people. The strategic location of the land cemented the concept from the beginning of time and the winds of legend swirled stories of war and warriors across the years of unwritten history.

Delores Albert-Jack, a Tlingit poet from Angoon, Alaska, has a feeling for this warrior spirit that could never be experienced by a non-native. She describes her feelings beautifully in a preface to a poem about America's failure to honor its Vietnam veterans.

Early naval commanders instituted a Native Police Force to maintain law and order in the villages. The program was successful as Natives were proud of their uniformed service for the U.S. Government and were loyal and effective.

"Since I was a youngster, soldiership was a subject that was handled with care. My ancestors impressed upon me that soldiers are treated with honor. Only they can dishonor themselves. Somewhere along the line, I was taught that I came from the land. Before the whiteman came, we held this mystery dear. Anyone who defends this land is highly recognized. Even if our warriors/soldiers returned unvictoriously they were treated with much respect. They put their lives on the line for the land which included us. Because of our belief, we greet and take care of our warriors/soldiers. Although Indians in general are called down, cut short and humiliated, they hold more dignity than most. They know what it means to fight, to lose, to win. The bottom line is that we take care of our fighting unit.

"When the situation called for it, our Tlingit people banded together for strength and number. We had an unwritten alliance with other Clans in Southeastern Alaska. The Plains Indians have this unspoken code also. I speak of a time when honor held its rightful place and was given when it was merited. Although I did not live technically in the times of old, it was instilled in me. I could close my eyes and look back to those times."

This inner strength or warrior spirit which carried native Alaskans through a sometimes violent unwritten history helped them survive an even more dangerous written history—the coming of the whites. The written history of Alaska began during the reign of Czar Peter the Great of Russia (1682–1725). Although Cossacks had been pushing towards Siberia for nearly a hundred years, it was not until Peter's time that the Russian Empire gained the foothold in Eastern Siberia that would make possible Vitus Bering's voyage of discovery to Alaska in 1741. Neither Peter nor Bering would live to see the settlement of Alaska, but within two years Russian traders pushed east along the Aleutian Islands and came in contact with the Aleutian people.

There may have been as many as 30,000 Aleuts at one time before the coming of the Russians. Many were robbed, murdered and enslaved and their numbers declined rapidly. Though often pictured as mild and helpless, they in fact were endowed with the warrior spirit and fought back when possible. They survived in a harsh sea world and successfully hunted in the world's most severe climate. Their skills were needed to keep the Russians in the New World.

Even before the Russians enslaved them, they practiced the techniques of war. They raided, feuded and fought amongst themselves and with others. It appears they used a sort of compound bow and poisoned lances in early wars and knew about metal. They also used a form of body armour along with clubs, daggers and battle helmets. They showed a special kind of courage but were no match for the Russians and nearly perished.

Realizing the value of these unique people, the Russians eventually made them a part of the Russian American Company venture for profit. There is some evidence that the harsh picture of the ruthless tactics used by the Russians has been overplayed. The Russians took native wives and left their names and their religion. The Russians taught and created as well as enslaved and pillaged. Today, Alaska is richer in language, architecture and in proper and geographic names for their having been here.

To the North, another people relied on part time soldiers to survive. The Eskimo communities along the north coast and inland were subject to raids by wandering groups invading hunting territories. Feuds often broke out and warfare was not uncommon. Karigi or kashims were men's houses where warriors might gather. Warfare survival techniques were learned at an early age. Umialiks (leaders with power) and Shamans (spiritual people) held major influences on village life and there were also trade and military leaders. These hunters lived off the land and made excellent soldiers then as they do today as members of the Army Guard's famed Eskimo Scouts. Warfare was violent and often extended up interior rivers where conflicts erupted between Eskimos and Athapascans over ancient hunting areas. It is said that this rivalry over hunting territory and the use of conflict extended down through the 1960s.

The Athapascans of interior Alaska practiced offensive and defensive warfare on a part time basis. They relied on war leaders during times of conflict—not unlike the present day National Guard. Boys were trained extensively to endure hardship and in hand-to-hand combat for that day they might be called upon to become temporary soldiers. Groups of Athapascans united by family or tradition would band together as a unit when fighting another group. Wars were fought over territory, for slaves or women and sometimes over insults of one group to another. The Athapascans evidently developed the buddy system where two warriors would support each other in battle.

There is record of continuing conflicts between Athapascans, Kutchins and Kobuk and Nunamiut Eskimos from the earliest of times through the 1870's in what is called the Koyukon Wars. The Nulato Massacre (about 1846) resulted in many deaths. In 1851, the Indians of the lower Koyukuk again subjected the post to warfare.

Perhaps the best documented warriors were those the Russians ran into in Southeastern Alaska. The Tlingit Indians were the wealthiest of all native Alaskans. They lived in a beautiful corner of Alaska rich in game and fish. There was less effort needed for survival in this mild climate so more time could be devoted to the creative fields of art and culture. They were true soldiers of the mists in this land of fog and rain. They could use hit and run techniques of warfare and disappear into the lush undergrowth and thick forests to fight another day. The Russians did not ride roughshod over these warriors.

The fighting unit revolved around the Clan. The Clan owned fishing and hunting areas and strangers in the land might be attacked and killed. The Tlinget men and women owed loyalty to the Clan and sometimes feuds broke out in which several Clans were involved. The wars between Clans were sometimes fought over slaves or territorial rights at long distances utilizing troop transports (the famous warboats of Southeastern). There is some evidence that some groups periodically increased in population and war would break out over an extension of territorial claims. Weapons were lethal and more often than not designed for close combat. Techniques of war included a form of basic training for young warriors, surprise night attacks, feints and amphibious landings. The Tlingit warrior was an efficient fighting machine. The Russians and the Americans, to some extent, learned this the hard way.

By 1850 it was becoming apparent the Russian American Company was losing its grip on Alaska. Yankee sailing ships began to dominate what was left of the fur trade and the whaling industry. The company was unable to stop the foreign ships in Alaskan waters and the fur trade declined rapidly. At home, the Czar lost a war. The Treaty of Paris in 1856, which concluded the Crimean War, left the British in control of one-fourth of the known world and with an appetite for even more. British naval forces had attacked Kamchatka in Eastern Siberia during the war and this convinced the Russian Government that Alaska, too, could become the victim of British expansion. Already, Hudson's Bay Company trappers were moving into Alaska along the Stikine and Yukon Rivers. Profitless years and a weakened military posture left little choice but to find a way out of the white elephant called Alaska. The Russians, who had been friendly towards Mr. Lincoln's government, felt they had less to fear from a divided nation than from the established powers on earth. A new player was about to enter the game.

The raising of the Stars and Stripes in Sitka on October 18, 1867, would signal another turn in the twisted timeline of events in Alaska history. But what of the warrior spirit? It never disappeared. The first decades after the U.S. purchase of Alaska brought fast changes as businessmen, prospectors, the U.S. military and the missionaries influenced the native citizens. The new government for Alaska stood on shaky ground and was uncertain of its role concerning Alaska's natives. Would this land and its native population be subjected to the same sorry policy that had destroyed so much of the Old West? There was one spark of hope. The warrior skills would be utilized by the Americans.

The U.S. Navy early on formed a Native Police Force, complete with uniforms, to maintain law and order in the villages. The plan worked well and by 1885, Governor Swineford was able to report, "I am convinced by my brief experience that no better or more economical system can be devised for the maintenance of order in the native settlements. The Sitkau native policemen are exceedingly proud of their blue uniforms, and being the recognized chiefs among their people, exercise a dual authority, which is universally respected and obeyed."

The American missionaries who converted and taught the natives throughout Alaska did not overlook the positive aspects of military life. Schools were established along the Yukon River and at Holy Cross, native boy cadets sported uniforms and drilled to learn self discipline. The Reverend Sheldon Jackson, a superintendent of schools as well as a missionary of the Presbyterian Church, established places of learning throughout the land. Again, self discipline was a highly desired trait for the young natives. Their warrior spirit, a love of physical fitness, a kindred spirit with nature and a sense of courage tilted their education towards a military bearing.

At the Sheldon Jackson School in Sitka, boy cadets drilled and stood with pride in military uniforms for their school picture. One needs only to study the faces to realize just how deeply affected by the warrior spirit were these young men. *The Thlinget*, the school newspaper of the Sitka Training School was able to report in its August issue of 1910 that, "Our school has always been on a military system. The sergeants looking after the conduct of the boys in the absence of teachers and serving in every way to preserve order. Drill occurs two mornings each week when weather and light permit. The gymnasium will allow this all year. The company was never so evenly sized or as well drilled as when the picture was taken. Mr. Beck has had command for almost fifteen years."

The efforts of the schools to keep alive a military tradition would pay dividends throughout the 20th Century. Whenever Alaska needed its warrior spirit it was there waiting to be used. The Aleut proverb "the wind is no river" referred to the calm periods between conflicts. It would be just as true and constant under the Americans as it had been in times of old. In their hearts, Alaskan natives maintained the warrior spirit for those future days they might be called upon to serve as American Soldiers of the Mists.

Student cadets at Sitka. The natives showed an interest in the military at an early age. The officers were teachers at the school. SHELDON JACKSON COLLEGE MUSEUM, SITKA, ALASKA

Student cadets took great pride in their Civil War-style uniforms and rifles. The inborn warrior spirit made them serious students of soldiering.
SHELDON JACKSON COLLEGE MUSEUM, SITKA, ALASKA

THE AMERICANS

FOR 126 YEARS, the Russians held Alaska. What the American government held for Alaska for the next 92 years until statehood was an attitude of indifference for a land holding vast wealth for the Republic. If the residents of Alaska thought a change of government would bring the blessings of liberty and protection under the law, they were in for a rude awakening.

The newly aquired Russian colony was placed under the War Department and the Army would govern Alaska for ten years. The Army was put into an unfamiliar role and short tempered General Jefferson C. Davis, an old Indian fighter, did not relish this added duty. Although Russian citizens were given a choice to stay or leave, even those who looked forward to becoming American citizens soon lost faith in the Army's ability to maintain law and order.

The desire to have a citizen army may have gone back to the very beginning of the American period. The American businessmen who came to Sitka following the transfer of flags in October of 1867 were not happy with General Davis' administration of the Military District of Alaska. Rather than protecting the Americans, former employees of the Russian American Company and natives, the soldiers seemed to disregard their responsibilities. When off duty, they harassed the citizens, deflowered the maidens, condoned stills, nightly reveled in the streets of Sitka and staggered from the effects of homemade hooch. The citizens yearned for protection, but appeals to Washington were, for the most part, ignored.

Early in 1875, the commander of the Western Division of the U.S. Army, General O.O. Howard, made an inspection trip to Alaska. At Sitka, he reported that, "Having been troubled by numerous newspaper charges concerning the present management of affairs at Sitka, I deemed it best to give those who are called citizens, consisting of Russians, Aleuts, Half Breeds, American and foreign traders now residing in the town the opportunity to see me apart from the officers of the garrison. The complaints did not prove to be of much importance; certainly not very grievous." The Army's supply of whitewash was unlimited.

General Howard made his views known in a report to the U.S. Senate and to Secretary of War William Belknap in June of 1875. Among other things, he showed concern about the monopoly enjoyed by the firm of Hutchinson, Kohl & Company of San Francisco and its mistreatment of Alaskan natives. He asked Major Campbell, the local commander, "To introduce a few police regulations and do anything humanity requires for the relief of a community, thus far, suffering from being within the limits of the United States, and yet absolutely without law." After the General sailed back to California, the Army began its withdrawl of soldiers from Alaska. The few troops that remained got their call to leave in 1877 with the outbreak of the Nez Perce Wars in Idaho.

If General Howard gained anything from his visit in 1875, it was a healthy respect for the warrior spirit of the natives and a concern for their welfare that would last a lifetime. He was the victorious general who finally defeated an outnumbered Chief Joseph, but he also fought for the Red Napoleon's return with his band of warriors to their rightful place along the Clearwater. His first lesson in humanity may have been learned in far off Alaska.

When the army withdrew from Alaska, only the customs collector at Sitka was left to administer the vast American holdings and to protect the citizens from a growing fear of an Indian uprising. Warriors bolstered by illegal "courage in a bottle" roamed the streets of Sitka and the citizens formed a militia in 1878 to patrol and to show solidarity since they had no other place to turn for help. The people took the old Russian philosophy that "God was in his heaven and the Czar is far away" and translated it to "Congress is in Washington and we must do for ourselves once more."

In February 1879, the citizens of Sitka sent a message to the British Government in Victoria, British Columbia asking for protection. There was talk of "joining Canada" and the Union Jack was shown as a reminder to Washington's indifference towards Alaska. The British sent a warship, *HMS Osprey*, to Sitka harbor and Captain A'Court of the Royal Navy stayed on station until an embarrassed American Government could get a U.S. Navy vessel to Sitka to protect its citizens.

The long coastline and the vast distances of Alaska were better suited to administration by the Navy than by the handful of soldiers stationed at Sitka, Fort Wrangell and a few other posts located in the southern half of the country. The Naval and Customs officials were able to improve conditions to some extent but the various Naval commanders

Wrangell, Alaska, circa 1880. Wrangell was an early site for a U.S. military base. The citizens of Wrangell organized a militia for self-protection in 1880 after the Army was called away to the Indian Wars in Idaho. U.S. ARMY

often found themselves involved in settling minor civil disputes that could have been handled more effectively by a local government. The need for a militia for defense grew during those years the Navy took the responsibility of running Alaska.

A gold rush in British Columbia made the town of Wrangell a booming port of entry almost overnight. Captain Beardslee and the *USS Jamestown* arrived there on January 25, 1880. He reported that the whole population was found under arms to guard against Indians. The Hoodchenoo Indians had visited Wrangell on a trading expedition. They had been drinking the liquor which bore the name of their band when they became involved with a band of Sucheen Indians whom they tried to suppress by force. A fight broke out and several warriors were killed and wounded on both sides. The alarmed whites stored their powder and ammunition in a storehouse and established a system of armed militia guards for the town. Guardhouses were set up by the armed militia and maintained until the crisis had passed.

A military code of sorts was established for the District of Alaska with the passage of the Organic Act of 1884. This act provided for a civil government for Alaska and appointed a governor who was made "the ex-officio Commander-in-Chief of the Militia." Although the act did little to advance Alaska's interests, it provided a platform upon which the governors could build a case for a National Guard or Militia.

The District of Alaska's first civil Governor, John H. Kinkead (1884–1885) arrived in Sitka on September 14, 1884. The following day, Lieutenant Commander Henry Nichols, commander of the *U.S.S. Pinta*, formally relinquished all civil authority exercised by the U.S. Navy to the new Governor. The Commander also discharged the Indian Police Force the Navy had paid for several years to maintain peace and order in the villages. At that moment, the Governor realized he was losing naval protection and what little civil protection Alaska possessed. He recom-

Governor Alfred P. Swineford (1885-1889) was one of the first government officials to push for a National Guard in Alaska. He was unsuccessful despite the growing need for an increased military role in Alaska. ALASKA STATE LIBRARY, JUNEAU

mended the Native Police Force be continued in his annual report for 1884.

For the most part, the Navy gave the early Governors support when called upon. In 1886, however, an attempt was made to blow up a house in Juneau in which some Chinese workers were living. The event was whitewashed by the local officials, but pressure began to increase during the summer to drive the Chinese workers from Juneau and Douglas. It reached its apex on August 6th when the Deputy Marshal of Douglas informed Governor Alfred Swineford (1885–1889) he was unable to control the mob that had seized the Chinese mine workers. The Chinese were rounded up and shipped out to Wrangell. The Governor called upon the Navy to return the Chinese to Douglas.

The commander of the *U.S.S. Pinta* sent several letters to the Governor containing a variety of excuses for not carrying out the request. In the absence of cooperation from the regular military, the issue of a Militia or National Guard to handle civil unrest took on a new importance. This incident may have influenced Governor Knapp (1889–1893) a few years later when he asked for and received $8,000 to procure arms for the Alaska Militia. In 1892, the Governor was able to report that Company A of the First Regiment, Alaska Militia was organized. The words Adjutant General, Militia, Guard and Chief of Staff would become a part of the Alaska Government vocabulary as the end of the 19th century approached.

The term Alaska Militia first became a distinct separate entry in the Governor's annual report in 1893. Governor James Sheakley (1893–1897) noted: "The militia organization in Alaska is in a state of disintegration. The migratory habits of the people will prevent any such organization from becoming permanent. Militia soldiers in Alaska could only be used as home guards, or for police duty in the immediate vicinity of their organization. To be of any service to the Territory at large, each organized company would be under the necessity of having and maintaining steamboat transportation for their full complement of men, there being no roads or land travel possible in the country." The Governor was not a visionary and preferred to rely upon the Navy.

The presence of a militia in Alaska became more probable during the tenure of Governor John Brady (1897–1906). This former missionary and close friend of the legendary churchman, Reverend Sheldon Jackson, held office during two world class events— the Klondike Gold Rush of '98 and the Spanish American War. Both events would advance the fortunes of the Minuteman concept for Alaska.

Alaska's image changed forever with the discovery of gold in the Klondike district of the Yukon Ter-

Governor John Brady (1897-1906) worked harder than earlier governors to establish a National Guard but the government in Washington, D.C., continued to ignore Alaska's needs.
ALASKA STATE LIBRARY, JUNEAU

ritory and the subsequent rush by thousands of adventurers through Alaskan ports to the rivers and mountain passes that promised access to fortunes. If Alaska had been overlooked by Americans for 30 years, it was now looked over by the world. The colorful mass of humanity that surged north on any floatable ships along the Pacific West Coast became bottlenecked at Dyea and Skagway, entry points to the Chilkoot and White Passes. Awaiting the newcomers at Skagway was the infamous Jefferson Randolph (Soapy) Smith and his gang of thieves, cutthroats, murderers and con men.

The story of the Gold Rush of '98 has been told well by Jack London, Rex Beach, Robert Service and thousands of miners who wrote home of their great adventure. A part of that story, but hidden to some extent, is the lesser known story of the Gold Rush and its influence on the founding of the Guard and Militia in Alaska.

The legend of Soapy Smith is still reenacted to this day for the thousands of tourists who visit the historical town of Skagway each summer. The exploits of Soapy and his gang have been presented in dozens of books and countless articles which have appeared since his death. The accounts, like Soapy himself, are controversial, contradictory and leave the reader with the feeling that Soapy in death is like Soapy was in life—part legend and part con. In Denver and Creed, Colorado, where he perfected his trade, he was cheered as a champion of civic responsibility and driven out several times as an undesirable con man. This dual status followed him throughout his career. He may have been the victim of a dual personality before psychologists understood that term.

Our interest here in Soapy Smith is not so much in his career as a benevolent despot but in his role as a military organizer. The title of Colonel was one of honor which many Southerners of questionable military background carried following the Civil War. Colonel Jefferson Randolph .Smith, born in Georgia in 1860, would exploit it to the hilt.

When Smith arrived in Skagway in 1897, following the news of the Klondike gold strike, he found an instant town with no organized law already full of confidence men, gamblers, some 70 drinking places and a Red Light District. Within a short time, he would control nearly every enterprise designed to separate men from their money.

Like Smith, the town itself had two faces. Many of those who passed through the muddy streets were only interested in obtaining a fortune and leaving the country. Others, like Harriet "Ma" Pullen, wanted to build a home, raise a family and live out their lives in the beautifully rugged land. The newspapers of the day reflected the two faces of Skagway. West Coast newspapers pictured Skagway as a "hell on earth" plagued with murderers, thieves and Soapy Smith's gang.

On the other hand, the *Skagway News* reported in December 1897, "There is no more orderly town in the world than Skagway. The town is without a legal city government simply because the Congress of the United States, in its wisdom, has seen fit to enact no laws which have been applied to the Territory which would give Alaska any measure of local government and the laws which have been applied to the Territory are wholly inadequate to meet any emergency. There has been a minimal supervision over the town by the Committee of One Hundred and One, a body of men elected by the people during the first great influx into this place. It was sort of a Committee of Safety, or Vigilance Committee, but this has fallen into a state of innocuous desuetude, for the very good reason that there is nothing for it to do. Law and order prevail and the absence of serious crime is notable."

The paper pointed out that the 120-day-old town had wide streets, good sidewalks through the business area, a school, electric lights and telephones. Soapy Smith would take up a collection to build the first church. The only enemies Skagway had, apparently, were the *Seattle Times* and the *Seattle Post Intelligencer*. The editor of the *Skagway News* noted, "The *Seattle Times & PI* continue to slander Skagway as they have from the beginning of our town and describe Skagway as a veritable death hole. It is to the effect that human life in this city is valued no more than that of the dogs that roam our streets. No hand of protest is raised and the Federal authorities are in co-partnership with murderers and thugs in Skagway according to Seattle newspaper accounts. Several tourists arrived on the steamer *Queen*. After reading the Seattle papers, they refused to get off in Skagway. Of course, these were only a few chickenhearted Easterners of the class who begin to look for wild, war painted Indians and bodies dangling from limbs of trees, the moment they cross the Mississippi on their way across the continent from their effete New England homes."

M.I. Sherpy, editor and owner of the *Skagway News*, delighted in reporting in 1898, "That miserable lying sheet the *Seattle Times* is being sued for libel by four citizens of Skagway for $25,000 each. Old man Blethen will discover that the worm will turn after a time and that he cannot forever continue his hellish lies about the people of Skagway without having to pay dearly for it."

There were many civic-minded citizens in Skagway who could be whipped up to a frenzy for a cause. Soapy Smith was aware of this when the Spanish American War broke out in 1898. He called for a volunteer militia to protect Skagway from a Spanish invasion which might be launched from Cuba or Manila at any moment.

This was not Soapy's first attempt at organizing a body of soldiers. That had happened back in 1896 when he had been invited to leave Colorado after fleecing one too many citizens. He drifted for awhile then came up with a brilliant idea. He made himself a colonel and wrote a letter of introduction to the President of Mexico, Don Jose de La Cruz Porfiro Diaz. Soapy went to Mexico City, met the President and proposed that he—Colonel Jefferson Randolph Smith, military organizer and suppressor of revolutions, organize a Mexican Foreign Legion. Jeff would recruit cowboys, gunmen and fugitives from justice and form the greatest body of fighting men in the world.

So impressive was Smith, President Diaz advanced him $4,000 and Soapy returned to Denver

Soapy Smith, King of the Con Men, led his Skagway Guards militiamen in the July 4th Parade in 1898. A few days later he was killed by city engineer, Frank Reid.
ALASKA STATE LIBRARY, JUNEAU

to set up a recruiting office. He promised the recruits they would be given a free hand in Mexico to loot the country. He was ready to begin training this Mexican Legion when he received news that President Diaz had learned the truth of his background and had threatened to put the Colonel in front of a firing squad if he ever came to Mexico again.

One of Alaska's oldtimers, Harry Suydam wrote, "As the war with Spain drew near, anticipating a call for troops, several National Guardsmen, I among them, joined a company of patriotic men who had wintered on the Arctic trail. The Indians called them Skookum, meaning strong and hearty, and they had earned the compliment." This was to be Alaska's militia but Suydam learned that Soapy Smith had obtained a commisssion as a Captain of Volunteers in the United States service. The commissioning papers were forged, of course, but Smith delivered patriotic speeches amid colorful demonstrations in support of the war and won the hearts of the war-inflamed citizens of Skagway. Although legend has it the volunteers entered a medical office for an induction physical, had their possessions taken from their cast off clothes and then were exited through a door into the alley naked as jaybirds, a goodly number did drill and marched in the huge Fourth of July parade in Skagway in 1898. Smith even offered his company of Brigands to the President and received a letter of thanks from the Secretary of War. Other militia companies also drilled in Alaska.

This interest in militia matters may have caused some concern on the Canadian side of the international border. The city of Dawson was overwhelmed by Americans during the gold rush and the Fourth of July celebration there was nearly as important as in Skagway. The Canadian Government sent a 200-man Yukon Field Force north to support the Royal Canadian Mounted Police in the Yukon city. These Canadian dollar-a-day militiamen even stepped foot on U.S. soil temporarily at Wrangell while awaiting transportation up the Stikine River. Much to their surprise they were given a hearty welcome by a detachment of U.S. Infantry on duty at Fort Wrangell.

The highlight of the year in Skagway was the Fourth of July parade. It would also mark the high-point of Soapy Smith's brief career as the King of Skagway. Again, two different views of this event attempted to analyze Soapy's place in history. Harriet Pullen remembered that Soapy had called at her home and had introduced himself. He informed her that he was to be the Grand Marshal of the parade and urged her to take part in the great event. She did not want to be a part of the parade but was "soft talked" into appearing by Soapy's masterful oratory. Soapy had boxloads of fireworks and flags sent in for

Soapy Smith's death was the result of a Klondike prospector named Stewart being robbed by gang members. Irate citizens formed a militia to oppose Smith and his gang. ALASKA STATE LIBRARY, JUNEAU

the big event.

The editor of the *Skagway News* reported that, "Skagway will have an Eagle in their parade. An American Bald Eagle has been captured and brought here from Haines Mission. It was lassoed while it was attempting to carry off a sheep from a large flock which will be driven over the Dalton Trail en route to Dawson. It measured ten feet from tip to tip and has a bill that could open a Senatorial deadlock. Mr. Smith will have his prize fastened to a perch above his silk American flag and together they will be carried in Monday's parade."

In the Fourth of July parade, Jeff Smith was in reality, the Marshal of the 4th division of the parade which consisted of: The Skagway Guards and the eagle named Fitzhugh Lee, the Man of War Float and Brook's Pack Train. Yet, popular histories picture him as an imposing Grand Marshal mounted on his horse ahead of his Klondike Battalion with the silk American flag leading the entire show. He did seem to be everywhere at once—riding here and there, shouting

orders, tipping his hat to the crowd and directing the progress of the parade. If there was a real grand marshal, he would be overlooked on that Fourth of July day in Skagway and forever in the hundreds of accounts of the event that have been written down through the years.

The militia, which followed Soapy Smith on the Fourth of July, would be a part of the Harbor Guards organized a few days later to hunt down members of Soapy's gang following his demise at the hands of one Frank Reid.

Evidence of militia action following the outlaw's death was noted in the *Skagway News* which told of a nervous town: "All last night the measured tread of the Guards could be heard as they patrolled the streets. All the haunts of any of those in any way connected with Soapy's gang were liable to be visited by the Guard. In most cases the birds had fled, however, quite a few were placed under arrest and are confined to the city jail."

Governor Brady had been invited to speak at the big parade on the Fourth of July. His personal thoughts on Soapy Smith on that day and the shoot-out that followed were not evident in the terse report he included in his annual report to the Secretary of the Interior for 1898: "At the first rush the bunco men and gamblers and prostitutes got in and became organized, and controlled matters pretty much their own way, and intimidated three United States Deputy Marshals. Matters came to a head early in July when a returning Klondiker was robbed of his dust in open day. The people were aroused, and they determined to endure it no longer. While many of the law-abiding citizens were assembled and considering plans of action, the leader of the lawless element undertook to pass the guard which had been stationed at the approach to the wharf. He was armed with a Winchester rifle loaded with explosive balls. When halted he became violent and pointed his gun to shoot. In a few seconds Frank Reid, the town surveyor, was shot through the groin and hip bone by the explosive charge from Jeff R. Smith's Winchester, and Smith fell dead with a bullet through his heart. This made the citizens determined. The U.S. Commissioner was sent for and committees rounded up the lawbreakers before him. While some were in favor of lynching, counsel from men of sober judgment prevailed, and there was no hanging. Some whose company was no longer agreeable were given free transportation out of the country. Skagway and Dyea are now models of good order."

That good order was made possible because the volunteer militia or Harbor Guards who rounded up the gang made it so. Never had the need for militiamen in Alaska been more evident than at Skagway in 1898. The incident would lead to further

The citizens of Skagway responded to the Soapy Smith crisis by forming a Militia Guard to rid the city of criminals. Some had served in Soapy's own Skagway Guards just a few days earlier.
ALASKA STATE LIBRARY, JUNEAU

The Skagway Harbor Guards rounded up Smith's men for deportation. The Soapy Smith incident pointed out a real need for a locally controlled National Guard. ALASKA STATE LIBRARY, JUNEAU

attempts to organize a home grown military force on into the early years of the 20th century.

Governor John Brady, missionary via the campus of Yale University, seemed more determined to form a National Guard than earlier governors had been. He notes in his 1899 annual report that, "He does have the power to cause all able-bodied citizens of the United States to enroll and serve as such when the public exigency demands." He stated that, "About ten years ago an attempt was made to organize the militia but the impression got abroad that it was more for show and parades than for organizing to meet ugly emergencies. The young men at Juneau and Douglas have organized companies. Mr. F.D. Kelsey of Juneau, a member of the Alaska Bar, who has had much experience as an officer of the National Guard in the State of Oregon, was appointed Adjutant General with the rank of Colonel. A beginning has thus been made. We hope that this matter will gain the hearty approval and cooperation both of the Interior and War Departments." This section of the Governor's report in 1899 was titled, The Alaska National Guards.

The former churchman again wrote a section on the Alaska National Guard in his 1900 report to the Secretary of the Interior. "A move was made last year toward organization but the matter is still in abeyance in the Departments. Of course the first step is organization, for there can be no calling out nor enrolling for service unless we lay the proper foundations for the service."

The Governor made a trip to Nome in August of 1900. While he was there, 104 men in Nome formed a militia unit and offered their services to the United States Government as volunteers, to assist in protecting the lives and property of American citizens in the Chinese Empire. Alaska Minutemen felt a patriotic duty to serve anytime, anywhere and the Boxer Rebellion was the nearest thing to a war they could find.

The Governor pursued an active interest in a National Guard unit for the Territory throughout his tenure in Juneau which ended in 1906. He left a record of letters sent to various community leaders in Alaska and to leaders throughout the nation concerning the formation of a National Guard unit. Although there would be no organized militia for some years, Alaskans had proven that even on a small scale they were willing to be part-time soldiers whenever an emergency threatened the stability of their community. They were ideal candidates to become National Guardsmen.

These isolated militia units scattered throughout the Territory during its early years would disappear into the musty records of history and be forgotten. Looming behind the scenes, however, was a much larger force ready to form a far greater militia. It would face the challenge of a great world war.

These new Soldiers of the Mists would come from nearly every hamlet and village in Alaska and they would form a militia that would mold forever the Minuteman image in the Great Land.

Muster of Company L, 7th Infantry at Fort Egbert, Alaska, 1900. Isolated frontier posts attempted to maintain law and order in Alaska. A local National Guard would have been more effective but the U.S. Government refused to fund Guard units. U.S. ARMY

The 30th Infantry Band entertains the citizens of Valdez at the turn of the century. A few years later the men of Valdez formed a Home Guard Militia Company when the Army left for World War One duty. U.S. ARMY

THE GREAT WAR

HOME GUARD MILITIA units had existed under several early governors during the later quarter of the 19th century for a variety of reasons. However, the true beginning of an organized militia on a grand scale took place in Alaska just prior to the Great War of 1917–1918. Diplomatic avenues to keep America neutral had nearly ended by the Fall of 1916. Although President Wilson had won reelection on the slogan "He Kept Us Out of War," America's payment for the price of freedom was about to begin. Many Alaskans realized early in 1917 that the war in Europe would involve America before the year was over. Feelings of insecurity on the northern frontier, due in large part to the vast distances involved and the indifference of the government in Washington, swept the Territory like wildfire. On April 2, 1917, J.F.A. Strong, Governor of Alaska, received in Juneau a letter written from the Hotel Coeur d'Alene in Spokane, Washington.

> Dear Governor,
> This is to inform you, that as an Alaskan, even though in the States on business, I hold myself in readiness to your command, and will respond thereto, at any time you deem it necessary to organize a military body to answer the call that I think our President will issue within the week.
> Yours respectfully,
> (Signed) George Goshaw

Governor John F.A. Strong (1913-1918) was a prospector during the Gold Rush of 1898. He organized and led Alaska's first large-scale militia, The Home Guard, during World War One. He was an effective leader who envisioned a strong National Guard for the Territory of Alaska.
ALASKA STATE LIBRARY, JUNEAU

The letter was written on March 26, 1917, eleven days before President Wilson asked Congress for the Declaration of War which brought America into the First World War. Although Goshaw was far from his home in Shishmaref he realized the significance of the world events unfolding before him and the implications for his beloved Alaska.

George Goshaw epitomized the patriotic feelings which would shortly sweep the Territory. Although the Distant Quarter was short on population, the men it produced were legend in talent and experience. Goshaw had served as a soldier in the United States Army at the turn of the century. In 1902, he left the Army in San Francisco to become a merchant in Nome. He met Amundsen when the famed Arctic explorer arrived in Nome after navigating the Northwest Passage and personally knew Brynsten, Lindberg and Linebloom. They were the trio who discovered the gold on Anvil Creek in 1898 that started one of Alaska's first large scale gold rushes. Goshaw sold goods to the miners, gamblers and prostitutes that poured into Nome. He shared Front Street with Rex Beach, Tex Rickard and Wyatt Earp. He recognized historical people and significant events when he saw them and wanted to take part in the action he saw was about to erupt on the American scene.

Goshaw volunteered in the Home Guard Militia when the war broke out but his spirit of adventure could not wait for a governor he felt was moving too slowly. He left the Territory and enlisted in the U.S. Army's 65th Engineers which ultimately became the U.S. Tank Corps. The commanding officer of this unit was a Lieutenant Dwight David Eisenhower.

Goshaw obtained a commission and worked as a personnel officer. He discharged thousands of soldiers returning from France at the end of the war. He returned to Alaska as a fur trader and would spend the rest of his life in the Arctic. When the Second World War came to Alaska in 1941, Goshaw would serve as an officer in the Alaska Territorial Guard.

The recipient of Goshaw's letter, J.F.A. Strong, had become Governor of Alaska in 1915. The popular governor had been a prospector during the gold rush and had founded the *Daily Empire* in Juneau. He leased the newspaper to a fellow prospector named John Troy when he became governor. John Troy would also serve as a Governor of Alaska.

The extent to which Alaskans responded in support of the war effort was almost unbelievable considering the small population of the Territory and its distance from the front lines in France—half a globe away. The responsibility for the defense of Alaska would ultimately be shouldered by a volunteer militia as young men left the Territory in droves to join the regular military services.

The manpower crunch eventually caused some mining operations and logging camps to restrict their productivity. The newly authorized Alaska Railroad's construction program saw its completion date delayed by several years due to the shortage of workers.

Alaska's wartime commitments could be roughly broken down into six major categories: the National Guard, the Home Guard Militia, the regular army, the Selective Service, the civilian war effort and the use of Alaskan resources for the nation. Interestingly enough, the Minuteman concept came first. The man who had to fit all the pieces together was Governor Strong. Ironically, he was not to see the project through to the end of the war. The man who did him in politically was John Troy, who was running Strong's newspaper. Troy discovered that the Governor of Alaska was not a naturalized citizen of the United States and the Canadian born Strong was replaced by President Woodrow Wilson on May 1, 1918. The new governor, Thomas Riggs, Jr., was equal to the task and carried on the programs which had been started by Governor Strong. The man who had ruined Strong's political career purchased the Juneau newspaper and used it as a power base which eventually brought him the governorship in the 1930s.

The issue of a National Guard unit for Alaska preceded the outbreak of war on April 6, 1917. As the stories of the carnage taking place in No Man's Land filtered back from the Front to every hamlet in America, Alaskan's became painfully aware of how unprepared the country was for war. Professional soldiers in the United States Army began to realize there was a wide gap between what was occurring in France and the tactics learned from chasing Pancho Villa along the Mexican border. By 1916, the big offensive mentality of the top brass in Europe who were chasing the phantom of one big victory was beginning to make inroads on American military thought. Once more the nation would have to gear up and train millions of citizen soldiers.

The attempt to organize a National Guard in Alaska had preceded the First World War by many years without success. Late in 1916, the idea surfaced again as huge armies pushed each other back and forth in France to gain or lose a few yards at a horrendous cost in human lives. As early as March in 1917, people in Alaska with a military background were aware that a bill to create a National Guard in Alaska was before the Territorial Legislature and that the position of Adjutant General would be available. Even before the Declaration of War, Governor Strong began to receive letters of application for the commander's job of the non-existent Alaska National Guard. One of the earliest applicants submitted a letter to the Governor on April 14, 1917.

D.W. Figgins had been the Adjutant General of Idaho under Democratic Governor Frank Steiunenberg during 1896–98. He held the rank of Colonel within the state when he formed the First Idaho Infantry, U.S. Volunteers. He resigned his office and accepted an appointment as a Major in the First Battalion when the Spanish American War broke out in 1898. He accompanied the regiment to the Philippine Islands where he served as Regimental Commander during the Insurrection. He was promoted to his former rank of Colonel before being mustered out. Figgins also wrote to Senators Heckman and Sulzer to advance his case and urged A.G. Shoup of Juneau to support his cause. The Ketchikan soldier would not get the job.

Fred C. Schiller, proprietor of "Fred's Place—The Place to Eat in Cordova," wrote to the Governor in March of 1917. He offered his services as a company commander based on his wartime services with the Second Massachusetts Volunteers. He had gained his experience while on active duty in Cuba. He urged the governor to consider a National Guard unit at Cordova and claimed he could muster between seventy-five and a hundred "Strong healthy young men." The proposed bill, however, would authorize only two companies of infantry—one at Juneau and one at Fairbanks.

The man designated to organize the first National Guard unit in Alaska was Major Peter W. Davison. Major Davison, a trained engineer, had spent some time in the Territory on road construction. When he received his order to organize the National Guard he was a member of the Alaska Road

The last 4th of July parade before World War One in Nome, Alaska, 1916. Many of the Nome men watching the parade would join the Home Guard Militia within nine months.
CARRIE MCLAIN MUSEUM, NOME, ALASKA

Commission. The Army Engineers had always furnished trained officers to the Territory. They had explored the land, manned the outposts, built the roads, constructed the telegraph lines and maintained the law and order as time would allow. No history of Alaska would be complete without the builders of the Territory such as Greely, Glenn, Allen, Steese, Taylor, Schwatka, Wilds Richardson and Billy Mitchell. Development of the Territory and the military had always gone hand in hand.

In March, 1917, Major Davison received a hand written Table of Organization from Headquarters, U.S. Army, Western Department in San Francisco. The plan was based on Guard and Militia organization from the manual published by the War Department dated October 26, 1916.

The official announcement of a National Guard for Alaska was printed in the *Daily Alaska* in Juneau in the morning issue of June 1, 1917. A front page article announced that, "The National Guard of Alaska is now virtually an established fact, word having come directly to the Governor's Office by cable—yesterday from Newton D. Baker, Secretary of War." Newton's letter to Governor Strong read, "With reference to your letter May 13, 1917, it is considered advisable to authorize organization of following National Guard units: one company Infantry, Juneau, one company Infantry, Fairbanks. Major Peter W. Davison will be detailed as inspector, instructor and Officer in Charge of military affairs. All details respecting these organizations will be sent by letter from the Chief of the Military Bureau." Once the announcement had been made, activity throughout the Territory and message traffic to the Governor increased by gargantuan proportions.

Major Davison sailed for Juneau on the steamer

Admiral Watson to set up his headquarters while Captain J.C. Mehaffey, another member of the Alaska Road Commission, completed a visit to Haines and neighboring points drumming up support for the National Guard. Other members of an office force were due into Juneau on the next trip of the steamer *Alameda* to set up the offices of the National Guard.

Juneau was in a festive mood and basked in the glory of being a headquarters city. The *Daily Alaska* ran an editorial that literally oozed enthusiasm:.

The Alaska Guard.

So, Alaska is to at last get her place in the sun, and one of these days we shall see real Alaska soldiers, well trained and fully equipped marching down the street to the music of the band. One hundred men are not many but a full company is quite an imposing little force in a city of this size and, perhaps, not many more could spare the time for the training.

It is pleasant to imagine that this force could be made distinctively Alaskan as it will be made up of the flower of Alaska men. It might, for instance, get the habit of wearing the Forget-Me-Not, Alaska's territorial emblem on big occassions if military rules would not forbid such decorations. The fact that Juneau and Fairbanks alone were mentioned in the cablegram from the Secretary of War to the Governor leaves us guessing as to what is actually intended. Such a force in Fairbanks could be of no use for defense but it is possible that the two companies will be made the nucleus of a greater force to come later. Anyhow, here's to the National Guard of Alaska.

On June 2, 1917, the Governor received additional information concerning the two companies of infantry from Brigadier General William A. Waun, Chief of the Militia Bureau. According to the Act of Congress approved June 3, 1916, the territory was authorized an Adjutant General and a staff to be located at Juneau, but under Section 66 of the act, the Adjutant General had to be a citizen of the Territory of Alaska. This effectively eliminated many of the letters of application flooding the governor's office. The two companies could contain no more than 150 individuals each and each was authorized three cooks and two buglers. The territory was to provide suitable armories or drill halls and was charged with protecting federal property in satisfactory storehouses.

News of the Alaska Guard was evidently leaked by the War Department in Washington before the official announcement was made in Juneau on June 1, 1917. Governor Strong received a letter one week after the Declaration of War in early April from the Century Autocycle Company of Chicago asking for an opportunity to display their machine once the Guard was organized. Evidently, war contracting was in gear before the war making apparatus was off the drawing boards. The Governor had to inform the Autocycle Company that no Guard unit had been formed in Alaska.

The Smith Worthington Company, manufacturers of saddles, harness, spurs and buckles, wrote in June. They asked for a mailing list of officers who might be interested in purchasing the Saumur type field saddle which they were manufacturing for the United States Cavalry. Perhaps they did not realize that horse cavalry would be of limited use for a couple of companies of infantry in a country little suited to cavalry warfare.

The Adjutant General's office received a letter, from the Justrite Manufacturing Company of Chicago requesting the names and locations of National Guard encampments in Alaska. They wished to sell acetylene hand lamps "suitable for camp purposes" for the officers personal use. Yankee Peddlers looking for wartime profits had abandoned their carts and were coming to Alaska via the U.S. Postal System.

Hundreds of letters coming into the governor's office from all over the territory requesting information on joining the National Guard worried the man in charge. On July 31, 1917, newly promoted Lt. Colonel Peter W. Davison wrote a letter on Road Commission letterhead stationary to the United States Army, Western Department, San Francisco, California. Davison stated that he had been charged by the Governor of the Territory to organize a National Guard. He requested that supplies of circulars, bulletins, etc., from the Militia Bureau be furnished as, "At this moment not one copy of orders, circulars or information letters on the National Guard are on file in this office and I am unable to give the Governor any information about this matter. There is at present no National Guard in Alaska and I would appreciate information as to how the first officers are to be selected. Also, I would like to know if there are any blanks for the enlistment of the men comprising the company." San Francisco sent the requested forms by return mail.

On July 3, 1917, President Wilson issued a proclamation through Secretary of State Robert Lansing.

"I do hereby draft into the military service of the United States as of and from the 5th day of August, 1917 all members of the National Guard and all enlisted members of the National Guard Reserve."
—Woodrow Wilson

This proclamation, the organization of the Selective Service System in Alaska and other factors delayed an Alaska National Guard until another generation organized the 297th Infantry in 1939.

The tempo of the war had increased so quickly that there was little need to organize two small companies of infantry in far off Alaska. At the national level the Guard was going to France—Over There—to fight the war to end all wars. Nationwide, mobility became the number one priority. The National Guard would write a glorious chapter of military history for the United States but the Alaskans once more felt like orphans of the government—destined to fade away into the mists on the fringe of the Arctic frontier.

The miners, trappers, lumberjacks, fishermen and laborers in Alaska were left with four choices: join the regulars, wait for the draft, make themselves scarce or organize themselves into a volunteer militia. Alaskans, according to their conscience, travelled all four routes to their personal adventures during the era of the Great War.

Although Alaska was not destined to have a National Guard in 1917, this did not become apparent in the beginning. Governor Strong assumed that Washington would make good on its commitment and continued to work on the National Guard issue. On June 11, 1917, he received a letter from Sergeant Wood, U.S. Infantry at Fort Gibbon, Alaska. The Sergeant wanted to assist in recruiting and organizing the new National Guard unit he had read about in the newspapers. He preferred being attached to an Alaskan organization. Although he was in the regular army he felt, "he was an Alaskan and that it was his firm belief that if an organization of Alaskans reached the front lines, they would make a proud record for the Territory of Alaska and the United States."

Governor Strong wrote to the Adjutant General of the Army requesting that Sergeant William E. Wood, on duty at Fort Gibbon, Alaska, be assigned for duty with the Alaska troops being organized at Juneau. Sergeant Wood was obviously smitten by the land and although Alaska would not get its Guard unit, Sergeant Wood would remain in the Territory to drill the Home Guard Militia.

Letters continued to flow into the Governor's office requesting information on the now defunct National Guard unit. Frank Foster, an attorney at law in McCarthy wrote to the Governor urging the formation of a company of miners who were "too old for the regular army being aged 35 to 55 but I feel by the nature of their work that the ordinary Alaskan is physically superior to most city bred men half of that age." Foster had served as an officer in the Washington National Guard and was anxious to offer his services in drilling those in McCarthy who had no training.

Letters from veterans of the Spanish American War came from Haines, Anchorage, Seward, Cordova, Petersburg, Wrangell, Fairbanks and as far away as Dutch Harbor in the Aleutians. Most of the veterans were too old for the regular army and the National Guard but they were to become the nucleus of the Alaska Home Guard, a volunteer militia.

As late as September 27, 1917, the Governor assumed there would be a National Guard. He wrote the Secretary of War and recommended Mr. Z.R. Cheney of Juneau as Adjutant General of the Territory. Cheney had been a member of Company D, 12th Minnesota Volunteers during the Spanish American War. He had worked as a civilian clerk in the office of Adjutant General Duncan in Manila, Philippine Islands in 1899. What soldierly attributes Mr. Cheney possessed were never clear from the Governor's correspondence. Politics would always be a consideration in the appointment of National Guard officers.

When it became apparent that the Territory would be left to its own devices in organizing itself for defense, the citizens explored their roots back through the ages and discovered the English heritage of an unpaid militia. It did not take long to form the Alaska Home Guard.

The first unit of the Home Guard organized itself a full month before war was declared on April 6, 1917. Alaskans knew the regular army would probably leave the Territory if war came. It had happened before when Chief Joseph had run the regulars ragged down in Idaho and later during the war with Spain in 1898. Although the government in Washington had initiated the paperwork to form a National Guard for the Territory of Alaska, the citizens could not wait. Ironically, as Home Guard units sprang up throughout the Territory, they undermined the efforts of the Governor to bring a National Guard to Alaska. The anomaly would dominate the military scene in Alaska all through 1917. In the long run, the Home Guard would prevail and create the foundation for the National Guard to build upon for a later generation of soldiers.

Early in 1917, the United States broke off diplomatic relations with the German government. A group of approximately 200 older men in Juneau met to form a Home Guard militia. In a letter to the Governor, they stated the reasons for organizing themselves into a military body. They felt they were justified in their actions and were looking for an official blessing. The Governor himself informed the Secretary of War in a letter dated March 13, 1917, that a Home Guard Militia had already been organized in Juneau and he requested 200 Springfield rifles

The Daily Alaska Dispat[ch]

JUNEAU, ALASKA, FRIDAY, JUNE 1, 1917

MEMBER ASSOCIATED PRESS

NINETEENTH YEAR—MORNING EDITION—PRICE TEN CENTS

NATIONAL GUARD IS ESTABLISHED FOR TERRITORY

Juneau Will Have One Company of Guard Infantry and Fairbanks Will Have Another

The National Guard of Alaska is now virtually an established fact, word having come directly to the governor's office yesterday from Newton D. Baker, secretary of war, stating that the government has considered it advisable to authorize the organization of companies of the Guard in the territory. Two companies are to be formed, one for Juneau, evidently with the intention of taking in other parts of the coast, and one for Fairbanks, to take in the interior. A military company in the United States at full war strength is one hun[dred] ed at the governor's office by Secretary Shorthill yesterday:

Washington, D. C.,
May 31, 1917.

To the Governor:

With reference your letter May 13, 1917, it is considered advisable to authorize organization of following national guard units:

1 company infantry, Juneau.
1 company infantry, Fairbanks.

Major Peter W. Davison will be detailed as inspector, instructor and officer in charge of military affairs.

May 25, 1917

TROOPS FROM POST WILL GIVE EXHIBITION DRILL IN SKAGWAY

With an exhibition in the afternoon by soldiers from Fort William H. Seward and a patriotic dance in the evening under the auspices of the Home Guards, tomorrow will be Military day in Skagway.

Major M. E. Saville, commandant at the post, cabled Dr. L. S. Keller yesterday afternoon that he will send a platoon of soldiers to Skagway Saturday afternoon. The drill will be held on the ball park, beginning at 2:30 o'clock.

Officers and soldiers of the post have been invited to attend the dance in the evening at Elks hall, and it is understood a number of them will attend.

Members of the Skagway chapter of the Alaska Women's Patriotic league are aiding the Home Guard by selling tickets to the dance.

The committee on arrangements has engaged Selmer's orchestra to play for the dancers.

MAKING PLANS HONE GUARD

Recommending the formation of a home guard in Skagway, the committee which has the project in charge, will report, tonight at a meeting of the Elks, under the auspices of which organization formation of the guard has been planned.

It is understood the committee will suggest that the patriotic meeting to begin recruiting for the guard be held tomorrow night.

WRANGELL ORGANIZES MILITARY COMPANY WHICH OFFERS SERVICES

Wrangell, April 10—Last night a patriotic meeting was held in this city which was attended by a throng of people which taxed the hall to overflowing.

The meeting was held for the purpose of organizing a military company, which was to be offered to the President through Governor Strong.

When the roll was passed for signature, 117 men signed their names to the roster. While the men were signing the roll, and a resolution was being drawn up offering the organization of the Wrangell contingent to the President of the United States through Governor J. F. A. Strong, W. H. Warren played patriotic and martial airs on the piano. When the last name had been signed, and the message which was to be cabled to Governor Strong drafted, several prominent citizens delivered speeches, among those being F. H. Bronson, deputy United States Collector of Customs and J. W. Pritchett, editor of the Wrangell Sentinel.

While the men were engaged in organizing the military company, the women of Wrangell organized a branch of the Red Cross society with more than one hundred charter members. Mrs. F. H. Bronson

The Daily

April 28, 1917

PROGRAM IS ANNOUNCED FOR PATRIOTIC RALLY

SENATE 57 TO 30 VOTES "NO" OI

Home Guard Will be Formed at Meeting Monday Night

Decorated with flags, the colors which the whole country is now bending its efforts to uphold as they have been since the days of the colonies, Elks hall will be the scene of a great patriotic rally Monday evening to form a home guard in Skagway.

The committee on arrangements, of which Mayor Howard Ashley is chairman, announced the program for the meeting this afternoon. It will include patriotic speeches, patriotic songs by the school children and patriotic airs by the Skagway band.

Auspices of Elks

Under the auspices of the Elks, and with the Eagles and Arctic Brotherhood co-operating, it is expected that the rally will be attended by an audience that will tax the capacity of the hall.

Members of the local lodges of Eagles and A. B., it is planned, will march from their respective clubhouses, with flags flying, to the hal The school children, forming their line of march at the school building, and carrying flags to be provided by the Elks, will parade down Broadway and thence to the Elks' clubhouse on Sixth street.

Mayor Ashley will preside at the rally. A request was sent this afternoon to Fort Wm. H. Seward that one of the officers from the post attend the meeting.

To Begin at 8:15 O'clock

The meeting will open, the committee announced, promptly at 8:15 o'clock. Following is the program

o'clock. Following is the program:

Introduction — Mayor Howard Ashley, chairman.

Invocation — Father P. H. Turnell.

"America"—Sung by school children.

Address — W. B. Batson, exalted ruler of B. P. O. E.

Address — Phil Abrahams, sec-

HAINES PLANS HOME GUARDS

April 11, 191

Haines, April 11—A meeting was called in the Arctic Brotherhood hall, yesterday evening by United States Commissioner J. J. Kennedy for the purpose of forming plans for the organization of a company of home guards. The meeting was largely attended, there being between seventy-five and a hundred present. Judge Kennedy called the meeting to order, and stated the object of the meeting. R. M. Odell was elected chairman, and B. A. Barnett secretary. Mr. Odell in a few well chosen remarks thanked the audience for the honor conferred upon him in making him chairman.

Judge Stout, Dr. L. S. Keller, Bruce Brown and several others gave short talks on the subject of forming a company of home guards.

On motion, the following committee was appointed by the chair, to perfect plans for the organization:

Bruce Brown, R. H. Ferry, Col. Sol. Ripinsky, N. G. Hanson, S. Sheldon, R. Combs and Frank Morris.

When the committee is ready to report, a meeting will be called for the purpose of perfecting the organization.

After a few more remarks had been made by some of the prominent persons present the meeting adjourned, subject to the call of the committee.

ARMY OFFICER TO DRILL LOCALS

Juneau, April 14—The final organization meeting of Co. "A" First Alaska Military Training Corps, was held last night at the City Hall and from now on the sessions will conform strictly to military meetings and regulatoins and the company and recruits will get down to work.

It was reported at the meeting by Captain George Irving, that upon reqest of Governor Strong, a non-commissioned officer from Fort William H. Seward, who has passed a high examination as a commissioned officer, has been appointed by the commanding officer of Fort Seward to come to Juneau to act as drill master for the corps until further orders. This officer, whose name was not sent to Juneau, will arrive on the Quartermaster steamer Peterson probably within the next few hours.

Non-commissioned officers for the company were appointed last night After Captain Irving stated to those assembled that only as many as are actually needed had been appointed and that the others would be appointed as rapidly as required and after the officers become better acquainted with the qualifications of the men.

A squad of men were put at work on the old Pacific Coast Company dock putting it in shape for company headquarters this morning. Lights are being installed by the Alaska Electric Light and Power Company. The members of the company extended a rising vote of thanks to the Alaska Electric Light and Power Company for lights and power, to the Pacific Coast Company for the use of the dock, and to the Pacific Coast Coal Company for a ton of coal and to Russell Casey for hauling.

The next meeting will be held in the new quarters as soon as they are ready. The call will be issued through the papers.

The non-coms appointed last night were C. P. O'Kelly, first sergeant; Walter Johnson, quartermaster sergeant; Otis Ross and P. E. Jackson, sergeants; A. B. Cole, Millard Murane, F. J. Hurley, corporals and Mr. S. Perkins, company clerk.

The Kake Rifles of 1917. Rare picture of the Kake Home Guard. Patriotic Alaskan natives were quick to volunteer when Uncle Sam needed them. DR. CHARLES E. SYDNOR COLLECTION, HELEN SKEEK, KAKE, ALASKA

for the unit along with official recognition from the War Department. The reasoning behind the formation of the Juneau unit a full month before the Declaration of War was that three large lode mines near Juneau hired about 800 Austrians, Germans, Bulgarians and other subjects of the Central Powers who had not been naturalized. There was fear among the citizens of Juneau that this body of aliens might attempt to loot the banks which held over two million dollars in gold or sabotage the mines. The Governor noted that outwardly, the situation was as calm as a summer sea. Should war break out this situation could change dramatically and the handful of soldiers at Fort William Seward, a hundred miles distant, would be unable to dispel problems at Juneau in a timely manner. Prior to the diplomatic break, pro-German sympathizers within the Territory had been quite vocal so there was good reason for putting together a Home Guard unit.

On March 19, 1917, John Hansen of Skagway, hearing of the Juneau unit, wrote Governor Strong concerning a Skagway Home Guard. He had served in L Troop of the 5th U.S. Cavalry and was willing to lead a militia unit. The men of Skagway wanted to guard the White Pass and Yukon Railroad in case aliens might be tempted to disrupt services to the mines along the narrow gauge route.

Word of the Juneau unit continued to spread and on March 26th, Dr. H.M. Craig, First Lieutenant in the Medical Reserve Corps on duty with the regulars at Fort William Seward, wrote the Governor. He wanted to volunteer for any Alaska unit, Guard, Reserve or Militia the Governor might be raising in the Territory. The Governor had to inform Lt. Craig that a state of war did not yet exist but he had contacted the War Department concerning a governor's role in organizing a militia.

Two days before war was declared, the Governor received a wire from Secretary of the Interior, Frank Lane. The Secretary said that officially the Governor could not be authorized to organize the militia, but unoffically, he should begin to organize and train a militia. On the same day Governor Strong issued a message:

To Whom it may Concern.

Mr. C.A. Bunch of Treadwell, Alaska is authorized to enroll volunteers for prospective military service, and to take such steps as may be necessary to drill and perfect the organization pending its official recognition by the United States Government.

Governor Strong.

On April 6, 1917, America entered the First World War. The Deputy Collector of the United States Customs at Ketchikan, Mr. Ernest Blue, was elected Captain and organized the Ketchikan Home Guard. Within a few days, the Governor received notice that the United Spanish War Veterans in Seward and Anchorage had held meetings to organize militia units in those municipalities.

Within two weeks of the Declaration of War, Home Guard units were formed in Fairbanks, Eagle, Douglas, Nenana, Sitka, Cordova, Dutch Harbor and Petersburg. Governor Strong had the beginnings of his army.

This sudden growth of military interest caused the Governor to seek guidance from the War Department and the Commonwealth of Virginia, among others, on the organization of militia forces. Naturally, the patriot soldier concept turned to the grand model of the minuteman—the National Guard. In effect, the Governor now had two reserve military organizations competing for manpower in the Territory with the regulars and the Selective Service.

Mass meetings for the formation of Home Guard units were held throughout the Territory. The Governor received a telegram from Wrangell on April 10, 1917. It was fairly typical of what was going on all over the Territory of Alaska.

Anchorage on Memorial Day, 1917. Although the war was less than two months old, Alaskans rallied around the flag. The large building across the street is Robard's Hall where the Home Guard Militia drilled. ANCHORAGE MUSEUM

"Resolved that we residents of Wrangell, Alaska, here gathered in public meeting approve and endorse the action of our country and its President in declaring a war against the Imperial German Goverment which action we believe necessary for the protection of our rights and people and for the preservation of our national honor and it is further resolved as proof of our loyalty and willingness to do our full share towards the carrying on of this war that we organize a military company to be drilled and trained in so far as our limited facilities allow and further that we offer this organization to the President and our country through his excellency J.F.A. Strong, Governor of the Territory of Alaska for such purposes as he may require them."

> J.W. Pritchett,
> Secretary of the Meeting.

One hundred and twenty-five men in Wrangell signed up for the Home Guard. Anchorage and Fairbanks held similar mass meetings. The local druggist in Haines organized a meeting and informed the Governor that the Haines Home Guard was organized and holding drills, but needed a uniform book of regulations to make sure they were conducting their military affairs in an acceptable form. The Governor had very little information to pass on, but did assure the Haines unit that a $10,000 war fund had been set up to pay expenses for rent, fuel, lights, etc., that Home Guard units might incur.

The Home Guard men of Seward had a particular reason for drilling. Because of the railroad construction in the area, aliens outnumbered Americans two to one. The engineer in charge of railway construction estimated 350 aliens were engaged in building the railroad with more arriving on each steamer seeking work. The Home Guard promised to protect federal and municipal property and to monitor alien traffic in and out of Seward. They asked for arms and ammunition and a regular army instructor to teach the proper drill techniques.

Fort William H. Seward furnished what soldiers it could to teach the drill but units of the Home Guard continued to be organized almost daily and the army could not keep up with the number of requests flowing through the Governor's office. Units from Nome, Dutch Harbor and Eagle had to rely on the Spanish American War veterans who joined their ranks.

The Fairbanks unit requested $2,500 as one-half the price to purchase an armory building. The Governor could not authorize Fairbanks one-fourth of his war chest. Fairbanks had to rent a drill hall from the Loyal League for $200 per month. Even this amount seemed excessive to the conservative governor and he recommended that the unit should appeal to the patriotic nature of the Loyal League and perhaps they would donate the hall rent free as they had done in Ketchikan, Juneau, Skagway and Seward. The Fairbanks unit would continue to have rental problems throughout the war. Long after the Fairbanks unit disbanded in 1919, bills from local merchants continued to flow into the Governor's office. In many cases, the Home Guard never did pay the bills presented by the local merchants.

The Home Guard militia units were often supported by the various Chambers of Commerce, Loyal Leagues, the Alaska Road Commission, the Pioneers of Alaska, local political leaders and, of course, by Governor Strong. There were logistical problems associated with an organization scattered across an area as large as all the States east of the Mississippi River. The units recruited, drilled and elected company officers. The officers were generally Spanish American War veterans, former National Guard officers or local professional men.

Skagway did more than its share for the war effort. Minerals vital for America's war machine came through the port. The regular army furnished troops to guard the White Pass and to watch the railroad bridges for saboteurs. The Home Guard was popular in Skagway and the local unit had a membership of over one hundred men. The shops of the White Pass and Yukon Railroad played a unique role. The U.S. Government did not furnish rifles so dummy wooden rifles were turned out in the Skagway shops of the railroad company and were sent to Home Guard units all over the Territory to be used for drill. During the summer of 1917, General Wilds P. Richardson visited Skagway to investigate the valley for food production for the Territory. Almost every ship sailing south from Skagway carried young men leaving the Territory to join the regulars. As the ships stopped at various Southeastern Alaska ports, more men joined the exodus from the Territory.

One of the unique military organizations formed during the First World War was the 10th Engineers (Forest). This unit included Alaskan lumberjacks and U.S. Forest Service personnel. They were to set up portable sawmills in France to manufacture timbers for bridge construction, trench and artillery needs. Many other Alaskans were involved in the procurement of Alaskan Spruce, a vital material in the construction of fighter aircraft. Those Southeastern Alaskans who were too old to take part in the American Army mission in France could still do their part as members of the Alaska Home Guard.

One of the major problems that developed dur-

OFFICERS:
FRANK B. HALL, President
GUY B. ERWIN, Vice-President
ROBERT W. TAYLOR, Secretary

JAS. E. BARRACK, Drillmaster
R. MYERSON, 1st Class Private, S. C.
G. B. ERWIN,
MACK SMITH,
P. J. RICKERT,
Assistants

FAIRBANKS HOME GUARDS
GENERAL ORDER NO. 1

You are informed that the Fairbanks Home Guard is now regularly organized and has been authorized by the Governor of Alaska to perform the services designated in Act June 14th, 1917, and that the Guards have the character of State Police or Constabulary.

It has been decided to use the Home Guard for patrol duty in Fairbanks and Garden Island during the night time. This patrol and guard duty will be started on April 1st, 1918, and will be kept up according to the schedule herewith for the period of four weeks, when the hours of guard duty will be shortened and a new schedule of names furnished.

The patrol will consist of six guards, two on Garden Island and four in town of Fairbanks, and the patrol will be relieved every two hours.

The object of the patrol is to guard and protect property, especially all warehouses containing food, and government property. The patrol on the Garden Island side will guard the warehouse district, railway depot and buildings and the bridge. The patrol in Fairbanks will pay especial attention to that part of town lying between First and Third Avenues and from Lacy Street to Wickersham.

The patrol will be armed with revolvers and are ordered to make arrests in the event of persons attempting to destroy property.

The guards will report for duty at the City Hall, where a book will be furnished for the entry of their names and time of going on duty and where they will be furnished with arms. The second, third and fourth relief, after reporting at City Hall, will relieve those on duty, who will hand over their arms, and when the fourth relief goes off duty at 5 o'clock in the morning they will return the arms to City Hall.

It is intended that each man shall stand guard two hours once each week. In order that the hours of duty be fairly distributed, each relief will be guided by and go on duty the first time in strict accordance with the schedule as printed. The second time their turn for guard duty comes around each relief will go on two hours later than they did the first week, and so on each successive week for the four weeks the schedule is intended to cover, which will give each relief patrol duty once for each of the four periods. In other words: Those who go on duty from 9 to 11 the first night will the following week go on from 11 to 1, and the next week from 1 to 3, and the fourth week from 3 to 5.

If there is any misunderstanding with reference to these instructions you are to call up any of the drill masters, who will put you right.

If for any reason you are prevented from attending to these duties at the hour fixed, it is expected that you will provide a substitute by changing hours with some other member of the Home Guard.

IT IS ORDERED THAT EACH MAN REPORT PROMPTLY AT THE HOUR NAMED.

The officers of the Guard look to the members to carry out this order in the spirit that it is for the best interests of all concerned. We are engaged in the bitterest war of all times; the safety of Civilization is at stake, and there is a debt of service due from every man to his country proportionate to the bounties which nature and fortune have measured to him. That you are willing and anxious to "do your bit" is not questioned — TWO HOURS EACH WEEK.

March 27th, 1918

By Order of Executive Committee

JAS. E. BARRACK,
Drillmaster.

9 to 11	11 to 1	1 to 3	3 to 5
GARDEN ISLAND			
Anderson, O. W.	Bloom, Robt	Joslin, W. H.	Hamilton, Ray
Bishoprick, F.	Bickford, J. B.	Boyer, E. H.	Brown, R. M
FAIRBANKS			
Bucci, J.	Bucci, T.	Bailey, H.	Bredlie,
Kelly, H. C.	Bidwell, J.	Buckley, J. J.	Cambridge, J. A.
Hess, L. C.	Beraud, G. E.	Clark, J. A.	Carlson, M. O.
Bernard, R. L.	Hess, S. R.	Love, Max.	Williams, A. J.
GARDEN ISLAND			
Levake, J.	Levake, Dave.	Raap, John.	Saulich, Milo.
Wolcott, Ed.	Kennedy, B. S.	Miller, Frank.	DeYoung, Harry.
FAIRBANKS			
Coleman, G. A.	Clausen, E. A.	Carey, Wm.	Cunningham, J. M.
Courtnay, Walter	Clark, F. R.	Conradt, Aug.	Drake, G. D.
Avakoff, H. B.	Cathcart, W.	Carlsten, A.	Johnson, A. J.
Gibson, Thos.	Coombs, D. F.	Carruthers, S. S	Wilbur, A. L.
GARDEN ISLAND			
Attich, Carl	Davis, Edby.	Kennedy, A.	Hayes, C. H.
Struthers, J. Fred.	Barrack, John.	Weir, H. A	Welch, Geo.
FAIRBANKS			
Dunn, John	Fairborn, J. A.	Graham, F. F.	Groes, John.
Davis, J. A.	Fortier, A. H	George, Chris.	Gillette, L. R.
Deal, T. H.	Fisher, Oscar D.	Groves, J. H.	Hall, F. H.
Evans, W. E.	Foster, T. H	Gellerman, E.	Hutchinson, G.
GARDEN ISLAND			
McCord, Abe.	Lewis, Fred.	Jankovich, M.	Davis, H. C
Soumers, R. J.	Hopkins, Paul.	Nerland, Andrew.	Heath, Jack
FAIRBANKS			
Hahn, C. S.	Krieger, O. F.	Landess, A.	Magnusson, S. L.
Johnson, Ed	Kramer, W. F.	Lumpkin, H. H.	Mehegan, J.
Kennedy, G. F.	Lavery, Robt	Miller, J. H.	Markus, Geo.
Fowle, J. R.	Lloyd, Reese.	Mack, E. H.	Marple, W.
GARDEN ISLAND			
Menzie, R. D.	Kelly, Robt.	Johnson, Theo.	Appleby, W. A.
Rose, Dan	Bryant, J. F.	Sheldon, R. E.	Smythe, E. J.
FAIRBANKS			
McKinnon, W. W.	Helmick, M.	Nerland, T. A.	Koon, Norman.
MacQuarrie, G. A.	McGinnis, D. L.	Pinkerton, W. T.	Parsons, T. A.
McDonald, Thos.	Newton, D. A.	Peterson, P. S.	Rhind, C. F.
McCrary, Frank.	Nerland, Andy.	Preston, Geo.	Rust, Jesse
GARDEN ISLAND			
Peoples, E. R.	Ross, H. H.	St. George, R. Y.	Selberg, C. S.
McIntosh, J. A.	McAdam, Ed.	Morrow, J. G.	Moyer, LeRoy.
FAIRBANKS			
Rolston, Ted.	Sherman, Ben.	Sells, Mark.	Tonseth, E. A
Roth, R. F.	Smith, Jos.	Smith, Jr., J. H.	Tull, H. R.
Steele, R. S.	Sea, Sam.	Taylor, R. W.	Wood, F. P.
Swan, T. T.	Sutherland, J. A.	Thompson, Ben.	Wooldridge, E. R.
GARDEN ISLAND			
Stroecker, Ed.	Sanderlin, E. L	Campbell, Wm.	Landerking, G. M.
Karstens, H. P.	Kubon, Ralph.	Lorentzen, Peter.	Lovejoy, Steve.
FAIRBANKS			
Copeland, A. L.	Fisher, Joe F.	Handley, W. H.	Hering, Ed.
Crawford, R. M.	Golden, Louis.	Harrais, Martin.	Hunter, Geo.
Brown, Harry W.	Grow, Harry L.	Heilig, Reed W.	Purdy, E. H.
Douse, Fred.	Hall, M. F.	Heacock, L. J.	Protzman, L. F.

OFFICERS:
FRANK B. HALL, President
GUY B. ERWIN, Vice-President
ROBERT W. TAYLOR, Secretary

JAS. E. BARRACK, Drillmaster
R. MYERSON, 1st Class Private, S. C.
G. B. ERWIN,
MACK SMITH,
P. J. RICKERT,
Assistants

FAIRBANKS HOME GUARDS
GENERAL ORDER NO. 2

As voluntary members of Fairbanks Home Guard you are required to file immediately with the Secretary your oath. You will therefore fill out and sign the hereunto attached oath, take it before a Notary Public or other officer authorized to administer oaths and swear to same and after such officer has signed and affixed his seal thereto, send or hand the oath to the Secretary. This is very important, and you must not delay in attending to it promptly. Any Notary Public in Fairbanks will swear you without charge.

By order of Executive Committee,
JAS. E. BARRACK,
Drillmaster.

April 8th, 1918.

OATH FAIRBANKS HOME GUARD

United States of America,
Territory of Alaska } ss.
Fourth Division.

I, ..., born in ....
State of ...., aged .... years, by occupation ....
do hereby acknowledge to have voluntarily enrolled as a member of the Home Guard of the Territory of Alaska for the period of the war; and I do solemnly swear that I will bear true faith and allegiance to the United States of America, and the Territory of Alaska; that I will serve them honestly and faithfully against all their enemies whomsoever; and that I will obey the orders of the President of the United States, and the Governor of Alaska, and the orders of the officers appointed over me, according to the rules and Articles of War.

....

Subscribed and sworn to before me this ..... day of ...., A. D. 1918.

....

A Notary Public for Alaska.

(Seal)

My Commission expires ....

GUY B. ERWIN, Vice-President
ROBERT W. TAYLOR, Secretary

~~~~~~~~~, John A Davis
P. J. RICKERT,
Assistants

FAIRBANKS HOME GUARDS
GENERAL ORDER NO. 4

The Alaska Territorial Council of Defense for Fairbanks District has requested that the Fairbanks and Garden Island patrols be continued for four weeks in the same manner as heretofore, except the 9 to 11 patrol be eliminated.

This new schedule will cover period beginning Monday, April 29th, and ending Sunday, May 26th.

The patrol will, as heretofore, consist of six guards, two on Garden Island and four in Fairbanks. There will be three reliefs, the first patrol going on duty from 11 to 1 o'clock, called the 1st Relief; the 2nd Relief from 1 to 3, and the 3rd Relief from 3 to 5 o'clock.

The patrols will go on duty the first week in strict accordance with this order. The second week, beginning Monday, May 6th, the patrol will go on two hours later, that is, the 1st Relief the first week will be the 2nd Relief the second week, 3rd Relief the third week and 1st Relief the fourth week, and so with the other Reliefs.

The patrol has worked out very satisfactorily during the past month and with few exceptions everyone has entered into the spirit of the matter and faithfully performed his two hours' service once a week.

However, it MUST be again impressed upon every member that this order MUST BE DEFINITELY UNDERSTOOD AND STRICTLY CARRIED OUT. Each one is required to put in full two hours' duty, and in no way relax the vigilance which is so essential in maintaining the morale of the movement. Report promptly at the hour fixed, date and sign the roll at the exact minute of your going on duty, and patrol your post for the full two hours unless relieved.

If for any reason you are prevented from attending to these duties at the hour fixed, it is expected that you will provide a substitute by changing hours with some other member of the Home Guard.

Dated April 27th, 1918. By Order of Executive Committee.

J. E BARRACK,
Drillmaster.

	1st Relief 11 to 1	2nd Relief 1 to 3	3rd Relief 3 to 5
MONDAY		GARDEN ISLAND	
	Anderson, O. W.	Bickford, J. B.	Morrow, J. G.
	Bishoprick, F.	Kubon, Ralph.	St. George, R. Y.
		FAIRBANKS	
	Bucci, T.	Hess, S. R.	Bredlie, A.
	Kelly, H. C.	Bailey, H.	Nordale, Alton.
	Bernard, R. L.	Buckley, J. J.	Kincaid, Emmett.
	Beraud, G. E.	Clark, J. A.	Gibson, Tom.
TUESDAY		GARDEN ISLAND	
	Wolcott, Ed.	Kennedy, B. S.	DeYoung, Harry.
	Weir, H. A.	Miller, Frank.	Wesch, Geo.
		FAIRBANKS	
	McCrary, Frank.	Rust, Jesse.	Graham, F. P.
	McGinnis, D. L.	Parsons, T. A.	Landaas, A.
	Peterson, P. S.	Koon, Norman.	Magnussen, S. L.
	Preston, Geo.	Mack, E. H.	Markus, Geo.
WEDNESDAY		GARDEN ISLAND	
	Struthers, J. F.	Lewis, Fred.	Heath, Jack.
	Davis, Edby.	McCord, Abe.	Hopkins, Paul.
		FAIRBANKS	
	Hahn, C. S.	Sutherland, J. A.	Handley, W. H.
	Kenney, G. F.	Rolston, Ted.	Hering, Ed.
	Moyer, LeRoy.	Lloyd, Reese.	Hunter, Geo.
	Sea, Sam.	Lavery, Robt.	Purdy, E. H.
THURSDAY		GARDEN ISLAND	
	Sommers, R. J.	Brido, Frank.	Landerking, G. M.
	Johnson, Theo.	Jankovich, M.	Lovejoy, Steve.
		FAIRBANKS	
	Coleman, G. A.	Newton, A. D.	Krieger, O. F.
	Clark, F. R.	Nerland, Andrew.	Marple, Wallace.
	Fairborn, J. A.	Fowle, J. R.	Lumpkin, H. H.
	Boyer, E. H.	Avakoff, H. B.	Carlson, M. O.
FRIDAY		GARDEN ISLAND	
	Bloom, Robt.	Joslin, W. H.	Appleby, W. A.
	Brigham, N. O.	Kelly, Robt.	Smythe, E. J.
		FAIRBANKS	
	Crawford, R. M.	Sells, Mark.	Kelly, J. H.
	Golden, Louis.	Tonseth, E. A.	Hutchinson, Geo.
	Hall, M. F.	Wood, R. C.	Tull, H. R.
	Fisher, Jos. F.	Taylor, R. W.	Wooldridge, E. R.
SATURDAY		GARDEN ISLAND	
	McIntosh, J. A.	Peoples, E. R.	Lorentzen, Pete.
	Ross, H. H.	McAdam, Ed.	Selberg, C. S.
		FAIRBANKS	
	Dunn, John.	Hiil, A. G.	Clark, J. E.
	Foster, T. H.	Steele, Ray.	Woodward, C. Harry.
	Groves, J. H.	Hamilton, Ray.	Brown, H. W.
	Gillette, L. R.	Brown, R. M.	Heilig, Reed W.
SUNDAY		GARDEN ISLAND	
	Menzie, Robt.	Rose, Dan.	Roth, R. F.
	Protzman, L. F.	Clausen, E. A.	Drake, G. D.
		FAIRBANKS	
	Coombs, D. F.	Smith, Joe.	Cambridge, J. A
	Thompson, C. L.	Sherman, Ben.	Cathcart, W.
	Wilbur, A. L.	Pinkerton, W. T.	Stein, Izzy.
	Johnson, A. J.	Hayes, C. H	Russell, Leith.
~~~~~~~~~

ing 1917 was the procurement of arms for the militia. The Governor was told that the War Department would only furnish arms to units of the regular National Guard. Since no units existed in Alaska, the Governor sought other avenues to arm his militia. When the Skagway Home Guard requested arms from the Governor's office, the Governor could only suggest that the Territory could not afford at this time the arms needed throughout the Territory. He did, however, suggest that organizations affiliated with the National Rifle Association (N.R.A.) were permitted to buy arms and ammunition from government arsenals at reduced rates. He enclosed a copy of the N.R.A. club by-laws and applications for membership. In July, the Congress finally passed an act authorizing the furnishing of rifles and other equipment to Home Guard companies. Eventually, the Alaskans were spared the embarrassment of being seen in public carrying wooden dummy rifles.

Within a few days of the Congressional action authorizing government rifles, correspondence between the Governor, the War Department and the U.S. Arsenal at Benicia, California began. The rifles to be furnished were the 1898 models and would be issued to the Governor of Alaska who in turn would authorize them to the various Home Guard units. The town of Anchorage had a special problem. It had two military organizations competing for funds and rifles. The Home Guard was organized primarily by the Pioneers of Alaska. The Loyal League unit was organized by the employees of the Alaska Engineering Commission. Each numbered 75 members. The Governor, being short of money in his war chest, wrote and urged the two units to act as one in renting a suitable drill hall.

The Sitka unit was fortunate in having two former U.S. Marine Corps First Sergeants to serve as drill masters—Joseph McNulty and F.C. Sherrod. The unit was able to drill at the Sheldon Jackson School with real rifles—old muskets that had been used by Boy Cadets for several years at the school. However, Mayor A.G. Shoup had one major problem at Sitka. He could muster at least thirty white men but the National Army Law would not allow Indians or half-breeds to register for service with the army. Shoup felt the natives were valuable men for any domestic service. If they joined the Home Guard it would tend to increase their self-respect and devotion to the country. Sitka would be glad to take them in the Home Guard as a section if it would not interfere with the unit getting official status.

By the end of 1917, the first shipments of arms from the Benicia Arsenal in California began to arrive at Seward. The Bill of Lading was made out to the Governor of Alaska. The shipments of the 1898 Model rifles, bayonets, slings, and cleaning kits were sent directly to the individual units from the arsenal. The Governor could only assume the rifles ended up in the right hands. Late in 1917, the Governor received a new form from the army that placed the full responsibility of all shipments to the Territory upon his shoulders. He was to take care of the arms and safely keep them and account for them. He was to return them in good condition when the war was finished.

During the build up of the Home Guard in 1917, the Governor continued to receive requests and offers from a variety of sources. George C. Johnson, an attorney at law from El Paso, Texas, tried to sell the Governor thousands of his booklets titled *Memoranda Court Martial Procedure*. He informed the Governor, "You have under your command a great Army that you are sending forth to battle under the Federal Service. You expect these stalwart sons that are coming forward with their lives to do honor to your state. What greater parting encouragement could you give than to place in the shirt pocket of every officer and enlisted man, a copy of this little pamphlet to remind him that not only at home are you interested in his welfare but also in his little troubles on his way to the firing line." The Governor could no doubt stare out his window at the rain in Juneau and ponder this "great army he was sending off to battle."

By September, 1917, local draft boards had been set up in eight communities in Southeastern Alaska and chairmen had been appointed to the other judicial districts of Alaska. The Territory would have its first drawing for the draft in November for 700 men. By this time many of the available men in the Territory had already departed to join the regulars or were governed by a draft board in the States. The number of men left to form a National Guard unit shrunk even farther. The Pocket Testament League requested a list of National Guard Chaplains in the Territorial National Guard. They were concerned about the spiritual guidance of the non-existent unit. A combination of the draft, increased enlistments in the regulars and the formation of the over-aged into a Home Guard doomed the establishment of an official National Guard for Alaska. The concept would fade into the mists to await a rebirth some twenty years later when the Territory once more would face the dangers of a world conflict.

Although the Governor technically was responsible for the formation of the Home Guard only, the war involved him in a range of military-related problems. In July of 1917, he wrote the Mayor of Douglas concerning a message he had received from Washington. Indians of mixed blood were to be exempted from the draft just as those of full-blood were not to be registered. Perhaps they could be used in the new Home Guard.

Early in the war, Councils of National Defense were set up in towns throughout Alaska. These were to promote patriotism and loyalty, carry out the laws of the United States and to promote the war work of the country. How would these councils relate to the Home Guard? The first test came when a mass meeting was held in Petersburg to organize against slackers in the war effort. The Governor had to remind the Defense Council that he saw no harm in a meeting but that no drastic action should be taken by the organization or the Petersburg Home Guard against alien slackers and urged that moral force be exerted without resorting to violence.

Defense Councils were formed wherever Home Guard units were formed in response to the large numbers of aliens working the canneries, mines and forests in Alaska. The fear of using the Home Guard against the alien population may have initially slowed the flow of arms from the U.S. Government into the hands of the Home Guard.

By the fall of 1917, Kodiak, Seldovia, Dutch Harbor and Eagle had completed the organization of their Home Guard units. The Defense Council letters of the period indicate that many communities in Alaska looked to the Home Guard to protect them against aliens in general but, "Germans, Bolsheviks, Swedes, Norwegians and Industrial Workers of the World (IWW) members in particular." The Skagway newspaper reported in August of 1917 that the local Home Guard and the Spanish American War veterans would be used to suppress I.W.W. efforts to sabotage the vital spruce timber industry in Alaska.

War fever stories of sabotage in defense plants on the east coast of the United States were featured in copies of the Hearst newspapers that worked their way North via the Alaska Steamship Company boats. The use of the Home Guard to monitor the activities of the I.W.W. Union would later fan the flames of union opposition to the formation of a National Guard in Alaska during the 1930s.

The Secretary of the Territorial Council of Defense in Seward, W.H. Whittlesey, sent a telegram message to the Governor on January 17, 1918 requesting U.S. troops be sent to Seward. He was concerned about the number of aliens coming and going through Seward and those found lingering on the government dock, the bridges and at the railroad warehouses. Strong replied by stating, "It is unadvisable at the present time to ask for regular troops at Seward as you have a Home Guard which is organized under the Acts of Congress of June 14, 1917. This military body, under that law is directly charged with the protection of the property of the United States, the protection of supplies in the course of manufacture for the United States, or the protection of transportation lines where necessary, including rights of ways, railroad bridges, etc."

Although Home Guard units were drilling and carrying out their assigned tasks of guarding property from Nome to Ketchikan and along the route of the White Pass and Yukon Railroad, the Governor found he was involved in other wartime matters. Getting Alaska spruce to the Boeing Airplane Company in Seattle was a priority. He was informed that Bruce Rogers, editor of the Nome newspaper, had been found guilty of seditious writing after a six-day trial and had been fined $300 and costs or 150 days in jail. Strong initiated a project to send 3,000 pounds of Matanuska Valley grown potatoes to the Food Products Company in Idaho Falls, Idaho, to experiment with on the manufacture of potato flour for the war effort.

The combined emotions of fear and patriotism created during a wartime climate created some unusual situations, particularly on the Last Frontier. The best sample of this came from the mining town of McCarthy.

> Hon. J.F.A. Strong
> Governor of Alaska
> Juneau, Alaska

> Dear Sir:
> I am writing what follows because I think it is my duty to keep you informed of all local conditions which in any way effect the defense of the Territory and its military establishment.
> The population within a radius of 20 miles of McCarthy is about one thousand of which 75% are foreign born laborers. I do not think that over 25% of our population is native born and not over 50% are citizens of the United States.
> Swedes and Finns predominate and constitute about 40% of the total. These are pro-German with but very few exceptions. In my opinion 50% of the population of this vicinity is pro-German. This condition is deplorable but is more so on account of conditions existing in the little town of McCarthy, formerly known as Shushanna Junction.
> In this little town of not more than 250 in population are four big saloons and from 15 to 20 houses of ill-fame all the latter engaged in the illegal sale of liquor. The saloons close at midnight and on Sundays and will go out of business January first but the other places have no closed seasons and I do not think will close on

New Years.

Let me here describe local conditions and set forth my reasons for believing that they will continue. The restricted or red-light district of McCarthy lies in a corner of the town, close to and right in sight of the Marshall's Office. There are from 15 to 20 houses in this district and one or more inmates in each. Drunkenness, robbery, fights and all manner of disorder occur here nightly. Last Spring conditions got so bad that the marshall had a high fence or stockade erected around this district. This was done to protect the inmates and to keep the public from seeing things which might cause complaint to be made. As would naturally follow, these dens are the headquarters for the criminal element including the I.W.W.s, gamblers and possibly German and Austrian agitators. There is no doubt that the criminal conditions which these joints naturally breed greatly aids the spread of sedition and German and Austrian propaganda. In support of this I will say that the so called sporting, gambling and rounder elements in McCarthy have been and are mostly Germans and Austrians.

As to conditions which will prevail after January first, let me say that a year ago last spring ended a year during which the town was nominally dry, there being no saloon licenses. Drunkenness was as prevalent as before or since and at no time during that year did the redlight houses stop selling booze. Last summer when the Kennecott strike was on the strikers, before they came down and located in the old town of McCarthy, asked for and had the saloons in Shushanna Junction closed. They asked for this for their own protection as they knew that if their members got drunk there would be much riot and disorder. In accordance with orders the marshall swore in several deputies and placed a guard at each saloon and also had the redlight district guarded. The strikers, however, were well acquainted with local conditions, they knew the marshall and that nearly all his guards watching the saloons and boot-legging joints were bartenders. Accordingly from the beginning to the end of the strike, the strikers themselves had out a strong guard picketing the marshall's guards and the town in general. They succeeded in locating caches of whiskey meant for them, had several arrests made and obtained the conviction of one prostitute for bootlegging. This was the only time that the town was really dry and free from drunkenness. A few days ago I had a conversation with Judge O'Conner on this same subject. He showed me a letter just received of which I enclose a copy. This letter shows the sentiment not only of the writer but of a large element in the town.

I know of the reputation of the women referred to in the letter and don't blame anyone for not wanting them as neighbors. Notice, however, that the writer don't want these women punished according to law but merely to be placed in the corral where they can continue to prey upon the young men of the community. This sentiment, that these joints, gambling and bootlegging are necessary evils, is increasing and the laxity of the officials in enforcing the law is largely to blame for this condition. Judge O'Conner is willing and anxious to have the law enforced but the marshall's office here refuses to cooperate and the sentiment above referred to prevents any complaints being made.

The Judge's record in Chitina where he effectually stopped bootlegging and created a sentiment against the saloons strong enough to have them voted out proves this. Therefore I do not blame him for conditions here.

You can readily see that before the draft occurs here it will be necessary to have a thorough cleanup. To have a large number of young men around subject to so many temptations will not be just to them or to the country.

Besides there is much veneral disease around. I am a father and have a son now in training at Camp Lewis. I have read with great satisfaction of the effective measures to clean up conditions around that camp. If this attitude is that of the government and I believe it is, do you not think we should begin the good work here? I believe this cleanup is absolutely necessary before the draft takes place but the question is how should it be done. If you think it advisable I will make an investigating trip as far as Valdez and while there lay these matters before the District Attorney.

Respectfully yours,
Peter S. Ericksen—Game Warden.

Another problem facing the Governor was the registration of young men for the draft. Inquiries came from draft boards in Pillar Bay, Treadwell, Thane, Hoonah, Excursion Inlet and Gambier Bay concerning proper forms and the problem of potential soldiers leaving the Territory without signing up. A letter was sent to the Special Agent of the FBI in Seattle informing him that one Don Lowdermilk of the Hoonah Packing Company had quit his job and had disappeared into Canada. The U.S. Commissioner at Chatham wrote to Judge Jennings in Juneau that he had 15 white people, some Philippinos and a couple of Chinese who needed draft forms. He was afraid they might slip away when the fish cannery closed for the season.

By September, 1917, Governor Strong, who took his job seriously, was sending messages to the U.S. Marshall in Seattle to pick up Territory men who were leaving Alaska without registering for the draft.

> "C.F. Skinner sailed from Juneau on steamer *Prince Rupert* last Saturday night for Seattle. Am informed he probably did not register for military service. He is described as an American about 26 years of age, height 5 foot 5 inches, weight about 160, dark hair & eyes, clean shaven. Request you take steps to find Skinner."
>
> Strong, Gov. of Alaska.

The Home Guard now had the additional duty of keeping its eyes on potential draft dodgers. The Governor continued his correspondence with the U.S. Arsenal in Benicia, California, which was still somewhat reluctant to send more targets, slings, ammunition and rifles north to Alaska. Even the famed Dog Team Doctor, J.H. Romig, wrote to the Governor on behalf of his son Robert, who was in the Seward Home Guard. Although the boy was patriotic and willing to serve in the regulars in any capacity, the father felt, "He would like to enlist in such service as will further benefit or prepare him for business when he returns . . . We thought perhaps the Quartermaster Department would be in line with his qualifications." Fathers have always been fathers.

The men who organized the Home Guard in 1917, along with Governor Strong, were going through the same basic process of forming a militia that Americans had been doing since Jamestown in 1607. The years had added complexity and paperwork but the end product—an organized militia—was similar in form. The pettiness, the politics, the amateurism, was probably as prevalent in 1607 as in 1917. However, the dedication and the patriotism associated with militia troops cut through two hundred years of history and the American fighting man came shining through the mists of time.

Governor Strong was relieved of the responsibility of returning every single piece of equipment to the U.S. Government at war's end on April 30, 1918. He was replaced as Governor by Thomas Riggs, Jr., who became Governor on May 1, 1918. It must have come as a shock to be so rudely removed from office. Strong had conscientiously experimented with forming an army and had met with success. His foundation could be built upon and Governor Riggs continued the war effort without a moment's hesitation. Aware that he was now in the Glass Palace in Juneau and subject to minute scrutiny, Governor Riggs moved quickly to establish his authority as the new Commander-in-Chief of the Home Guard. As units continued to be formed throughout the Territory, the Governor encouraged the expansion of the militia. He had himself bonded and insured by the Maryland Casualty Company for $25,000. The Baltimore company charged a fee of one hundred dollars a year for the policy, but the Governor felt the pressure of being responsible for the U.S. property that would have to be returned at the end of the war. He in turn required each Company Commander of the Home Guard units be bonded and responsible for the equipment under his command.

Governor Strong had created something of a problem for Governor Riggs concerning the Home Guard unit in Fairbanks. Strong had questioned the motives of the Fairbanks citizens organizing for the defense of the Interior. When the Fairbanks unit sought Strong's approval, he fired back a letter informing them that, "The Home Guard seems to be a fraternal society organization; therefore, it is impossible to use Territorial funds for the purpose mentioned. To do so would create an undesirable situation and serve to invite the formation of similar bodies by other fraternal societies."

Several prominent businessmen in Fairbanks had invested in a local building for drill and had hoped the Territorial Government would help pay for the building through high rents. The former Governor had refused to do this so the investors wasted no time in contacting Governor Riggs, a hometown favorite. On the Governor's very first day in office he received a letter from W.F. Thompson, editor and manager of the Fairbanks *Daily News-Miner:*

> Dear Gov,
>
> Welcome home. It's about our armory. There's a mortgage due by the time you get this and Strong cut us off the payroll because Caskey or somebody wrote him that they were not drilling there during the winter.
>
> Put us on the payroll again, Tom, the payroll the armory was on when you were here. Times are hard and everything goes for war, and we just can't take any money out of town for

armory balances if we can help it. You know it is a good and proper cause, worthy of Territorial support. All our investments in it, of course, are gone but it is for the camp and the country's good.

Wishing you and the rest of the family the best of luck, and promising to stand behind you whether you are right or wrong,

Sincerely,
W.F. Thompson

Governor Riggs enjoyed no "Honeymoon Period" upon his ascent to the position of Commander-in-Chief. The pressures of office were intensified because of a thousand projects traceable directly to the war. Communications took up a disproportionate amount of his days and the tasks to be accomplished must have seemed overwhelming. Letters and requests competed for the Governor's time.

The National Civic Association, the Special Aid Society and the Negro Books for Negro Soldiers movement all requested the Governor's help. The American Victory Garden Commission, the American Victory Union, the Aerial League of America, the Women's Liberty Loan Committee, the American War Mothers and the National Economic League competed with a dozen better known national organizations for the Governor's favor. These were the positive organizations. The negative ones created an even greater problem for Governor Riggs.

One of the Governor's major concerns involved the Alaska Territorial Council of Defense. Nearly every town had a branch of this patriotic organization. Home Guard members often served on the boards and it soon became apparent that the militia could be used to monitor the activities of the many aliens who held jobs in the Territory.

Aliens were not required to sign up for the draft which caused them to be special targets of the Loyal League and other patriotic organizations. During 1918, some of the aliens wrote to the Governor requesting protection from the Loyal League and the Governor's own Home Guard. Even long time Alaskans and men of the cloth were not immune to such attacks:

Dear Sir:

I am informed from reliable sources that my name appears on a list of Anti-Americans, made up by a member or members of the Council.

As the observance of the golden rule "Keep the law & keep your mouth shut," has always been my policy in the past, I am amazed that such an action could be taken by a member or members of the Council. To my mind it appears as the insane act of a diseased brain, inspired by ill-adviced, over-zealous, ignorant or pin-headed bigotry. A man in my position will not stand for any base underhanded work nor allow his good name or character to be aspersed by suspicious insinuations or unproven charges. As an American citizen of long standing, I bid members of said council beware, as I shall know, if needs be, how to assert my rights to prosecute & confound any would be traducer.

Yours very truly,
Rev. Paul P. Kern

The letter was sent from the Church of the Holy Name in Ketchikan, Alaska, on January 26, 1918.

The Home Guard continued to grow in size and influence. The units continued to drill in ordinary civilian clothing, but demands for a uniform came in from units all over the Territory. Governor Riggs wrote a letter of inquiry to Washington D.C. but was informed by the Adjutant General of the U.S. Army that no uniforms could be issued or sold by the federal government as there was a shortage of wool cloth. Wool cloth was a priority item for the manufacture of uniforms for the regular army. There was no objection to the wearing of a uniform by Home Guard units as approved by the Chief of Staff, but the Territory would be responsible for uniforming its own militia.

The Governor wrote a letter to Governor Lister of Washington State asking if the Washington National Guard had any of the old blue Spanish American War uniforms it might give to Alaska. Governor Lister replied that the Washington National Guard had been called up and the old blue uniforms were to be used by his own recently organized State Militia. No uniforms were ever worn by the Alaska Home Guard during the Great War.

The expenses of organizing a Home Guard Militia continued to be a matter of concern for the Territorial Government. The Governor sent blank vouchers to various units for materials purchased from local venders. Rents for drill halls went to various fraternal organizations. The Robard's Hall in Anchorage cost $65 a month. Bills run up by the Home Guard continued to flow into Juneau as late as 1926 and some, like that presented by the Fairbanks Lumber Company, were never paid by the Territorial Government. The Federal Government was more insistent on being paid. Bills from the Federal Arsenals were promptly paid as well as those presented by the Pacific Steamship Company. A box of rifles shipped from Seattle to Juneau which was 12 cubic feet in size cost the Territory one dollar and fifty cents. However, the Territory was exempt from the War Tax charges so was reimbursed five cents by Uncle Sam.

The Home Guard began receiving its 7.62 mm Russian Rifles with equipment in October of 1918. Seven hundred arrived in Juneau and were held by the bonded Governor until he made sure his unit commanders were also bonded and had a place to safely store the weapons. The initial shipment came from the Rock Island, Illinois Arsenal. Subsequent shipments would be sent directly to the local Home Guard units from the Benicia, California Arsenal, the Watervliet Arsenal in New York and the Springfield, Massachusetts Arsenal. It was up to the Governor to recover the equipment at war's end and return it to the Federal Government.

The Home Guard units provided safe storage for the borrowed arms. Juneau had 100 rifles in the Arctic Brotherhood Hall. Fairbanks stored 60 rifles in the Masonic Temple while Anchorage held 80 in the Alaska Building. Sitka and Eagle held 20 each and they were stored in the Pioneer Home and the Customs House Building respectively.

Often, the units had the rifles but no ammunition and Ketchikan did not receive its shipment until four days before the Armistice was signed in November of 1918. At least the men were now drilling with real rifles and they looked impressive around town.

One of the most active units was the company organized at Cordova. Captain John Gillis was able to report to Governor Riggs on July 6, 1918 that, "The Home Guards of Cordova number 125 men, the average attendance during the summer is 65 and drills are held on Tuesdays and Fridays of each week. The drill period is one and a half hours. The object of this organization is to preserve law and order and for the protection of government property. We will perform such guard duty as we may be called upon to perform, presumably from your office. So far we have no special guard duty, but the appearance of the Home Guards, composed of the best citizens of the community in line of march, has provided a strong factor in maintaining order, especially during the cannery season."

The City of Fairbanks continued to have problems with the Home Guard issue because of factions vying for power. The Tanana Rifle Club element informed the Governor that they planned to build a new 600-yard rifle range commencing in front of the grandstand at the racetrack and running in a southerly direction across P.J. Rickert's homestead. There was no shortage of Fairbanks men willing to respond to the call of arms. The Governor's old friend W.F. Thompson once more wrote to Juneau to point out that the Masons were hogging the glory of a Home Guard unit and were pushing to receive the rent money allocated for Fairbanks to benefit the Masonic Hall. Thompson felt it would be a victory for Masonry. He suggested the Governor stall on the question of money for the renting of the Masonic Hall because the Eagles would want the contract for the next year, then the Catholics, etc.

The editor of the Fairbanks *Daily News-Miner* reminded the Governor that the armory deal had fallen through, although Riggs himself had been one of the buyers. He pointed out that Governor Strong had filled all the desirable places with "aliens" before he left office and that Riggs had no excuse for firing them. As for a position for himself, Thompson concluded, "Appoint me game warden, now that there is a vacancy and the warden is expected to do nothing—the day the time comes to get out into the bush to "warden" I'll resign, the salary in the meantime would pay cigar money—there's no beer here now anyway!"

Despite the inter-fighting taking place in the Fairbanks Home Guard, it proved to be one of the best led and best organized units in the Territory. Indeed, the whole First World War effort by the Territory of Alaska was amazing considering the short 19-month duration of the war. Much had been accomplished under the leadership of two very different Governors. Long hours and dedication by aroused citizen soldiers had overcome disorganization, politics and seemingly insurmountable problems. An organized band of warriors stood ready to defend the Great Land if called upon. The 280-year Minuteman tradition had carried through from Massachusetts to the Bering Sea and America was all the stronger for it.

On November 11, 1918, word came from France that the War to end all Wars had itself come to an end at 11 A.M. The great war machine which had been created throughout the nation would be dismantled. In time, the memories of one of the world's most devastating wars would soften as the distance between the reality of horror and the comfort of old age security (that thing we call history) became a fact of life for the participants who had survived.

As the years rolled by and the Alaskan Home Guardsmen of 1917–1918 marched off towards eternity, they unknowingly left a legacy of duty, patriotism and honor behind—sturdy foundations for the Minutemen who would come swarming out of the mists for a new call to duty in 1940.

The Juneau Home Guard on the city dock on June 4, 1918. The wooden drill rifles were made in the Skagway shops of the White Pass and Yukon Railroad.

THE RUSSIAN RIFLES

Shortly after entering World War One in April of 1917, the United States Government agreed to send shipments of rifles to the Imperial Government of Russia. The Russians had lost heavily against the forces of Kaiser Wilhelm of Germany almost from the moment the Czar cast his lot with the Allied Powers. The Battle of Tannenberg had been a disaster in 1915. The Czar's personal intervention in the direction of the Russian Army led to even greater losses.

In the October Revolution of 1917, the Bolsheviks under Lenin set up a Communist form of government. Its priority was to make peace with Germany and pull Russia out of the war. Considering war-weary Russia's situation and the risk of establishing a new form of government born in revolution, this would have been a logical political move to unify the people.

The United States immediately cancelled the order for the rifles bound for Russia. Some of these so called "Russian Rifles" were among those shipped to Alaska for use by the Home Guard in 1918. The 700 Russian Rifles that Alaska received from the United States Army Arsenal at Watervliet, New York, were 7.62mm Remingtons which had been manufactured by the Bridgeport plant. Seven hundred bayonets and slings were included in the shipment.

The Territory of Alaska paid the transportation costs for the shipment North and back again to the arsenal when the war ended. The rifles had been marked "Packed for Russia" when they arrived in Alaska. The rifles had changed routes and instead of ending up in Europe, they came to Alaska only 50 years after the United States purchase of the Territory from Russia in 1867. The former colony had been called Russian America until 1867. The Russian Rifles were returned to the U.S. Arsenal but there may still be some of the Enfield and Springfield rifles from the Home Guard shipments scattered around Alaska today.

BETWEEN THE WARS

AS THE TWILIGHT of an era set in across the nation following the Great War, social consciousness grew in the gap of time between the distant battlefields and revisionist historian's accounts of the conflict. As Americans pondered those triple devils of blame, guilt and profit, they sought to rid themselves of those distractions by launching their generation headlong into that wonderful madness called the Roaring Twenties.

Not so in Alaska. The frontier population rolled up its sleeves, logged and returned to the mines and fishing boats. The construction gangs of the Alaska Railroad headed north and south towards the little river town of Nenana where the golden spike would be driven in 1923. Alaska was still Alaska. The gold was still there for the digging, vast coal deposits could be found and the salmon still ran by the millions. There was talk of liquid black gold seeping to the surface at Katalla and in the Arctic, portentously marking the course of Alaska's future.

Let the gangsters control Chicago. Let the youth dance the night away or become members of the Lost Generation. Alaskans had better things to do than feel guilty, become flappers or to speculate in the stock market. A vibrant frontier society set to work building a territory towards that day it could proclaim statehood and the citizen rights and responsibilities that would accompany that coveted status.

Pilots bought surplus Jennies still in the crates from the government, put them together with the help of backstreet mechanics and taught themselves to fly in the most dangerous sky in the world. Those who were successful created the legend of the Alaskan bush pilot.

Co-partners with the men who built Alaska between the wars were the pioneer women. Skimpy flapper dresses were not as evident on the Last Frontier as pants and flannel shirts. Instead of rolling silk stockings down below the knees, they rolled their sleeves up above the elbows and set to work. Their bobbed hair was for a practical reason, not for style. They were hard working women who matched the men who matched the mountains. Down the road fifty years, their granddaughters would join the National Guard and learn to shoot and march with the best of men.

Alaskans never forgot their military heritage. The Fourth of July parades in the small towns throughout the Territory continued to be the social highlight of the year. Home Guard veterans became local leaders in Alaska for a decade or more. The '20s and '30s were lean years for the military services as isolationism stalked the land, but in Alaska the Guard and Militia dream never completely dissolved. The Minutemen simply stepped back into the mists to await a more opportune moment.

The Home Guard Militia continued to exist in various forms for some time following the conclusion of World War One. Some units disbanded almost immediately while others continued to drill. The Cordova unit under Captain Hazelet held on for years after most other units were gone. Many of the units began to die from a lack of attendance. The unit at Eagle got down to just seven members before it disbanded. Many members, not unlike the ancient Roman general Cincinatus, simply returned to civilian life once the danger of war had passed.

Mr. Charles W. Bush, manager of Brown & Hawkins Outfitters, wrote to Governor Riggs from Anchorage on January 15, 1919: "It is impossible to get the boys out to drill since the war ended. I see no reason to continue paying rent for Robard's Hall. If there has been any rule pertaining to the Home Guards, please advise."

G.F. Cramer, Secretary to the Governor, corresponded with nearly every Home Guard unit concerning bills against them that continued to pour into Juneau. The White Pass and Yukon Railroad sent a bill for $53.20 against the Territory for freight charges on three boxes of rifles consigned to the Governor himself for the unit in Fairbanks. Bills came in from lumber companies, hardware stores, steamship companies and the Federal Government.

The Governor received a letter from Brigadier General H.M. Lord informing him that U.S. ordnance property could be demanded by the Chief of Ordnance on 30 days' notice. Governor Riggs was well aware that he was personally responsible for Uncle Sam's rifles. On February 4, 1919, Riggs sent a wire to the Chief of Ordnance in Washington D.C.

"Territory has 325 Russian rifles issued by War Department for Home Guard purposes not needed now. To whom shall these rifles be returned?" Washington answered that directions would be sent from the supply officer at Fort Mason in San Francisco as to where the Russian rifles should be sent.

One of the major problems concerning the federally owned rifles was the transportation costs of returning the weapons to the federal arsenals. The various Home Guard units found that the steamship

Governor Thomas Riggs, Jr. (1918-1921) tried to keep the Home Guard intact following World War One. His efforts to form a National Guard and an Alaska Ranger Force were unsuccessful.

At the 19th Annual Convention of the National Guard Association of the United States in Richmond, Virginia, November 1919, each state and territory was assessed $25.00 to help defray expenses. Alaska did not respond because it did not have a National Guard or an organized militia. Territorial government had been in force some eight years but colonial status still abounded. The frustration of being a part of the Grand Union without political clout would continue unabated for another 40 years.

These were the years the National Guard itself was struggling for its separate place in the sun. The Association had earlier in 1919 issued a news release from New York City. It favored the compulsory universal military training of every young man in the country and called for "the overthrow of the military dictatorship which has used but never considered the National Guard (Re: the regular army)." It opposed any form of compulsory service that would "thrust young men into the regular military household at an age when they were not yet fully qualified to decide for themselves to lead the life of professional soldiers with all its temptations, and with the narrow influences which broad men know that a soldier's life is filled with." The National Guard Association felt, "It would be better for a boy to receive universal military training to give him a deep sense of obligation to his country, and to any opportunity that may be offered him for patriotic service; but do not let us tempt him to go into the regular army and adopt as his career the life of the professional soldier. Train him in military matters in small doses over a period of two or three years, then with the foundation well laid, graduate him into the citizen soldiery of the nation—the National Guard."

The statement issued by the National Guard Association concluded by saying, "It is important at the outset for the people to understand that the National Guard Association has no quarrel with the personnel of the army, but that it demands that the pernicious system, which has been the outgrowth of the military bureaucracy of Washington, which has dwarfed officers and made them unwilling tools of a self-perpetuating body, must be abolished and its supporters driven out of power." The American debate over standing armies was clearly alive and well in 1919.

While Alaska did not have a National Guard during the years between the wars, the interest in such an organization remained. There were in the Territory many men who belonged to the Reserve Officers Association and the National Guard Association of the United States. Some attended national conventions and others maintained contact through the mail. The lifestyle and the nature of the land attracted a large number of veterans to Alaska. The

companies demanded shipping payments prior to delivery. The Russian rifles were separated from the Springfield rifles and were finally shipped to California on the Pacific Steamship's *City of Seattle* on March 7, 1919. A week later, Riggs sent a letter to the remaining Home Guard units informing them that there were no appropriations available to kee Home Guard units going.

Eventually, there was only one holdout from the disappearing militia army. Captain Calvin C. Hazelet informed the Governor that Cordova would like to continue its unit. Although attendance was down because of the flu epidemic, the 45 remaining men had formed a new organization with stateside militia by-laws. These by-laws were being sent to members of the next Territorial Legislature in hopes favorable Home Guard legislation would be enacted. The Cordova Guards also requested a machine gun. They would find an instructor among the returning veterans who could show them the proper techniques to operate the weapon, "as a moral persuader in case of any Bolsheviki trouble among our foreign laboring element (of which we have had a few rumors) it would hold high rank."

basic ingredients for the building of a Minuteman Force were in place on the Last Frontier.

A rather unique problem developed following the Armistice of 1918. There were still Alaskans in the military service who thought they would never be civilians again. The Governor was asked to use his position to get the Alaskans home. The majority of these men were miners and fishermen who could envision a whole working season slipping away while they sat idle at a military camp. The requests for help came from as far away as Ponteux, France, where Private Stanley G. Thomas lamented, "Could you use your influence to secure my release from the Army? During the period of the war the 20th Engineers operated a sawmill just behind the lines on the Alsace Front. Our company is operating one of several mills in a large area of burned timber and our chances of getting home soon does not look very promising. We never complained during hostilities but now that hostilities have closed, we feel entitled to a return to God's country. It is a fact that Alaska is short of men for the mines and canneries."

There were many Alaskans who volunteered for another uniformed service called the U.S. Guards. This organization called for prior servicemen to volunteer to serve at military bases in Alaska. The U.S. Guards would take men up to the age of sixty and many old time Alaskans, particularly miners and fishermen, put on uniforms for the duration of the war. Company A was assigned to Fort William Seward while Company B served its time at Fort Gibbon.

Second Lieutenant James H. McCarron had joined the U.S. Guards in San Francisco after leaving Seward. He was trained at Angels Island and served in Company A, 6th Bn, U.S. Guards at the Presidio until he was assigned to the 30th Bn, U.S.G. at Fort Gibbon, Alaska. He owned mining property near Seward and hoped to go overland by way of Nenana while the trail was good if the Governor could obtain his release in April, 1919. When he found out a discharge was not forthcoming, he dropped a bombshell on the Governor's desk. He informed the Governor that some of his friends in the U.S. Guards at Fort William Seward were virtually prisoners of the army and his own discharge was being held up at Fort Gibbon.

Governor Riggs held informal hearings with eight discharged Alaskan soldiers concerning their friends still being held by the U.S. Army. They testified that the commanding officer, a Major White, had indeed used devious means to hold on to Alaskans in his rapidly shrinking command at Haines. The War Department circular concerning discharges was read at reveille and then posted on the post bulletin board, but the all-important Circulars 86 and 186, which outlined how to get a discharge, were withheld from the men. When the Alaskans realized what the army was doing, they retaliated by having their plight published in the public press.

One of the requirements for discharge was a letter from an employer stating a position existed for the soldier. Immediately, the Alaskans prepared wires to prospective employers within the Territory. The army responded by creating new rules. All mail in any way soliciting outside aid to obtain discharges was censored and wires being sent off post had to be cleared by the post adjutant. All communications from the post by soldiers concerning discharges were stopped. Major White said no more men could be spared by the command.

Private Thomas Running prepared his wire and found it in an outgoing basket five weeks later. He went to the Company Commander who said, "I'll send it through now but I'll mark it disapproved." The Private replied, "That's just what I want you to do; I just want to find out if you can hold me here any longer." He then sat down and wrote a letter to the Governor. Perhaps the Governor could make a trade off with the U.S. Army—Alaskans in exchange for the return of thousands of venereal disease pamphlets which had arrived for the Home Guard long after the war was over. The pamphlets were colorful affairs titled: VD, U-Boat #13—A Modern Attack on an Old Enemy.

Governor Riggs was eager to put the army and the wartime problems behind him. There was an attempt to have the Legislature strike a medal for Alaskans serving in the military during the war, but the Legislature voted it down because of the expenses involved in the program. Riggs did appoint a well known Alaskan, Harriet "Ma" Pullen, as War Mother of Alaska. Ma Pullen operated Pullen House, a resort hotel dating back to the gold rush era in Skagway. She was the mother of the first Alaskan appointee to West Point. Colonel D.D. Pullen was Commander of Tank Corps 781 and was highly decorated for gallantry near Bois de Cuisy, France. Her other son, Major Royal Pullen of the U.S. Army Engineers, also served in France.

In 1919, the Governor had no militia or Territorial Police to enforce law and order in the Territory. There were 55 Marshals and Deputy Marshals in the Territory under the Department of Justice. There were about 35 wardens of various sorts, such as fish wardens, fur wardens, forest rangers, game wardens and special liquor agents. With the demise of the Home Guard, the Governor clearly needed a military-type force for the half-million square miles of his area of responsibility. There was not much prospect of the National Guard being established in the near future, so the Governor looked for other solutions for his problem.

Mr. Fredrick Zorn of Seattle wrote to the Governor concerning the lack of any armed body for the protection of Alaska's citizens. He and several other prospectors had been ambushed in the interior of Alaska the previous year. His son was killed and buried in a trailside grave while he himself had been shot and beaten. He urged the formation of a militia, which would be organized like the Royal Canadian Mounted Police in the Yukon Territory. He pleaded with Governor Riggs to make the hills and fields of Alaska safe for the prospectors who were the trailblazers and forerunners of civilization. He also wrote to Teddy Roosevelt, Woodrow Wilson and William Howard Taft to urge proper legislation to control the destructive elements infesting the Territory.

The Governor lamented the fact that the four judicial units he controlled had only a handful of officials whose primary function was to act as process servers. A few towns hired one or two policemen but Alaska had virtually no protection for its 30,000 white and 25,000 native peoples. In a letter to the Superintendant of the New York State Police, the Governor admitted there was a radical element colonizing the Territory with the avowed purpose of "disrupting industry." He hoped to offset this movement by organizing the Americans in every community into vigilance committees but felt even this organization could not be maintained. He needed a federally paid force for the protection of the citizens. Thus the concept of the Alaska Rangers Force came into being to replace the disbanded Home Guard Militia.

The Governor felt the Alaska Rangers should be patterned along the lines of the famous Texas Rangers. The proposed organization would be placed under the Secretary of the Interior. The Rangers would perform the function of the Militia in putting down civilian disturbances and would enforce the law, act as coroners, do rescue work and prevent looting during natural disasters. The Governor felt the Rangers should attract only the best-qualified men and to fight the temptation of corruption, the officers and men of the Rangers should be highly paid with the security and status of at least that of the U.S. Army. The Royal Canadian Mounted Police would serve as a role model. In lieu of a National Guard this was what the Governor sought.

To perfect his Alaska Ranger Bill for Congressional consideration, the Governor wrote to Major E.F. Koenig, 21st U.S. Infantry at Fort William H. Seward seeking input. The Major consulted with Captain Bell of the Royal Northwest Mounted Police detachment in Whitehorse, Yukon Territory. Bell suggested a clause in the proposed bill that would permit the Rangers to obtain data from arrivals into Alaska as a means of scaring criminals away from the Territory. A detachment would be assigned to Seattle to supervise the passenger lists of all vessels sailing for Alaska. Fingerprints would be taken of all suspects, and a cooperative clause between the Alaska Rangers and the RCMP would create an international force against crime. The remnants of the Home Guard Militia would be organized as a backup force for the Rangers.

Major Koenig suggested that the Rangers should be highly mobile and organized along military lines. All promotions would come from the ranks to keep morale high. Since there would be no cooks, buglers or medics, each man hired would have to be inovative, self reliant and have the ability to command any local militia that may be called upon to assist the Ranger. The Major closed his letter by noting, "with a quite to be expected degree of egotism, I have left the position of Commanding Officer open for myself. I believe, that whatever my faults may be, the person originating the bill is most apt to carry out the spirit of the legislation."

The Governor considered his bill carefully and corresponded with the Department of State Police in Albany, New York. He also wrote law enforcement agencies in Lansing, Michigan, and in Chicago. With his bill now written up, Riggs sought one more opinion before submitting it via the Congressional Delegate to Congress for consideration. A copy was sent to the Adjutant General of the State of Texas in Austin. The letter was forwarded to Captain R.W. Aldrich of the Texas Rangers who found the plan favorable and returned it to the Governor, along with a copy of the rules and regulations governing the Texas Ranger Force.

The only major criticism the Governor received on his proposal came from the Superintendent of the New York State Troopers. He forsaw trouble in mixing a civilian constabulary with the military. Michigan had tried that concept and there had been trouble with its program. He was also against the Governor's idea of saving money on uniforms by using those of the U.S. Army, slightly changed. He suggested that if the Alaska Rangers allowed the transfer of officers from the regular army service into its ranks, the army men would wish to control the force and make it a complete military organization.

At the beginning of 1920, Governor Riggs left Alaska for a three-month visit to Washington D.C. He hoped to secure Congressional legislation for his Alaska Ranger Force. On February 24, He wrote home that he expected to get his bill introduced within a week but felt, "I cannot hope for a realization of my ideas this session of Congress." It was quite apparent that Alaska needed both a civilian law enforcement agency and a National Guard. Congress did not authorize the appropriation to set up a civilian Ranger Force for Alaska. The cause was lost when the Governor failed to get support from his own Congressional Delegate.

Although Governor Riggs failed to get his Rangers he kept alive the idea of some type of force in the Territory. His desire to establish either a militia or a federal law agency for the protection of Alaska attracted worldwide interest. Wilber J. Watkins, 2nd Lt., U.S. Infantry, read about the Alaska Rangers in the *London Daily Mail*. He applied for a position based on the fact he had worked in Iditarod, Ruby, Fairbanks, Circle and Dawson and had trapped two winters on the Chandalar River out of Fort Yukon. He reinforced his argument by stating he was a 32nd Degree Mason and Shriner and had won a commission from the ranks during the war. Even these sterling qualifications would not bring him home from Europe. The magical hold Alaska exercised on young adventurous men could extend thousands of miles without noticeably weakening. Clearly, the Lieutenant was homesick for the northern frontier and did not intend to remain at Toulouse University to become a part of what Hemmingway would call the Lost Generation.

There was one tiny flicker of light left concerning the National Guard. The War Department had written the Governor at the end of 1919 to extend an invitation to the non-existent Adjutant General of Alaska to attend the Adjutant Generals Conference in 1920. The State Adjutant Generals of the United States National Guard were ex-officio directors of the National Rifle Association of America and were expected to introduce a resolution to the Assistant Secretary of War to promote rifle practice in the United States. Although Alaska did not have a National Guard, perhaps the remnants of the Home Guard could hang on as organized gun clubs. The idea interested the Governor because he, as Chief Administrator of the Territory, could approve the charters of the gun clubs in the absence of an Adjutant General. The NRA could make available cheap government rifles and inexpensive ammunition. The NRA followed up by offering copies of their publication, *Arms and the Man,* to all militia and gun club members at two dollars per copy.

Gun clubs began to be formed all over Alaska. In many places, the Home Guard members simply switched over to the local gun club and continued to meet as a group once a week. The Anchorage Home Guard was one of the first to form a gun club. In 1919, the Governor received a request for an Alaskan rifle team to take part in the National Rifle Matches at Caldwell, New Jersey. The Territory was authorized 17 positions on the proposed team and

expenses would be paid by the Federal Government. Several Home Guard veterans showed interest, but August was a busy time in the mining and fishing industries and the Governor was unable to field a team.

The War Department encouraged the formation of gun clubs throughout the nation and they became extremely popular in Alaska. Charters were approved by the Governor for the Tanana Club in Fairbanks and for an auxiliary, the Fairbanks Boys Rifle Club. Although charters were approved for clubs in Nome, Cordova and at Ketchikan High School, the Territory again failed to field a team for the 1920 Olympic Team tryouts which were held at the U.S. Marine Base in Quantico, Virginia.

The interest in gun clubs as a means of training potential militiamen continued unabated between the wars. The most interesting application for a charter came from J.J. Quiwegon, Secretary of the Kodiak Rifle Club. He enclosed the ten dollar application fee and penned an interesting postscript to his letter—"PS: The Japanese will find us prepared!" The date on the letter was February 9, 1921.

Governor Scott C. Bone (1921-1925) sought to organize a National Guard Unit under the Army Reorganization Act of 1920. The Federal Government would not allocate money for an Alaska National Guard during the 1920s.

The National elections of 1920 brought Warren G. Harding to the Whitehouse and boosted Alaska's hopes for a larger role in American history. The Alaska Railroad was completed in 1923 and Harding became the first President to visit the Territory. In the glow of a well-publicized trip, the President hinted that statehood could be obtainable in the near future and Isolationists talked of a place for Alaska in the creation of a Fortress America. The President appointed a new governor shortly after assuming office.

In 1920, Congress passed an Army Reorganization Act which in part read that the Chief of the Militia Bureau would be a National Guard officer appointed by the President from a list of officers nominated by the governors. Although the law did not provide for endorsements by Territorial Governors, the new Governor of Alaska, Scott C. Bone, had reason to believe the Bureau might consider a National Guard unit for Alaska. In December, the Adjutant General of the U.S. Army sent a letter to all governors throughout the Nation. Under Section 3A of the Army Reorganization Act of 1920, the location and designation of units of the National Guard "entirely comprised within the limits of any State or Territory shall be determined by a board, a majority of whom shall be reserve officers who hold or have held commissions in the National Guard and recommended for this duty by the Governor of the State or Territory concerned." Governor Scott Bone realized the mechanism to organize a National Guard unit now existed under law.

The citizen-soldier concept received an additional boost with a letter from the Secretary of War. A month's course in the Citizens' Military Training Corps for 10,800 men had been set up for men between the ages of 16 and 35 years. The Secretary felt that these camps were a vital asset in the "broad scheme of National Defense because they advance the upbuilding of the National Guard and the Organized Reserves." It was his belief that the camps would teach the privileges and responsibilities of American citizenship and stimulate interest in the importance of military training. He urged the Governor to spread the word to young Alaskans.

On March 30, 1925, Governor Bone wrote to the War Department for information concerning the steps necessary to establish a National Guard in the Territory of Alaska. The Chief of the Militia Bureau, Major General George C. Rickards, informed the Governor that he was not authorized to alter in any way the allotments of Guard units to the states. He did, however, forward Governor Bone's request to the Adjutant General of the Army.

The War Department through the Militia Bureau replied to the Governor's letter on May 19, 1925. Governor Bone had requested information because he felt a National Guard could be organized in the Territory with an enlistment of 1,000 men out of a total population of 55,000. The War Department made no allotment for Alaska but would "study the proposition and get back to the Governor when the study was completed." Governor Bone would not remain in office long enough to see the fruits of his work.

George A. Parks was appointed Governor of Alaska by President Calvin Coolidge and took office on August 16, 1925. He continued the effort to establish a National Guard for Alaska. It was true that the Citizens' Military Training Camps were training up to 35,000 men per summer throughout the nation, but Alaska's distance and travel costs virtually eliminated Alaskans from participating on any large scale. The Governor pushed hard for a National Guard unit. On January 19, 1926, he received a letter from Major General Hamond C. Creed, Chief of the Militia Bureau. The Secretary of War had considered Governor Park's request for a National Guard for Alaska but there were no funds for fiscal year 1927-28.

Governor George Parks (1925-1933), himself an Army Reserve Captain, fought to establish a National Guard for Alaska. The Federal Government ignored his concerns for Alaska defense.

The interest in a reserve military organization never waivered in Alaska during the remainder of the 1920s. Some ambitious Colonels in the Territory viewed the National Guard as a way of obtaining the single star of a Brigadier General and the prestige that accompanied that rank. While traveling in the Interior during the summer of 1926, Governor Parks received a letter from his secretary, Harry Watson, who was holding down the fort in Juneau.

James Steese, an able army engineer, requested that his designation be changed to Territorial Director of Public Works and that he be appointed Brigadier General and Adjutant General of the Alaska National Guard. He would serve without compensation since there was no Guard in Alaska and felt the title would be "merely for appearance and added dignity for my term of employment." The Governor went along with the appointment as Director of Public Works, but was unsure of appointing an Adjutant General for a National Guard which had never existed. He asked Watson to research whether there was a precedent for the appointment suggested by Colonel Steese. By the time the Governor arrived downstream on the Yukon River to the small village of Holy Cross, an answer awaited him from Watson. He could find no precedent for appointing Steese to the rank and position of Adjutant General. The decision was based on Chapter 53, Act of May 1894 which outlined the duties of the Governor as ex-officio commander of the militia. Steese would earn his star on the merit of his work as an engineer and take his rightful place in Alaska history.

The nearest thing to having a trained military force to back up the regular army in Alaska during the '20s was the assignment of the 549th Infantry Battalion to the Zone of the Interior. Major Henry R. Sanborn, an Army Reserve infantry officer from Ketchikan, wrote to Governor Parks on February 2, 1927. He had met the Governor in Washington D.C. a few weeks earlier and had now been called back to the War Department. A Colonel Parsons informed Sanborn that the mobilization section of the General Staff had allocated the 549th Infantry Battalion to Alaska. The Governor was to nominate three reserve officers to meet as an allocation board for the assignment of the new unit to various cities in the Territory.

The official letter from Major General J.L. Hines, Commanding General of the Presidio of San Francisco, arrived in Juneau on January 10, 1928. It informed the Governor that the War Department had indeed assigned the new unit to Alaska. Under the National Defense Act of 1920, a board would be assigned by the Governor and it would serve in an inactive status. Major Sanborn, Captain Harry DeVighre of Juneau, Captain Marion Sanders of Ketchikan and Lieutenants Frank Medcalf and D. Mayrven of Juneau would serve on the board.

The reserve officers met to assign members of the battalion to various locations in the Territory. There was some objection by one member of the board to the decision of splitting the machine gun unit into two platoons. Because of the long distance that separated Southeastern Alaska from the Railbelt Area, General Hines felt the suggested division was justified.

It would provide an infantry company and a supporting machine gun platoon along the Alaska Railroad. The General pointed out that in an emer-

Gun Clubs replaced the Home Guard Militia units between the wars. The Nome Veterans held midnight shoots during the longest days of the Arctic summer during the 1920s.
CARRIE MCLAIN MUSEUM, NOME, ALASKA

gency it would be necessary to have a complete organization in that section because it would be one of the first points of attack in the Territory.

As far as can be determined, the 549th Infantry was a phantom battalion that existed on paper—one of many attempts to study Guard and Reserve mobilization plans between the wars. The important point is there was in those years, a pool of Alaskan reserve officers that had helped create the foundation for new interest in the military at the local level. Among them was a Captain George A. Parks, Chemical Warfare Corps, who happened to also be the Governor of Alaska.

Governor George Parks continued to work the National Guard issue during his eight years in office. Between April, 1933 and December, 1939, the problem was handled by President Franklin D. Roosevelt's appointee to the governorship, John W. Troy. The new Governor, a former newspaper owner, had been around Juneau during World War One. He had seen the coming and the going of the Home Guard Militia. He was aware of the unsuccessful struggle by his predecessors to establish a National Guard for the Territory. He had his work cut out for himself and had to accomplish it on a depression-era budget.

The Governor early on realized that Alaska was nearly defenseless in an ever growing hostile world. In his report for 1933, Governor Troy pointed out the need for the building of an international highway through Canada to link Alaska to the rest of the Nation. He asked for the construction of a major air base. The Governor said, "The importance of Alaska's position on the shortest route to the Orient would give it command over the sea and make impossible the hostile movement of fleets of warships or transports against the American Pacific Coast." This Governor would be no more successful in preparing Alaska for war than earlier governors had been.

During the 1920's and 1930's Americans saw the Army and the National Guard used to break up strikes and to dissolve the Bonus Army march on Washington D.C.. In Alaska, the fishing, mining and labor lobbies combined to fight any attempt to establish a National Guard. The Soldiers of the Mists would not reappear until a large amount of real estate had fallen into the hands of Adolf Hitler without a shot being fired.

The slow awakening of an isolationist giant continued at the national level. In Alaska, a remarkable politician would help establish the Alaska National Guard. Governor Ernest Gruening would change the course of Alaska history forever and succeed where others had failed for over seventy years.

INDUCTION OF GUARD ON SEPT. 15

Date When Alaska Boys Will Leave Made Official by Stimson

The Alaska National Guard will be inducted into active duty September 15, it was officially announced last night in a telegram to Governor Ernest Gruening from Secretary of War Henry L. Stimpson.

The order is to affect "all federally recognized elements of th First Battalion, 297th Infantry (the National Guard of the Units States of the Territory of Alasl and all personnel of both the a tive and inactive National Gua assigned thereto," according to t message from Secretary Stimpsol

The move will see control o approximately 300 guardsmen Juneau, Ketchikan, Anchorage i Fairbanks shift from the Terril to the federal War Department ~~minute after midnight on~~ tember 14.

10 Days Later

In less than 10 days after order becomes effective, the will leave for training base Chilkoot Barracks or Port ardson, Maj. Jesse E. Gr Army instructor for the / guard units, said here today

During the period from Se ber 15 until the men leav their training posts, complet sical examinations will be m each man and preparations made for equipping the sold

"Due to poor armory f men living in Juneau may mitted to sleep at home the preparation period befc ing for the training base. ed such arrangement does terfere with his military Major Graham said. Men side Juneau will be prov bunks in the armory, he added. The company will be fed in local restaurants.

Transportation

Although no definite arrangements have been made as yet for transporting men to the training bases, it is hoped that a boat will be available to pick up Company B

Juneau Empire,
August 6, 1941.

KETCHIKAN NAT. GUARD SWORN IN

First Company in Alaska Is Inducted in Federal Service of U. S.

KETCHIKAN, Alaska, Sept. 18.— The first National Guard company in Alaska was inducted into Federal service last night when 59 men were sworn in by Major Jesse Graham, Commanding Officer of Alaska's National Guard.

Gov. Ernest Gruening and Mayor Harry G. McCain participated in the induction of the company.

The Governor pointed out that the American Army is responsible to the American people. He compared the privileges of free men 'in the Army service as free people with those forced to obey "a Fuehrer despot and tyrant."

The Guardsmen are expected to receive their uniforms and guns in about a month. However, they will start drills on Thursday night.

Other National Guard companies will be inducted later at Juneau, Anchorage and Fairbanks.

Daily Empire,
Sept. 18, 1940.

The Alaska National Guard—World War Two

WHEN GOVERNOR GRUENING took the Oath of Office in Juneau on December 6, 1939, the Second World War was already three months old. The new Governor was no stranger to Alaska. The New York born graduate of the Harvard Medical School had found government service more exciting than medicine. He was serving as the Director of the Interior Department's Division of Territories & Island Possessions when Franklin Roosevelt chose him to become Alaska's new governor.

Doctor Gruening had made the grand tour of Alaska with Secretary of Interior Harold Ickes in 1936 and was aware of how unprepared the Territory was for war. Little did he know in 1936 that his future would be linked with Alaska's future. He was destined to become a Governor, an author, a U.S. Senator and an Alaskan for the remainder of his life.

Governor Troy had continued to push for a National Guard during his years in Juneau and had met with some success. The various Rainbow Plans developed by War Department strategists included Plan Orange which dealt with a Pacific War scenario and Alaska. On October 21, 1939, the 297th Infantry Battalion of the Alaska National Guard was constituted. It would take almost two full years to organize it into a fighting force, but Alaska at last had a real National Guard. Preliminary plans were being drawn up by the time the new Governor took office.

Governor Gruening had no honeymoon period when he first took office. Old-time Alaskans, lobbyists and labor unionists looked upon Gruening as merely another outside politician who would be followed by another outside politician. They were alarmed by his views on taxation, fish traps, lobbying tactics by Stateside interests and on the military. They did not realize this Governor of Alaska would have an impact on the country like no other Governor before him.

At the national level, the United States made preparations for the coming war. The Selective Service System was put into effect. The industrial plant started to gear up for war. The military budget began to grow and both the regular military and the National Guard strength authorizations were increased. Joint military war games were carried out in the southern states and Lend-Lease became law. For the first time the United States would enter a major war with a relatively large army (1.6 million in 1941).

The Last Frontier was not a part of this military buildup. As usual, there was a reluctance by the federal government to authorize anything for Alaska. Most defensive preparations had halted with the Naval Disarmament Treaty of 1922. Alaska's Delegate to Congress, Anthony Dimond, fought a losing battle to gain military appropriations for the Territory. He predicted the war would come across the Pacific to Alaska but had no more success in warning the nation than General Billy Mitchell had during the 1920s. Dimond, Gruening and General Simon Buckner, the ranking military officer in Alaska, continued to ask for a military buildup, but could only watch the valuable months slip away while war came ever closer to Alaska and the Nation. Alaska's major military complex—Fort Richardson and Elmendorf Field—was not approved until Hitler's Spring Offensive had overrun much of Western Europe in 1940.

The National Guard's 297th Infantry started out on a very small scale. Some young men around town who had the education or experience to become officers found themselves invited to dinner at the Governor's Mansion. Conversation inevitably led to patriotic duty and the National Guard. Gruening himself urged young men in the streets of Juneau to join the new unit. He had some good material from which to fashion his little army.

Early in 1940, two regular army officers, Major Jesse Graham and Chief Warrant Officer Hamilton Bond, appeared in Juneau to recruit and organize Company A of the 297th Infantry. There were well-educated young men, some with a reserve officer's background, available in the capital city. They would become officers in the new infantry company, the medical detachment and the headquarters detachment. Captain William Redling, a paymaster at the AJ Mine, became Commander of A Company. He would later leave the 297th and become a career officer in the U.S. Army. He would eventually retire as a Major General. Captain Gerald McLaughlin, a

The first muster. The men of Company A.
297TH PHOTO ALBUM

Early Juneau Guardsmen drilled at the city baseball field, before Pearl Harbor. There was no armory. 297TH VETERAN'S ASSOCIATION

Juneau school teacher, joined the unit. He would stay with the 297th in Alaska throughout the war and return to the Territory after law school to become a U.S. Attorney in Anchorage.

Myron Christy was urged to join the 297th by Governor Gruening, among others, and for a time would become Post Commander at Chilkoot Barracks in Haines. He would specialize in logistics and would serve on General Simon Buckner's staff. His experiences during the war in the field of transportation would help him become President of the Western Pacific Railroad.

The first Guardsmen set up a training center in a corrugated iron building in Juneau which had been used for the Southeastern Alaska Fair. Enlistments were pushed and the Juneau company attracted talented soldiers from the area that would serve with distinction in many theaters of the war.

The regular army representatives then moved on to Ketchikan to organize B Company. Here, Captain John VanGilder became Company Commander and organized a fine unit from the townsmen, fishermen, loggers and miners in the area. The soldiers, for the most part, were outdoorsmen or athletes and were in excellent physical shape. Among those who enlisted in Ketchikan were several Japanese Americans who became very special soldiers during World War Two.

To the north, a third authorized company was organized in Fairbanks. Not only were merchants, prospectors and laboring men available for the National Guard, but a pool of college educated men could be found up the road at College Station. Here, Doctor Charles Bunnell was shaping the future University of Alaska. Captain Don Adler became the commander of Company C. Lieutenant Earl Beist-

Lt. Myron Christy remained in the Alaska Theater and rose to the rank of Lt. Colonel. He was a member of General Buckner's staff and was Director of Transportation during the war.
COURTESY MYRON CHRISTY

line would have a career with the University and become a mining consultant following the war.

One of the students at the college, Sherwood Stutz, joined Company C on October 10, 1940, as a charter member. He would stay with the Company until late 1943. He became bored one day while walking guard duty on the Lend-Lease aircraft at Ladd Field destined for Russia. He volunteered for officer training and parachute school and was never

297th Infantry, Alaska National Guard on the road near Haines before World War Two. The Guardsmen were called up on September 15, 1941.

returned to the 297th. He would serve with the 11th and 82nd Airborne Divisions during World War Two and become a Company Commander with the 7th Division during the Korean War. He would win a Silver Star, a Bronze Star and a couple of Purple Hearts before becoming a senior professor of wildlife technology at Penn State University.

In Anchorage, Company D came under the command of Captain William Niemi. He would retire from the Alaska Road Commission following the war. First Lt. Charles Aylworth of Anchorage would be killed in action in the South Pacific. Another Company D soldier, John Hellenthal would become a successful attorney in Anchorage after the war. Many prominent Alaskan natives would become members of the Anchorage unit.

The original authorization order for the Alaska National Guard provided for four companies of infantry, a headquarters detachment and a medical detachment. The Governor asked for a fifth company for Nome but it was not granted. A 129th Observation Squadron was to be organized as an Air Corps arm of the Alaska National Guard, but it never materialized.

The 297th from the beginning was a unique organization made up of colorful Alaskan charac-

ters. They were an independent lot who could do just about anything that was asked of them. At first, there was a fight over whether they would be funded or not. They trained with no weapons at the beginning, but eventually they received boxes of '03 Springfield rifles, then M-1 rifles. The Alaskans preferred the Springfields because they were marksmen. Hitting a standing target was simple compared to hitting a charging bear, a fleet deer or caribou or moose on the run.

The companies drilled as separate small units one night a week at local halls with virtually no contact with each other before the activation in September 1941. The typical drill lasted about three hours and Guardsmen received a couple of dollars for their efforts. Many would recall years later that the training they received made them better soldiers when the big war came along in 1941. There was no annual training period—just the local weekly drills. The Alaskans were physically and mentally suited to become good soldiers. Most of the young men knew war was coming and were enthusiastic about soldiering but felt they would remain in the Territory. There was great comfort in having friends close by. When war did come, many of the original members of the Alaska National Guard would scatter to the four corners of the earth and the 297th ranks within the Territory would be replenished with Alaskan draftees.

On May 17, 1941, Executive Order Number 8756 amended Executive Order 8633 which had been issued on January 14, 1941. These provisions would be the basis for the induction of the Alaska National Guard into federal service on September 15, 1941. By the summer of 1941, Major William R. Mulvihill, a Railway Express agent in Skagway, had set up offices in Juneau and was functioning as Adjutant General of the Alaska National Guard. Things were beginning to move. In August, Lt. Myron Christy began grading papers of officer candidates and Guardsmen were made aware that the call up could come at any time.

The nearest federal military post for the Southeastern companies was at Chilkoot Barracks near Haines. The small, turn of the century military post with its large barrack buildings, parade ground, officer's row and washerwoman's alley harkened back to the more leisurely era of frontier army post life. The mule stables, blacksmith shop, commissary, post exchange, dry cleaning plant, bakery, rifle range and Post garden area made the installation nearly self-sufficient. From the parade ground, the soldiers could view the rugged majestic mountains looming up from the beautiful blue bay. Whales could be seen playing below the free-wheeling eagles who kept track of such things, while occa-

297th drills on the parade grounds in front of Officers Row. The dog was probably the company mascot. 297TH VETERANS ASSOCIATION

The turn-of-the-century barracks at the Haines Post were spartan but adequate. This was typical throughout the U.S. Army before World War Two. 297TH VETERANS ASSOCIATION

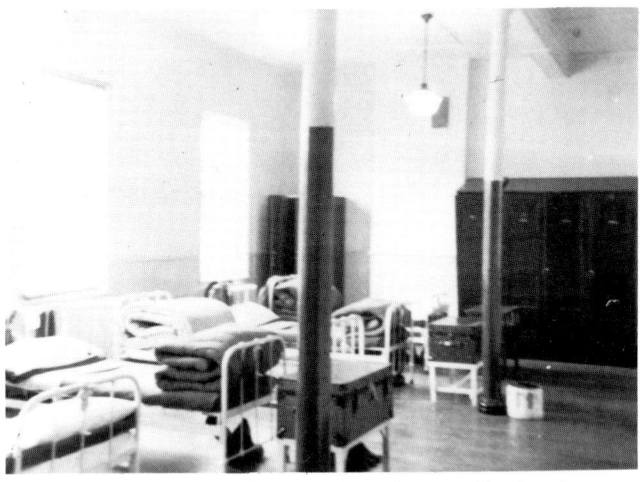

The 297th was called to active duty on September 15, 1941. Companies A and B went to Chilkoot Barracks while C and D went to Fort Richardson near Anchorage. Here, 297th men stand inspection at Chilkoot before World War Two.

COURTESY WM. H. SMITH

The 297th in training at Chilkoot Barracks. Note the World War One style uniforms and equipment. A few months later, the original members of the unit would be scattered all over the world.

297TH VETERANS ASSOCIATION

Company B, 297th was from the Ketchikan area. Here the men fall out for inspection.
297TH VETERANS ASSOCIATION

Two months before the Pearl Harbor attack, life seemed secure at Chilkoot Barracks. Capt. Bill Redling (in jacket) and Lt. George Willey of A Company enjoy a sunny fall day. Captain Redling started out with the Alaska National Guard, remained with the Army after the war and retired as a Major General. COURTESY MYRON CHRISTY

Many of the photos of the early Guardsmen were taken by Wm. H. Smith and Bill Lattin. They left a visual history of the early Alaska Guard. Here 297th men enjoy stories around a campfire.
297TH VETERANS ASSOCIATION

Alaska Guardsman guards approaches to Chilkoot Barracks following the attack on Dutch Harbor. COURTESY MYRON CHRISTY

sionally a fishing boat would slip out of the small town of Haines. On Sundays, soldiers could climb the mountains, fish from the army dock or hike up the old Dalton Trail towards the Canadian border. They could explore the scenic Chilkoot and Chilkat River Valleys, talk to old-time prospectors and marvel at the Tlingit legends that abounded in the country.

During the fall of 1941, the Alaska Guardsmen arrived and settled into garrison life along with the handful of regular army personnel who inhabited the post. They had come north by boat—some on the fifty-plus-year-old army boat, *Fornance*—and were amazed they had completed the trip in one piece. Many of the Alaskans had never been north of Juneau and indeed, some had no idea where Chilkoot Barracks was located when they were called to duty.

During the crisp days of autumn, the newly arrived soldiers of the 297th Infantry Battalion began to learn the finer points of soldiering. The sounds of close-order drill and the rifle range echoed across the post to the water and rebounded from the mountains. They observed the first touch of winter's hand on the highest mountain peaks and watched the white line of snow advance down to the golden line of trees which reached up the backbone of the Coastal Mountains. The two lines would meet briefly, then winter would dominate and the post would settle down to a train and drill routine. The young Guardsmen were as near to heaven as they could come before the swollen God of War would touch their lives and lead them to far different fields. Fifty years later, they would remember fondly those prewar months they spent at Chilkoot Barracks.

To the north, the other half of the 297th Infantry received their marching orders. They reported to a partly built Fort Richardson near Anchorage. Here, the frenzied construction efforts of an almost-too-late government were creating a boom economy for the railroad town on Cook Inlet. Again, the beauty of the land overshadowed a drab army post where Guardsmen learned the techniques of war.

At eye level, the soldiers marched through trails of yellow leaves clinging to white birch trees and patches of willow interspersed with scrubby green spruce. The clear clean air was perfumed by the strange musty smell of overripe highbush cranberries. Lifting their eyes, the Guardsmen saw the upper meadows of the rugged Chugach Mountains turn to a blaze of red as frosts touched the unending carpet of wild blueberries. Here the bears fattened themselves before the long sleep of winter, while overhead, long lines of Canadian geese aimed their V formations south seeking a new comfort zone. The wild geese would never know the color-

ful Northern Lights that would dance across the winter skies for those who stayed.

In 1942, some of the Guardsmen from Chilkoot Barracks would join the men of C and D Companies at Fort Richardson. The 297th Battalion would perform an amazing variety of missions throughout the Territory during the war. They would leave a chapter of history which was practically forgotten for half a century, except in their own minds. What they did for Alaska and the Nation was essential to assure a victory in 1945.

At Haines, Companies A and B would fall out in front of the barracks each morning for roll call and inspection. After breakfast, the soldiers would train and drill. In their spare time many of the men took part in athletic events. There were basketball games and boxing matches on base, while a few soldiers sought entertainment at a local tavern in Haines where illegal card games often took place upstairs. Relations between the soldiers and townspeople were amicable. The military pay was a welcome addition to the small town's economy and some townspeople worked on the post. On Thanksgiving Day in 1941, a full-course dinner with all the trimmings was served to the men of the 297th. They would be at war two weeks later.

By December, the weather had turned cold. The bugler still blew reveille at 6 A.M. but his lips sometimes stuck to the mouthpiece and an imperfect melody would drift across the parade ground to awake the troops. The army supply boat which brought food for the troops did not shown up for a while that winter. A company cook got a little drunk on vanilla extract at the mess hall one morning. He made a comment to one of the KP's on duty: "Have you noticed there are a lot less army mules on post now than when we first arrived in September?" The steaks served to the Guardsmen that evening were left untouched. The next day the steaks were cut up and added to a stew which the Guardsmen ignored. What was left of the meat was ground up and served in a soup that night which was finally eaten up by the hungry Guardsmen.

On December 7, 1941, Corporal Max Lewis was out skiing with some other soldiers. Earlier that morning, Lt. Myron Christy had been awakened and given a message that had just come in from the Alaska Communications System network. It informed the post: "Japanese negotiations have broken down—a Japanese task force is on the high seas— fire on any target within the three mile limit." The serious tone of the message convinced the Lieutenant he should awaken Colonel Graham. The colonel read the message and commented, "I don't think our .30 calibers will reach that far."

At 10 A.M. Sergeant Pat Hagiwara was forming

up the guard for a change at 11 A.M.. Private Jimmy Tatsuda of Ketchikan was one of the first soldiers to hear the attack message at the PBX Center. He took the news to the Post Commander. Private Larry Butke came running outside shouting, "It's on the radio—Pearl Harbor is being bombed." Some of the men gathered in the barracks around a radio and listened to the news. As the casualty list was read, it was reported that an Ensign Ervin Thompson of Ketchikan, Alaska, had been killed on the USS *Oklahoma*. Pat Hagiwara heard the name, turned and saw the Ensign's brother Chris, a 297th cook standing behind him. Chris Thompson turned without a word and walked out of the barracks towards the parade ground. War had become a personal thing for the men of the 297th—not some far off historical happening.

Colonel Graham called for a meeting of all the officers and non-commissioned officers at the base gym and informed them, "Pearl Harbor has just been bombed. We are at war with Japan. We must organize our defenses." The old army steamer *Fornance* was cranked up as it had the largest gun at Haines mounted on its bow—a 57 MM tank gun. The rest of the weaponry consisted primarily of rifles, .30 caliber machine guns and some .50 caliber machine guns with no ammunition. There were some anti-tank guns but no ammunition for them. Men off post were called back to duty.

Private Vince Anderson of Juneau was on guard duty. When Corporal Max Lewis returned from skiing, he was ordered to halt and give the password. One of the guards informed him that Pearl Harbor had just been bombed. "Where is Pearl Harbor?" asked Lewis. "I don't, know," answered the guard."Have you ever hear of it?" the Corporal asked. "No," answered the guard.

War had finally come to the distant frontier. Isolationism had become a liability and unknown Alaska would become a household word as hundreds of thousands of men and women would pass through the Territory during the course of the war. One golden age of adventure had ended as another began. Many young Americans would discover a land of beauty and opportunity while others would only recall the bleakness of the Aleutians, the mosquito-infested muskegs and the bitter cold. Some would pay the supreme price of war and never return home. Whatever their draw in the gamble of war, they left their mark on a land that would never be forgotten again.

Within a short time following the outbreak of war, Alaskans began to adjust to a new style of life. All the wasted years came back to haunt communities preparing for war. Alaskans knew full well the Great Circle Route to the Orient shortened the war distance in both directions. Blackout curtains became a part of interior decorating from the Arctic to Ketchikan. Civil Defense and air-raid drills became commonplace. Alaskans with skills in boating, construction, transportation or knowledge of permafrost, hidden bays, inlets and places suitable for airfields became very employable. Many who qualified were already in the military. They were members of the Alaska National Guard.

At Chilkoot Barracks, outposts were set up around the perimeter of the post. They were manned by three eight-hour shifts of guards. When the snow fell, the men went to the sites on snowshoes. For some reason, the sergeants had larger and better snowshoes than the private soldiers. The men of the 297th were used to guard a variety of facilities early in the war.

Corporal Max Lewis was sent with his twenty-two ski students to Skagway. They were put up in the roundhouse of the White Pass and Yukon Railroad. Their job was to guard every culvert and bridge on the railroad up to Crystal Lake. The corporal spent long hours organizing and deploying his men. He returned to Skagway one night after going without sleep for 34 hours. He had just taken off one boot while sitting on his bunk when a sentry came in and interrupted his long awaited sleep.

"Are you Lewis?" asked the guard.

"Yes," replied the sleepy soldier.

"Put on your boot. You are leaving on a boat immediately for Fort Benning and Officer's School."

Max Lewis would never again see some of his 297th friends and he would not meet up with others for 44 years. His war would be fought in far-off Europe. He would return after the war with a chest full of medals, an English war bride and scars on his body he would carry for the rest of his life.

Going the opposite direction was Charles Johnson who had joined Company C in Fairbanks in May, 1941. He, too, went through Officer's School in April, 1942, and would serve in the 71st and 89th Divisions in the Pacific during the war. He became a member of the 5307th, which was known as "Merrill's Marauders" and fought in the battles of North Burma. Another member of Company C, Herman Rosenstein, would win his Silver Star in North Africa. It is interesting to note that every single Guardsman of the original Company B, 297th Infantry, Alaska National Guard, became an officer or non-commissioned officer during the course of the war.

One of the more unpleasant duties performed by the 297th was the rounding up of Japanese-American families living in Alaska. Private Vince Anderson took part in this operation. Some of the Japanese-Americans, including the owner of the popular City Cafe in Juneau, were held for a time at the Haines Military Post. Anderson had to march the interned at gunpoint to a cafe in Haines to get them fed. The Juneau soldier knew some of them as personal friends. Another Guardsman, Sergeant Pat Hagiwara, helped to guard fellow Japanese-American citizens while they exercised daily on the post parade ground. Some of Japanese-Alaskans were sent to Anchorage, then to Puyallup, Washington. From there, some went to Idaho, California, Chicago and New Mexico. Those families living in Southeastern Alaska were gathered up and sent south by ship.

The Alaska National Guard had several second generation Japanese-Americans within its ranks. Because they were first of all Americans, then Alaskans and then soldiers, they earned a very special place in the history of the National Guard. Their story is unique, yet almost unknown by most citizens of Alaska.

Pat Hagiwara's parents owned the Alaska Home Bakery in Ketchikan. They were one of several highly respected, hard-working Japanese-American families in town. In 1940, Captain VanGilder of the National Guard convinced the well-known local athlete that if he joined up, other friends would also join the new unit. Pat's father was reluctant at first to let his son join, but he had always stressed to his sons that they should do their part for their country, so Pat became a Guardsman. By the time the Juneau unit was called to federal service in 1941, he had become the company Drill Sergeant. The Tatsuda boys in Ketchikan also became members of the unit.

While the company was still drilling in Ketchikan, an Immigration Officer stopped Pat one day and said, "If there is a war with Japan, who will you fight for?" He was asked the same question in October of 1941 at Chilkoot Barracks by an FBI Agent. "I was so naive," said Pat, "that I thought—what a stupid question. I am an American soldier, I'll do my duty." The Japanese-Americans of the Alaska National Guard would more than "do their duty" during World War Two. By Thanksgiving Day, 1941, they were shooting at targets on which had been painted faces of Hitler and Tojo.

Early in 1942, Captain VanGilder learned that his Japanese Guardsmen were being shipped out. Lieutenant Cochran went to the Commander to argue against the decision. "I'm losing my best soldiers," said the Lieutenant. The popular soldiers would be put on a boat and shipped south. The ship stopped briefly in Ketchikan where the Guardsmen went ashore to check on their families. The fathers were being held in confinement on Annette Island and Pat Hagiwara managed to see his father before going on to Fort Lewis, Washington. They were not allowed to remain with the 44th Division and were shipped out again. Pat Hagiwara and Jimmy Tatsuda went to Fort Sheridan, Illinois, where Pat drilled 6th Services doctors and nurses and Jimmy served as a company clerk. Another Japanese-American Guardsman from Wrangell went to Cairo, Egypt, to train dogs for the K-9 Corps.

In December of 1943 Pat was reassigned to Camp Shelby, Mississippi, as a drill sergeant. Here he joined a new replacement unit of Japanese-American soldiers who would become members of an elite force. The 442nd Regimental Combat Team would become America's most decorated organization during World War Two. In March, the Ketchikan soldier was assigned to Headquarters, Second Battalion, Anti-tank Company of the 442nd.

The Camp Shelby scene was a strange one. The Japanese-American sons from Hawaii did not mix well with the Mainlanders from California. They resented being told what to do by the Mainland training cadre. The Hawaiians were looked upon as being rich and spoiled by the Mainlanders and fist-fights were an everyday event. At first, the locals in Mississippi discriminated against the Japanese-American soldiers. The Hawaiians seemed to have an unlimited supply of money sent from home and became known as big spenders. They often left a five-dollar tip for a three-dollar meal. The Alaskans were probably the poorest of the lot but quickly allied themselves with the free-spending Hawaiians and were treated royally by the locals. Once the 442nd organized and shipped out, they unified and became one of America's premier fighting teams.

The 100th Battalion of the 442nd had already fought its way through North Africa, Salerno, and the battle for the Abbey of Monte Cassino before Pat arrived in Italy. The 100th was the famed Purple Heart Battalion. Pat's brother Mike was wounded at Hill 140 in Italy on July 4, 1943. The 442nd was a close-knit organization. So many brothers, uncles and cousins served in the organization that when the outfit was pulled out of the lines, survivors would look up relatives in the rest areas to see if they were still alive.

Pat went into combat on June 26, 1944. He asked a 442nd veteran, "How accurate is German firepower?" He was told, "You open up your back pocket and the Germans will put a mortar shell in it." He would end his war on the French-Italian border. From the basketball court of Ketchikan High School through the fighting in Italy was quite a stretch of the legs for the young Ketchikan soldier.

Two brothers from Ketchikan, Jimmy and Charlie Tatsuda of the 297th Infantry also contributed to America's victory. Jimmy Tatsuda served

Sgt. Pat Hagiwara and friends enjoy a rare sunny day in downtown Ketchikan, October 1941. Two months later they would be caught up in World War Two. COURTESY PAT HAGIWARA

in the famed 442nd Regimental Combat Team. He was in on the Lost Battalion Mission where some of the heaviest fighting took place and served as a Staff Sergeant and Platoon Leader in Company K. Of the 250 men in his outfit, only 17 had escaped death or injury by war's end. Jimmy Tatsuda earned three Purple Hearts. He was wounded in the shoulder in Italy, in the leg in France and picked up schrapnel in his ankle when the unit went back to Italy towards the end of the war. The slight Ketchikan soldier saw the bodies of Mussolini and his mistress hanging from a lamp post in Northern Italy. After the war, he returned to Ketchikan to become a much-beloved figure in the wet Gateway City of Alaska.

Charlie Tatsuda's wartime career took place on the other side of the war. This 297th veteran was a graduate of the University of Washington. A poll was taken following Pearl Harbor to determine the least prejudiced section of America. Fort Snelling, Minnesota, was judged best and became the home of a Military Intelligence School. Charlie was trained here and became an intelligence officer for the U.S. Army. He would parachute into Luzon with the 11th Airborne Division. The Major's greatest fear was that of being found in an American uniform and shot as a spy by some uninformed American G.I. One can only speculate how vital Charlie Tatsuda's efforts were in shortening the war in the Pacific. He would return to Minneapolis to a successful law career after the war. These citizens all proved to be great American soldiers and they were all proud to be Alaskan Guardsmen.

One of the other great Alaskan soldiers to come out of the Second World War was a wiry bundle of energy from Juneau named Max Lewis. He was the son of a famous sculptor and would become an art

Pat Hagiwara in training with the 442nd Regimental Combat Team at Camp Shelby, Mississippi. A few months later he saw his first action against German soldiers in Italy. COURTESY PAT HAGIWARA

Sergeant Pat Hagiwara. The young Ketchikan Guardsman was one of several Japanese-Americans from Alaska who fought with the famed 442nd Regimental Combat Team in Europe. Photo was taken somewhere in France in 1944. COURTESY PAT HAGIWARA

Corporal Max Lewis (nearest curb) and friend. The young Guardsman from Juneau was a superb athlete. He graduated from OCS, became a combat scout in the 95th Division and fought in General Patton's 3d Army. COURTESY MAX LEWIS

Max Lewis, combat scout in training before being sent to Europe. He won a Silver Star in Patton's Army but was severely wounded near Metz, France. COURTESY MAX LEWIS

Captain Max Lewis and his English war bride were married at Salisbury Cathedral in 1945. The couple live at Thane, near Juneau where they raised a family. The highly decorated Guardsman is a retired Juneau-Douglas High School teacher. COURTESY MAX LEWIS

teacher at Juneau-Douglas High School after the war. The father designed the famous statue of a gold rush prospector, which stands in front of the Sitka Pioneer Home. Max helped his father cast the statue.

The model was to be the likeness of George Carmack, the prospector whose discovery of gold kicked off the great Klondike Gold Rush of 1897–98. The old prospector's first wife had been an Indian princess. After she died, Carmack took a second wife and Max could remember her coming to his father's studio while the statue was being worked on. She sort of looked like one of the old-time dancehall girls that once graced the streets of Dawson City.

After the statue was completed, the Seattle Yukon-Alaska Pioneers Lodge which was footing the bill, insisted on a likeness of one of its members— Skagway Bill Fonda. Max and his father carefully removed George Carmack's head from the statue and attached the sculptured head of the former real estate agent. No one was the wiser, the commission was paid, and the body of one man with another man's head gazes out at the beautiful Sitka water front year after year for the benefit of Alaskans and tourists visiting the former capital of Russian America.

The father did statues of Presidents Wilson and Hoover in Washington D.C. and Max accompanied his father to Nome when he was 13 years old and met Roald Amundsen. They were there to unveil his father's statue of the famed polar explorer.

Max Lewis put a 150 percent effort into every-

thing he attempted and made an excellent soldier. After completing officer's training, he was sent to Europe to the 3d Battalion, 379th Infantry of the 95th Division. Because he was an Alaskan and an athlete, it was determined he should be a Combat Scout in Patton's Third Army.

He won a Silver Star with the Division, but near Metz, France, a round of artillery fire landed at his feet. His Sergeant, Jiggs Ritter, was severely wounded. The Lieutenant from Juneau had all the ligaments cut out of his right knee. His colon was torn out, four ribs broken, lungs and chest filled with schrapnel and both eyes were split open. He was sent back to a hospital in England to heal and was told he would be sent back to the States for a medical discharge.

When the soldier heard his unit was involved in heavy fighting at the front he skipped out of the hospital, hitched a ride to Southampton and made it across the channel. He caught jeep and truck rides across France and reported to his Battalion near Aachen, Germany. His Battalion Commander said, "Lewis, you are supposed to be dead. There is no way you could have survived that." With wounds still draining, he asked to command his Combat Scouts again. The Colonel said, "No way—you run around out in front of the lines too much." He was made Commander of L Company and Captain Lewis fought through three more major campaigns—The Bulge, The Rhine and The Rhone. General Patton called the 95th Division the Iron Men of Metz.

The old soldier came home to a 27-year teaching career. He enjoyed hiking and skiing in the beautiful mountains around Juneau despite his war wounds and inspired generations of young people to enjoy the good life of physical fitness.

"I would have volunteered for Operation
Desert Storm if they would have taken me."
—Captain Max Lewis
Age 76—1991

By the spring of 1942, many of the original Guardsmen of the 297th had departed to become a part of the history of other army organizations. Those who remained in Alaska were joined by draftees to take part in some of the most unusual missions of the war. Colonel William C. Walther remained as Commander of the Battalion. He said, "The men of the 297th were especially talented, self-reliant and innovative, and able to do anything required of them. Outstanding personalities and characters? The battalion was full of them."

General Simon Buckner came to rely on the 297th increasingly as the war in Alaska progressed. If a mission needed to be carried out he would often turn to the Alaskans because they knew the land and possessed the skills to complete the assignment. The only negative argument concerning the 297th was their tendency to downplay the strict military discipline the regular army seemed to enjoy trying to enforce. One frustrated regular army officer lamented, "You Alaskans are all alike—you are too damned independent." Had he studied history, he would have known he was mouthing a two-hundred-year-old universal complaint which had been lodged against all American Frontiersmen.

Many of the Guardsmen from Southeastern Alaska had grown up around boats and the fishing industry. Mountains of supplies had to follow the military forces engaged in dislodging Japanese forces occupying the Aleutian Islands. The operation would have been a logistic nightmare without an organization called the Harborcraft. A fleet of

Many men from the 297th served in the U.S. Army's Harborcraft. They ran a variety of ships, barges and tugs to carry supplies and personnel wherever needed. The seagoing soldiers worked constantly in dangerous conditions.
297TH VETERANS ASSOCIATION

army boats which included tugs, power barges, landing craft, container reefers, tankers, and the wooden hulled ship "Brown Bear" kept freight and passengers moving during the war. Guardsmen familiar with boat operations were assigned to the Harborcraft unit.

At one time during the war, there were between 600–700 personnel assigned to the Harborcraft. Among those army sailors was Vince Anderson, 297th machine gun operator and Juneau fisherman. He had been drafted in 1941 and was at Chilkoot Barracks when the war started. He was sent back to Juneau to pick up his fishing boat, then fished for the army to add variety to the messhall fare. His boat was once held in port because a crewman had run up a tab at the local house of ill-repute. When the lady of the house was paid in full, the boat was allowed to proceed on its government mission.

One of the Harborcraft skippers had a still aboard his boat which was hidden inside a metal fire extinguisher. An army inspector picked up the

Vince Anderson became a skipper in the Army's Harborcraft. He sailed the dangerous waters of the Aleutian Islands and fished for the U.S. Army during the war. He still captains his own tug between Seattle and Alaska at 75 years of age.

fire extinguisher and discovered the still. He was told the apparatus was used to distill water for the boat's battery system. The naive officer noted in his report that all Harborcraft boats should have a similar setup.

Anderson skippered his boat throughout the war, often sailing from Seward or Seldovia out to the Aleutian Islands through some of the world's worst weather. Often, the Harborcraft had to make it into a hidden bay to ride out a storm. Some boats and crews never made it. Long days and nights were spent by the army crewmen who sailed the waters of the Aleutians. Ice often had to be chipped from the boats lest they became top heavy and capsized in the rough seas. Tug service was essential during the Aleutian Campaign.

Vince Anderson established a historical first for World War Two. He was the only army skipper to be court-martialled and busted for sneaking a woman out to the Aleutian Islands. The woman had talked her way into the trip at Seward. She cut her hair and dressed up like a GI for the trip. The boat was inspected at every port on the way to Adak, but the woman was not detected until they reached the final stop. The 297th skipper was up for promotion to Warrant Officer but lost his chance to ever become an Officer and a Gentleman.

The world of Harborcraft was dangerous but vital. The Army Transport Service had power scows at Massacre Bay during the Aleutian Campaign.

They lost a liberty ship and the U.S. Attack Transport *Cleveland* blew up in Yakutat. Three medium tugs were lost going around Cape Spencer and a T-2 tanker broke up. The stern of the *Sackett Harbor* continued to float so the Army Transport Service hauled it up to Anchorage where it was used to house a power plant for the city. Wherever the Harborcraft sailed, there were 297th men who served the Nation from highly unlikely duty stations.

Early in the war, the decision to build the Alaska-Canada International Highway was arrived at following a series of lengthy meetings of the International Commission. Governor Gruening had favored an "A" route. He felt this route was less costly, shorter and closer to the Territory. Side roads could be built to Southeastern Alaska's isolated towns on the coast. The Canadians pushed for a more eastern route to open up a huge section of their North-western Frontier. Route "C" was chosen because the Canadians had built three airports they wished to connect by road—Fort St. John, Fort Nelson and Watson Lake. Although Gruening lost out on his choice of a western route, he did convince the Corps of Engineers they should extend one branch road across the mountains to the port of Haines. The 297th played a major part in selling the Corps the idea of a Haines cutoff road. The battalion contributed to the building of the main Alcan Highway as well.

As men left Chilkoot Barracks, the remaining 297th personnel began to be used for a variety of jobs. Captain Myron Christy sent 297th men to Skagway to unload material being sent in for the construction of the Alaska Highway. They worked alongside a black Port Company and pulled guard duty along the railroad. Some 297th men went inland to the Alcan Highway construction sites. Captain Christy did an inspection trip during the winter of 1943. He came across two black engineers warming their hands over a small fire.

"Where you from Sergeant?"

"Mississippi, Sir."

"And what do you do on the Alcan Project?"

"Mostly try to keep warm, Sir."

The hard working black troops played a significant role in the completion of the huge project. They also unloaded ships in the Aleutians during the shooting war.

As conditions became more crowded in Skagway and vital material began to back up on the docks, Captain Christy and Colonel Graham got the idea of extending the old Dalton Trail out of Haines as an alternate route to the Alaska Highway. The 297th cut logs on base and built an extension on to the army dock so that larger ships could be

297th men helped in the construction of the Alcan Highway. Two 297th officers shake hands at the Alaska-Canada border.

tion of greater responsibility. He would be promoted to Major and become Assistant Chief of Staff for General Buckner in Anchorage.

A half dozen 297th men went off to become members of Colonel Lawrence V. Castner's Alaskan Combat Intelligence Platoon. They would perform legendary feats in daring reconnaissance missions during the Aleutian Island Campaign. They were called "Castner's Cutthroats" or simply the Alaskan Scouts. A few others, like Pete Esquiro of Sitka, transferred to the Army Air Corps' 924th Emergency Rescue Boat Squadron which became part of the USAAF 10th Rescue Group. They picked up downed pilots in PT-type crash boats during the Aleutian Island war.

Major Christy reported in to General Buckner at Fort Richardson on June 18, 1943, and became a member of his staff. The Guardsman became so indispensable to the General that when Buckner moved on to head up the invasion of Okinawa late in the war, he requested Christy by name to join his staff in the Pacific. Buckner's replacement needed Lt. Colonel Christy to continue as Chief of Transportation so the Guardsman finished out the war in Alaska. He may not have survived Okinawa. General Buckner and some of his staff died on the far distant island.

The Alaska Guard officer found General Buckner easy to work with. For the most part, he was quite friendly and informal on a day-to-day basis. He was often accompanied by his two Springer Spaniels when off-duty and was well-liked by his staff. He was a soldier's soldier and made it a habit to get up front to visit his troops. The General loved four things beyond soldiering: Mrs. Buckner, duck hunting, Bourbon & Branch and Alaska. He had plans to return to Alaska after the war to live out his life. Much of his appreciation for Alaskans came about by his association with the "can do" 297th Battalion.

Initially, the 297th Infantry was 100 percent Alaskan. Native Alaskans who were drafted into military service did their basic training with the 297th at Fort Richardson. Some stayed with the Battalion in Alaska for the duration of the war. Others were reassigned and served throughout the world. Non-native Alaskans also trained with the 297th and many remained in the Territory with the battalion. Later, outside draftee replacements filled in the ranks.

Whenever an odd job came up in Alaska for the military, General Buckner would say: "How about the 297th?"

"Well, there are no quarters available for the troops there."

"That's alright," the General would reply, "they

unloaded at Haines. A couple of 297th natives from the village of Klukwan near Haines were familiar with the country towards the Canadian border. They accompanied a civilian from Skagway on horseback to map and survey a route for the Haines cutoff. A proposal was written up by Captain Christy and accepted by the Army. Captain Christy, who was now working with the Department of Public Roads, was there in November of 1942 when the McDonald Construction Company began building the road.

The 93d Black Engineering Regiment moved to Chilkoot Barracks in November 1942 and worked until March of 1943. They would move out to the Aleutians to do their share in pushing the Japanese out of Alaskan territory. By now, the 297th was pretty well scattered all over the Territory. Captain Christy, too, would leave in June of 1943 to a posi-

will build their own."

As a result, the 297th Infantry saw more of Alaska than any other group of soldiers during the war. They guarded the Richardson Highway and salvaged rail from the abandoned Chitina-Copper River Railroad. They guarded the bridge at Carcross in the Yukon Territory and the north end of the Alaska Highway. Company C guarded Lend-Lease aircraft at Ladd Field in Fairbanks until Russian pilots could fly them on to Siberia. 297th men also guarded the Alaska Railroad tunnel at the Port of Whittier and the Canol Pipeline that brought vital petroleum to the war effort. They roamed Alaska from Ketchikan to the Arctic. They served in the Aleutians, at remote sites in the interior and guarded seals in the Pribilof Islands in the Bering Sea.

When the 297th was not being used for guard duty, it unloaded ships, helped build military bases, fished, ran boats, tested equipment, and trained soldiers. It performed search and rescue missions and carried out hundreds of other vital assignments throughout the war.

At Valdez, the Headquarters detachment, the Medical detachment and most of Company C unloaded ships and helped construct a garrison site near town for troops assigned to the area. A ski patrol got caught on Valdez Glacier and survived a series of avalanches and a severe storm, but one soldier fell into a crevasse and remained buried forever in an icy grave. Private Edward Jackinsky was awarded the Soldier's Medal for heroism for his part in a rescue effort. The presentation of the medal was pure 297th. It may have been the first such ceremony ever performed by American soldiers on snowshoes.

Some aspects of military life were actually enjoyed by the Alaskans. They could usually find time to fish and hunt wherever they were sent and were accepted as fellow Alaskans by the locals. They did not have to get used to the weather like outside troops and enjoyed the opportunity to see new parts of their vast homeland. They could enjoy nature and the beauty of the country without daydreaming about a far-off hometown. They could only wonder at the stateside GI's who cursed the land and counted the days before they could return to Chicago, Flatbush, the wastelands of New Jersey or Cripple Creek, Nebraska. Their world was one of peaked mountains, white silence, wildlife, Northern Lights, clean air and blessed room enough. The Northland magic would work on the spirit of thousands of outsiders as well and they, too, would become Alaskans when the war ended.

One of the 297th men stationed at Northway for the construction of the airfield there "salted" a gravel pile with a gold nugget. After his "discovery" was announced, the gravel pile was attacked by hundreds of GI's with shovels seeking their fortune in the Far North. Certain platoons of the 297th moved around a great deal. There were jobs to be done in Galena, Portage, Nenana, McGrath, Attu, Excursion Inlet and at Moses Point on Norton Bay.

One of the most unusual missions during the war occurred when Company B, 297th Infantry departed Chilkoot Barracks on August 7, 1942, for Moses Point, Alaska. A Japanese task force had been reported in the Bering Sea area and it was feared a landing might be attempted at Nome or in the fur-rich Pribilof Islands. The men were to spend 43 crowded, cramped days at sea on this journey to the Seward Peninsula. The first platoon remained at Moses Point while the rest went on to St. Paul Island. Another small group went on to St. George Island. They would remain on this isolated duty until September, 1943.

When the 297th men arrived in the Islands, they discovered the Navy had evacuated the natives and had given the inhabitants only a few hours notice they were leaving their homes. Household goods were left as if the people would soon return and there were some indications Japanese may have briefly visited the Islands. The buildings on St. Paul Island would be used by the 297th soldiers and some regular army troops. The tour consisted primarily of guard duty, sitting and waiting, inspections and close order drill. The weather was bleak most of the time and the men were kept busy with routine army life to keep up morale and to pass the time.

The small group sent to St. George Island for a year found even less to do. They did fish for halibut and set crab pots to vary the army rations diet. At one point during the tour, the group at St. Paul (which felt sorry for those few at St. George) sent a barge with food, tobacco and other supplies to St. George in the dead of winter. It was a good 40-mile trip across an unfriendly sea and perhaps a foolish thing to do. They had motor problems, then the sea grew rougher. The barge almost made it but lost its cargo just before it reached the St. George men.

On St. Paul, a young lieutenant fresh from California insisted on going out on patrol during a whiteout. A couple of Alaskans were sent out to look for him but he was never found. He probably wandered out onto the inshore ice and disappeared into the Bering Sea. One of Captain Gerald McLaughlin's toughest jobs was writing a letter to the missing man's mother.

Duty was boring in the bitter winter weather on the far side of civilization. A heavy weapons platoon became an anti-aircraft unit and would

Company C, 208th Infantry Battalion (separate) at Ladd Field in May 1944. Companies C and D traveled all over Alaska during the war to do everything, everywhere. 297TH VETERANS ASSOCIATION

search the skies day after day for enemy activity. An inspecting officer was sent out from Fort Richardson. He was appalled at the unit's lack of knowledge about camouflage techniques. He ranted and raved and wondered why the 297th men just stood there listening to the chewing out with a grin on their faces. He never did figure out he was standing on top of their cleverly hidden and camouflaged still.

Guard posts were set up at strategic locations around the islands. The guards did 30-day and sometimes 60-day stints on St. Paul Island. The men on the two islands were separated for almost a year. Once, the army forgot to send food to the islands, so the men shot reindeer and survived from the sea. At one point in time, the men ate canned beets three times a day for nearly a year. The food situation became so bad the men threatened to go directly to the Commanding General of Alaska. The army finally sent a barge out with food along with a paymaster because the men had not been paid for nearly a year. However, a storm sank the barge and the paymaster and the pay went down with the ship.

Mail was another problem. Letters were frequently a year old. Once, an arrangement was made to fly the mail out to St. Paul Island. The 297th men were so anxious to receive their mail that they lined the airstrip and waved at the pilot as he flew low to have a look at the landing strip. To the men's great disappointment, the plane turned and flew off. The pilot had been instructed if the landing strip was too soft to land on he would be waved off.

The men of the islands left in September of 1944 after spending a year on isolated duty. The war had moved on while they manned their lonely outposts. About the only thing that had changed was their name. The 297th Infantry Battalion (Separate) had been designated the 208th Infantry Battalion

Duty was desolate, harsh and boring in the Aleutian Islands for the men of the 297th. This is a typical field quarters for the men. Note the igloo entrance (1943). COURTESY C. MIDDLETON. 297TH INFANTRY

(Separate) on January 26, 1944. The name change had not modified their daily routine. Their war had been one of survival and boredom. However insignificant their contribution may have seemed at the time, it was an important junction that had to be manned on the road to victory. The footprints would vanish from the sands and muskegs of Northwestern Alaska, but the accomplishments would be

Five of baseball's best visit the troops in Anchorage in 1944. Left to right: Hank Borowy, Frankie Frisch, Stan Musial, Dixie Walker and Dan Litwhiler. COURTESY C. MIDDLETON, 297TH INFANTRY

recorded in the memories of others who had or would serve as Soldiers of the Mists on the Bering Sea frontier.

Christmas of 1944 was spent at Attu. Even Attu seemed an improvement over where they had been. The food was better and there were things to do. The soldiers could explore the Japanese fortifications and listen to the music and talk of Tokyo Rose on the radio. Somewhere beyond Attu there was still a war and some of them would shortly head in that direction.

The Battalion had been scattered throughout the Territory of Alaska almost from its inception before the war. Towards the end of 1944, the elements began to centralize towards Anchorage to become a unified command for the first time. However, the 208th Infantry Battalion would not remain in Alaska. Portions of the unit were moved to Camp Earle, Alaska, then left on the hospital ship

Dorthea Dix and arrived at the Seattle Port of Embarkation on February 25, 1945. The men spent a couple of days at Fort Lawton, Washington, then moved on to Camp Gruber, Oklahoma. By April 28, 1945, they had moved by troop train to Camp Shelby, Mississippi—the last stop of a long historical journey.

The 297th men who had served out the war on the boats of the U.S. Harborcraft, in many cases, took Alaska discharges and simply went home. Many of the boats were gathered in a bay at Seward and sold as surplus for very low prices. The 297th Skipper from Juneau, Vince Anderson, was ordered to take the old army boat, U.S. *Fornance* south to be broken up. It was a tense trip as the old boat had been condemned before it left Alaska. The Alaska Guardsman nursed it all the way to Jacksonville, Florida.

On May 16, 1945, the 208th Battalion was inactivated at Camp Shelby, Mississippi. The men who were there were reassigned and scattered all over the globe as parts of other commands. Once more, Alaska's soldiers disappeared and the Territory lost the remnant of its National Guard. It did, however, have a militia on duty at home. Some former 297th men remained in Alaska when the Battalion left the Territory; and the numerical designations 297th and 208th would return someday after a prolonged fight. Governor Ernest Gruening would see to that.

New Soldiers of the Mists were emerging to serve Alaska almost from the moment the original National Guard was called to Federal Service in September of 1941. When the Governor sent forth a call for defense, it would be answered by an unpaid militia, just as it had been during the First World War. This new force would be called the Alaska Territorial Guard.

Founding fathers of the Alaska Army National Guard. 297th infantry veterans return to Anchorage, Alaska, in 1989, nearly 50 years after entering military service. Some had not met since 1942. They saw action all over the world. OFFICIAL ALASKA AIR NATIONAL GUARD PHOTO

The Alaska Territorial Guard

ACROSS THE BLEAK featureless terrain moved a team of huskies followed by two men. The figures seemed to appear briefly, then would merge almost mirage-like into the white mists of a raging Arctic ground blizzard. The tall man moved cautiously, but with the same self-confident gait that had carried generations of his kind ever westward as frontiersmen and conquerors of a continent. He followed the lead of a shorter stocky man whose walk was one of authority, honed by generations of inherited knowledge and experience. This was his home ground. He was the product of a process that stretched back thousands of years in one of the wildest, most isolated lands in the world.

The two men pushed through the snows with an urgency born of a wartime necessity. They were on a special mission for the Governor of Alaska. The Governor had been authorized to organize a two-branch militia by the 77th Congress of the United States which had passed a military code for Alaska on December 31, 1941. The organized militia—the Alaska National Guard—had already been called into Federal Service. Section 7 of the code had provided for an unorganized militia "during such time as the Alaska National Guard, or any part thereof, is in active Federal Service." The formation of the "unorganized militia" or the Alaska Territorial Guard (ATG) in the Arctic portion of Alaska was the reason for the historic dog team journey late in 1942.

The journey along the Arctic coast was a natural part of life for the Eskimo, Sammy Mogg. Much of Sammy's expertise came through the eyes. At a glance, he knew the land and could detect minute signs never seen by his travel mate that guided them from one point to another and secured survival.

For the tall man, Major Marvin Marston of the Army Air Corps, this journey would be a rare opportunity to be a part of a land little-known to members of his race. He came from a different world and possessed his own unique talents. He would become a student of the Arctic and learn much from the native peoples he came to admire. He would also become an Alaskan and a legend. The combined efforts of the two men and this historic trek would help produce the famed Eskimo Scouts of the Alaska Territorial Guard.

The need for a Territorial Militia became apparent more than two years before Marston and Mogg's organizational trip in December of 1942. In July of 1940, Governor Gruening received a confidential telegram from Royal Gunnison of Fairbanks. He had completed a trip to Nome on June 28, where he had picked up some information. There were stories circulating about the Japanese mapping activities along the coastline of Alaska.

A few months later, the Governor received more news from Father Cunningham, the flying priest. He and a merchant had circled Big Diomede, had noted new Russian activity on the barren island and had learned about the construction of new Soviet air bases just south of St. Lawrence Bay. A Big Diomede Eskimo had told the priest a Soviet supply ship had brought lumber to the island to build a radio and weather station. The reports caused some concern because the Soviet-German Non-Aggression Pact was in effect. Western Europe had just been overrun by Hitler's Blitzkrieg Army and the Allies had their backs to the Atlantic wall. Clearly, the world was changing very quickly and the impact was beginning to be felt on America's Arctic frontier.

With a woefully undermanned military presence, a small four-company National Guard subject to active duty and war looming ever larger on the horizon, the Governor's thoughts turned to the defense of America's longest coastline. Would Alaska become a battlefront and would Alaskans once more be called upon to furnish a home defense force for the protection of a half-million-square-mile area?

In 1940, the Alaska National Guard was beginning to drill in the population centers of the Territory but the Governor realized it would almost certainly be called up and would leave at the first sign of trouble. Should fighting break out, the regular army would leave the backwaters of the Arctic to be utilized in a more critical theater of a general war. The Governor began to lay plans for a Territorial Guard.

The first task Gruening faced was the selection of an Adjutant General. There were several candidates to choose from in 1940. First Lieutenant

Governor Ernest Gruening organized the Territorial Guard after the Alaska National Guard was called to active duty during World War Two. Dr. Gruening served longer than any other Governor and became a U.S. Senator when Alaska achieved statehood.

Alvin C. Welling, a regular army officer, was considered for the job. He had been assigned as Professor of Military Science & Tactics at the Territory's Agricultural College near Fairbanks. Lt. Colonel Harold Collins, Coast Artillery, was on a six-month leave of absence from the Alaska Railroad when he applied on June 12, 1940. He could offer 30 years of service in the U.S. Army, the National Guard and the Army Reserves. He was a 1937 graduate of the Command and General Staff College at Fort Leavenworth, Kansas.

On July 29, 1940, William R. Mulvihill, the Railway Express Agent from Skagway, wrote a terse letter to Gruening listing his qualifications. He had been born in Trail, British Columbia, but had spent his childhood in Skagway. He had enlisted in the Coast Artillery in 1917 and had served in the 161st Motor Transportation Company of the Washington National Guard. He received his commission in 1926 and had left the National Guard as a First Lieutenant in 1934. He still retained a reserve officer's commission in 1938 and was willing to serve again.

Probably the most unusual application was that of a Colonel Mitchell. On paper, the candidate looked so good that Gruening took his suggestion of contacting the superintendent of the Copper River and Northwestern Railway in Cordova. The candidate had dropped the railroader's name as a reference. The Governor received an answer to his inquiry a few days later:

"I do not know anything regarding his qualifications for leadership or as to his physical condition. He made an application to me for a railroad position two or three years ago. Upon investigation, I found that he was too free with liquor and too anxious to accept credit and am told that he leaves creditors wherever he lights. The gentleman, in my opinion, would set a poor example. Therefore, in my opinion, he would not be the proper person to serve as Adjutant General of the National Guard of the Territory of Alaska."

The Governor appreciated the Alaskan characteristic of "telling it like it was." The Colonel was not heard from again. On August 8, 1940, Governor Gruening appointed William Roy Mulvihill, now Express Agent at Juneau, Adjutant General of Alaska. He would serve the Territory well, but shortly after the National Guard left Alaska, Major Mulvihill, too, would be called to duty and serve on the far side of the world as a transportation officer for the U.S. Army. The ATG would have a new Adjutant General, Jason P. Williams, to carry it through the war to the dawn of a new Alaska National Guard during the post-war years.

Under the provisions of the Congressionally approved Alaska Military Code of 1941 and paragraphs 5 and 11 of Army Regulation 850–250, the Commanding General of the Alaska Department became involved in the organization of the Alaska Territorial Guard. General Simon Buckner was eager to help form a local militia and pledged support to Governor Gruening within a few weeks after the Pearl Harbor attack. He was to provide instructors to the ATG, if available, to assist in equipping the Guard, insofar as supplies were available, and to assist in training and developing the Guard. He was to conduct inspections of the training and to account for the maintenance of Federal property issued to the Territory. The organization, training and missions of the ATG were to be the responsibilities of the Governor or his appointees.

A problem developed when General Buckner, who was entirely sold on the ATG plan, submitted a list of vulnerable targets throughout the Territory his thinly strung forces would be unable to defend. He felt a fully paid militia could successfully take on the mission allowing the regular army to concentrate on offensive operations against the enemy.

Colonel Jason P. Williams, Spanish-American War and World War One veteran, served as adjutant general of the Alaska Territorial Guard during World War Two. ALASKA NATIONAL GUARD

This 800-plus-man militia would be paid for from Territorial funds which would mean some sort of tax on the only revenue makers in the Territory—mining and fishing. The other alternative to the problem of internal security was the assignment of regular military police battalions to do the job.

It was soon realized that Alaska's long coastline could be easily penetrated by a determined enemy. Neither a small paid militia nor a military police battalion would offer the protection needed for such a vast territory. None of the officials involved in the formation of the Alaska Territorial Guard could envision the 6,000-man force of patriotic Alaskans which would serve home and country during the course of the war. The Minutemen were just beginning to appear from out of the mists of the land, just as earlier generations of Alaskans had done, to answer the call of duty. The forces would swell as the war heated up and they would serve as honorably as those earlier warriors had served. The organizers once more underestimated the resolve of the Alaskans.

Before war was declared on December 8, 1941, Governor Gruening had become determined that every able-bodied male in Alaska not otherwise in the National Guard, the regular military or involved in essential to war employment, would be enrolled in a Territorial Guard and kept at home for the defense of Alaska. To form such an organization from a people so diverse in thought, interests, culture and experience would require an effort just short of a miracle.

A large part of the ATG would be comprised of Alaskan natives who had never been given the full benefits or responsibilities of U.S. citizenship. Ironically, they would respond to the call to become "Uncle Sam Men" at an almost 100-percent rate in this unpaid army. They would become the most remembered part of the ATG legend following the war. Their service to Alaska and the Nation would open broad avenues to a better life which had been out of their grasp for so many years under the American flag.

The white ATG members would also benefit from serving and would grow in their understanding of the land they loved. Their contribution to the war effort would be largely ignored by historians and almost forgotten by the people they served. Together, the two parts of the ATG formed an almost impossible entity, given the odds against success early in 1942. But the Soldiers of the Mists appeared from the smallest fishing hamlets in Southeastern Alaska and from the towns in the interior, from the river settlements, the islands and the Arctic lands and the mountains of a half-million miles to produce the most unusual militia ever formed by Americans. Nowhere else was there such a mixture of people with an uncommon background living in a raw land of many time zones, climates and terrains. To make it all work and to work well, a variety of personalities would have to be the movers and shakers. Alaska was never short of those characters.

The Adjutant General of the Alaska Territorial Guard was Jason P. Williams. His administrative abilities would carry the ATG through the war and create a foundation for the return of the National Guard when the war was finished. Williams had grown up in Wisconsin, but the great outdoors pulled him ever westward and in 1904 he came to Alaska to become a part of the Boundary Commission Survey Team that Teddy Roosevelt used to settle a border dispute between Canada and Alaska. He surveyed and hunted the area of the Chilkat Valley and found a home in the rugged forest-covered mountains of Southeastern Alaska. After a stint as a forest ranger at Wenatchee National Forest in Washington State, he returned to the wet climate of Southeastern Alaska to cure an asthma problem. He became a timber cruiser, a big game guide and had been Chief Forester of the Tongass National Forest when Gruening asked him to assume the

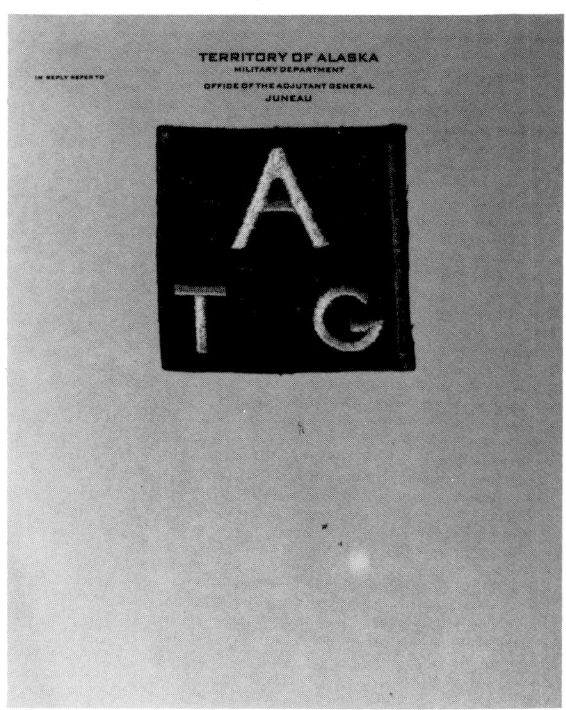

The members of the Guard wore the distinctive cobalt blue patch with the golden stars of the Big Dipper. PHOTO BY KRISTINE SCHUSTER

LEGEND OF THE LITTLE MEN

One of the most unusual stories to come out of the Arctic during World War Two was that of the "little men." There were several ATG reports concerning these leprechaun-like figures who would appear on the outskirts of villages along the rivers of western Arctic Alaska. They were pictured as being mischievous troublemakers who would steal meat and fish, sabotage boats and campsites, then would disappear when confronted.

One Nome woman reported they had been seen many years earlier at a fall hunting camp when she was a small girl. The men had gone down river to hunt. During the night, the little men came to the campsite whistling and shouting; frightening the women and children. The next morning, tiny arrows were found stuck in the door of the cabin.

Muktuk Marston reported "little men" incidents in his wartime diary: "Left Kotzebue 28 April (1945) with Johnny Schaeffer, an Eskimo, and 13 dogs for Noatak in response to urgent letter received from Charles Bailey, Captain of the ATG unit at Noatak. Reference: 'Little Men' or Koyukuk men. Up to now I have not taken this problem seriously, but letter of 7 April 1945 caused me to take seriously these 'little men.' They appear in the fall of the year and are interferring with the hunting and fishing activities of the natives, causing them to leave the camp and return to their village before finishing their fishing and hunting. Only these villages of Noatak, Kiana, Noorvik, and Selawik take these 'little men' seriously and to such an extent that they interfere with their livelihood. The occurrence of the Japanese balloons augmented this fear of them. Hence, I made this extensive trip by dog-team into these villages to allay this fear among them and to tell them about the Japanese balloon situation.

"I started out from Noatak on 29 April through the Baird Mountains. We ran into deep snow and ran out of food for dogs and men and it became necessary to hunt caribou. We made seven camps in the mountains, pushing the dogs through deep snows ten hours per day until they were worn out. On the seventh day we came out at Kiana. This is a big beautiful valley and about half-way down from the divide the lowland is covered by forests. Spent two days at Kiana resting up and feeding the dogs. Had a meeting with the ATG and talked over their problems as to the 'little men,' or Koyukuk men. Many years ago the Indians from Koyukuk area raided the Kobuk area and as a result these stories have been cropping up year after year. Archie Ferguson (bush pilot) reported seeing strange men dressed in white at Selawik this winter. In the winter of 1942, I covered the entire Seward Peninsula by dog-team and on two occasions I saw mirage dog-teams and men that did not exist when we approached them. This is one explanation of the occurrence of strange men in these parts—'little men' or koyukuk men."

Lieutenant Colonel William Wortman of the present Alaska Army National Guard spent several years in the Nome area. He, too, has heard stories of "little men" but points out that children are sometimes told not to lay their mittens down in the snow; the little people might take them. Parents sometimes told children not to stay out late because little men might seize and detain them for several years—although the time of captivity would seem like only a few hours to those being held. The little men can be used as a learning tool for surviving in the Arctic.

Raider, elf, bogeyman or fable, the "little men" have existed as part of the lore of the Arctic for a long period of time. Perhaps there is a northern branch of the famed leprechauns of old Ireland.

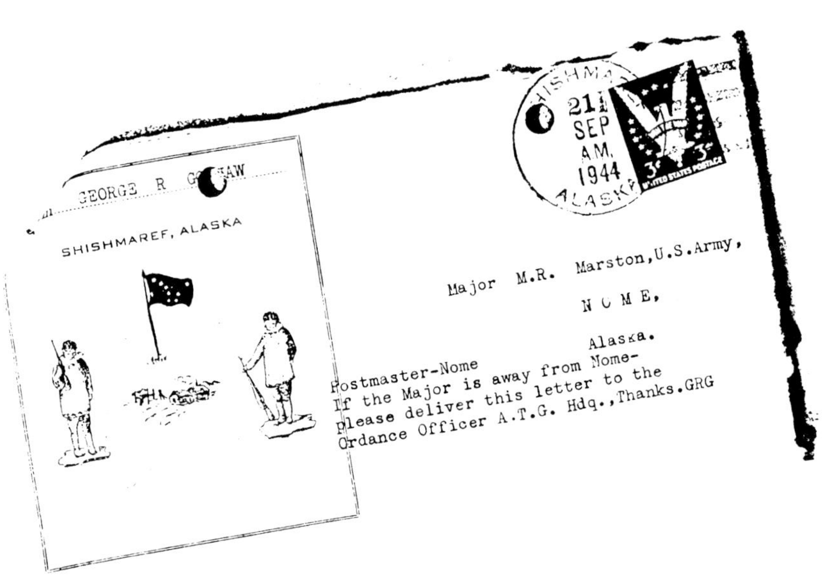

COURTESY UNIVERSITY OF ALASKA FAIRBANKS ARCHIVES

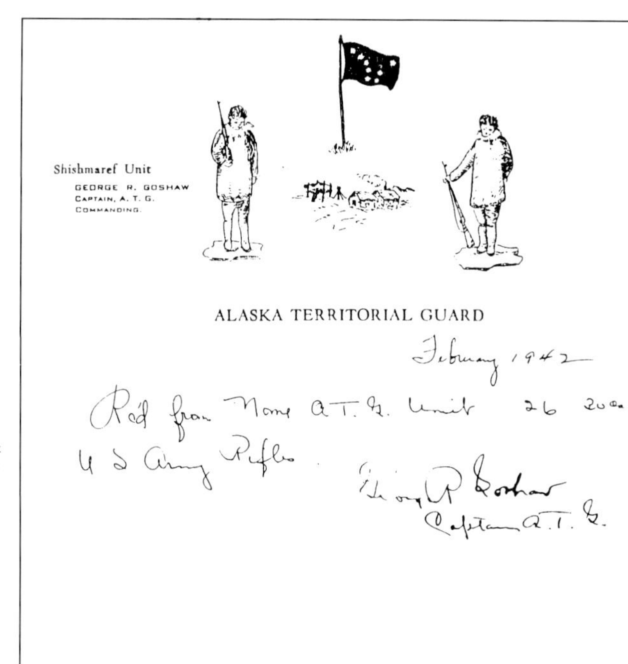

ALASKA TERRITORIAL GUARD

OATH AND CERTIFICATE OF ENROLLMENT

I, CURTIS HOMER SHERWOOD aged 45,
(First Name) (Middle Name) (Last Name)

a citizen of the United States, resident of Glacier Highway; Juneau, Alaska,

do hereby acknowledge to have voluntarily enrolled this tenth day of

August, 19 42, as a soldier in the Territorial Guard of Alaska, and
I do solemnly swear (or affirm) that I will bear true faith and allegiance to the United States of
America and to the Territory of Alaska; that I will serve them honestly and faithfully against all
their enemies whomsoever; and that I will obey the orders of the Governor of Alaska and the
orders of the officers appointed over me, according to law.

Signature _Curtis Homer Sherwood_
(First Name) (Middle Init) (Last Name)

I certify, that the above oath was subscribed and duly sworn to before me this tenth

day of August, A. D. 19 42. I further certify that this soldier was minutely
inspected by me prior to his subscription to the oath; that I found him entirely sober and in full
possession of his mental faculties; that to the best of my judgment and belief he fulfills all legal
requirements, and that in enrolling him into the Territorial Guard of Alaska I deem him a thoroughly worthy and dependable person. I further certify that the above oath, as filled in, was
read to the applicant before his subscription thereto.

John G. Osborn   John G. Osborn, Company
(Signature)   (Name typed)   Commander.
Captain Infantry

Glacier Highway unit of A. T. G.
(Fill in Town)

APPROVED:

Ernest Gruening
Governor of Alaska

COURTESY UNIVERSITY OF ALASKA
FAIRBANKS ARCHIVES

duties of Adjutant General.

Jason P. Williams was a Spanish American War veteran and had served in World War One. He had just retired from the U.S. Forest Service and had turned 65. The challenge of running a far-flung army was just too great to turn down and he served as Adjutant General until he was 70 years old. He worked well with his field commanders and acted as a negotiator between the Governor and General Buckner—two strong personalities who did not always see eye to eye. His rugged constitution and years of living in the woods put him in superb condition for a man of his age and he proved to be effective and efficient.

Gruening had been assured he would be given two military aides to help him form the ATG. The first of these was Captain Carl Scheibner, U.S. Army, a World War One veteran. The captain worked out of Juneau and organized Southeastern Alaska and everything east of the 158th Parallel. He was familiar with army regulations and procedures and outlined field defensive tactics for the units under his command. He traveled extensively during the war, but was relatively unknown compared to the flamboyant Air Corps Major who organized the ATG west of the 158th and in the Arctic.

Marvin R. Marston was born before the turn of the century in Tyler, Washington. He grew up in Seattle, but left home at 15 for Nome, Alaska, where he worked for a short time. Later, while attending college in Illinois, he enlisted in the National Guard and became a company commander in 1911. He moved to California after World War One and speculated in oil and real estate. He spent 13 years in northern Canada in the mining industry and when World War Two broke out, he was given a direct commission as a Major in the Army Air Corps and sent to Alaska. He became Morale and Recreation Officer at Fort Richardson and stepped on a few official toes during his efforts to build recreational facilities for the troops.

The highlight of his assignment at Fort Richardson was the 9,000-mile-long USO Tour he arranged for the famous comedian, Joe E. Brown. It was during this tour throughout Alaska to entertain troops that Marston first became aware that Western Alaska was defenseless. He realized there could not be a massive army stationed along the western fringe to protect the Territory, but he had the feeling that the people who survived the Arctic on a daily basis could be organized into an efficient guerilla army.

When he returned to Anchorage, he drew up a plan for such an army and presented it to General Buckner's staff. At first, the plan drew comments, but worked its way to the bottom of the agenda as more pressing wartime decisions were considered. The bombing of Dutch Harbor in the Aleutian Islands in June of 1942 created a new interest in Marston's plan.

The plan not only organized the natives into the eyes and ears of the Arctic, but Marston envisioned a guerilla force throughout the Territory should the Japanese take the major cities of Alaska. He wanted to establish small camps in isolated spots to act as lookout posts with main camps located to the rear at timberline to take advantage of the mountain

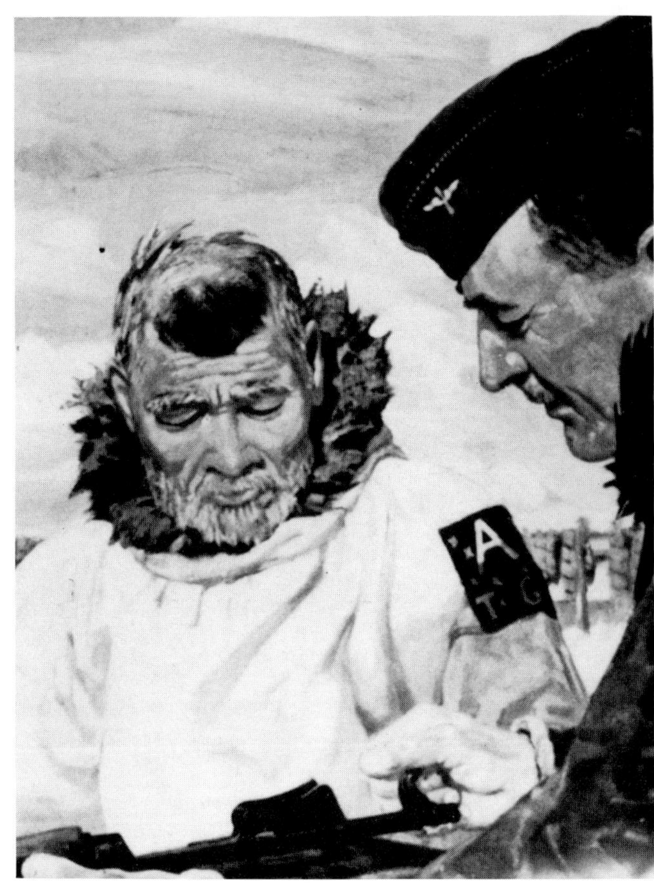

Major Marvin "Muktuk" Marston traveled by airplane, boat and dog team throughout the Arctic to organize the famed Eskimo Scouts during World War Two. U.S. ARMY CENTER OF MILITARY HISTORY COLLECTION, WASHINGTON D.C.

ranges. The natural protection of the country would afford several exit routes to the hinterland. The first camps would be located in the Chugach Mountains near Anchorage. They would be stocked with ammunition, dynamite, caps and fuses, clothes, snowshoes and rations.

Other camps would be established in the Susitna Valley and the north slope of the Alaska Range. The camps to be established between the Susitna and Kuskokwim drainages would be stocked by

Muktuk Marston enjoyed his years as Commander of the ATG in the Arctic and formed a permanent bond with the Eskimo people. OTTO GEIST COLLECTION, UNIVERSITY OF ALASKA, FAIRBANKS

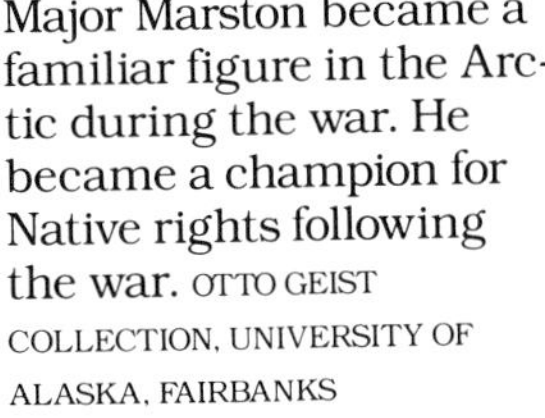

Major Marston became a familiar figure in the Arctic during the war. He became a champion for Native rights following the war. OTTO GEIST COLLECTION, UNIVERSITY OF ALASKA, FAIRBANKS

light planes landing on the numerous small lakes in the area. He wanted the main body of guerillas to be scattered through the great valleys south of the Alaska Range and east of the Talkeetna Mountains centered at the Tyone River.

The guerilla army would be formed from natives of Alaska's interior villages, and would include prospectors, homesteaders and trappers. They would be used to slow down the enemy, to aid the army in evacuation through mountain passes if it became necessary; and they could ferry passengers across rivers and provide food caches along interior routes within Alaska. This was to be the grand strategy of the Alaska Territorial Guard. Two hundred forty copies of an article on guerilla warfare at 17 cents each were ordered from *The Infantry Journal* on July 27, 1942.

Marston also proposed the use of a small Air Force of Pipercub, Taylor and Waco aircraft to supply caches located in strategic locations in the areas around military posts on the mainland of Alaska. They would be self-supporting camps located in good game and fishing areas and would be disguised as logging, fishing or mining operations. The guerillas could strike back at the enemy from these camps. The ATG would operate day and night

Major Marston appoints a local citizen as Company Commandant of an ATG Eskimo Scout unit. Many future Eskimo leaders were developed by the Territorial Guard. OTTO GEIST COLLECTION, UNIVERSITY OF ALASKA, FAIRBANKS

Governor Gruening had been assured by General Buckner that Marston was a top man. Later, a staff officer confided that Marston was considered a trouble maker and was "no damned good." Gruening had been impressed by Marston's accomplishments and attitude and realized that he had a special gift in dealing with the natives. The Governor, who could be a rebel with a cause and the Major, who could buck army regulations and accomplish much, became kindred spirits. Gruening was perfectly happy to have the Air Corps Major help him organize the ATG.

By early 1942, militias were operating in all the States since most of the National Guard had been called to active duty. The War Department issued a confidential letter on February 14 that listed each State's authorized strength, the number of men mustered and how many militiamen were on active duty guarding vital installations. Ironically, the Territory of Alaska (part of the 9th Corps area) had been authorized 2,000 militiamen but could muster none and had none listed on active duty. Alaska had 3,000 rifles but no Territorial Militia, while the Territory of Hawaii had 1,227 militiamen on duty, but had not received any rifles as of two months after the Pearl Harbor attack.

The Governor made several trips around the Territory during the summer of 1942. In June, he began to organize his militia in the major cities and throughout Southeastern Alaska. He was accompanied by Captain Scheibner. Later in the month, he flew to Anchorage. He and Marston flew on to Bristol Bay and up the coast to the Arctic villages. It was the Governor's first look at this part of Alaska and the Eskimos' first look at a real live Governor. Marston and Gruening were well received in every village. Usually, they would appoint the local minister or teacher as the village Company Commander. As Marston explained in his book, *Men of the Tundra*, there was a standard speech at each village to explain the purpose of the ATG, followed by the actual enlisting of the men.

on the enemy by cutting supply lines, destroying communication and rail links and by blowing up bridges. The patriots would live off the land and keep the enemy off-balance with hit-and-run tactics. The enemy would be hard-pressed to just survive in the hostile environment and the logistic supply line from Japan through the Aleutians to the mainland of Alaska would be long and vulnerable.

Marston was probably not the man to sell the program to the Army Brass. He was brash, he was direct and he cut through red tape as if it didn't exist. He got things done and was exactly what the Governor was looking for. Marston embraced the philosophy of the branch of soldiery he was a part of—the Air Corps. They were, for the most part, free spirits who seemed to soar through hidebound army regulations as easily as they soared through the sky. That pragmatic philosophy, which still today marks the basic difference between airmen and soldiers, was basic Marston and this did not set too well with the traditional, by-the-book army officers he dealt with on a daily basis.

"The President of the United States and the Governor of Alaska have told me to come and ask your help. The Japanese have bombed Pearl Harbor.

They have dropped their bombs on Alaska at Dutch Harbor. They will come with more bombs. We do not know where they will strike next. They want to drive you out of your villages so they can take the fish, the whale, and the seal for their people. Uncle Sam does not have enough soldiers to watch all your coastline. Will you help keep the Japanese out? Will you keep a look-out along your shores? If you see a strange boat, or a strange airplane, or a strange man anywhere around your village, will you send a message to the army at Nome? We will give you guns and ammunition. If the Japanese comes here and lands his boat will you shoot him quick? You men who will help your country against the Japanese, come forward now and sign your names here on this paper."

The response was almost automatic. The native men would make their mark and thus began the famed Eskimo Scouts. These loyal Americans signed up by the thousands. The Arctic mists were lifting on a glorious chapter of Minuteman history. Later, Marston would expand his recruiting program to nearly every Arctic village he could reach by boat, airplane, dog team or shanks mare. He would carry rifles and ammunition and always, a supply of the bright blue shoulder patches with the gold stars and the white ATG letters. Eight thousand patches had been ordered from M. Hoffman & Company of Boston in October of 1942, but were soon gone. An additional 4,000 were soon ordered. At 14 cents each, the patches were a small investment for the pride they created. The Empire Printing Company of Juneau created the ATG Oaths and Certificates of Enrollment.

While Marston was creating the Tundra Army in 1942 and 1943, Captain Scheibner was traveling almost as much while creating the lesser-known half of the ATG. In March of 1942, the Governor received a letter from the District Ranger at Mt. McKinley National Park, John C. Rumohr. He pointed out that there was a large group of older Alaskans, past 45 years of age, that were physically fit and willing to serve the country. If they were indeed a part of an unorganized militia, they were anxious to be trained to do their share as members of "Gruening's Guerillas." He urged the Governor to act immediately.

Captain Scheibner organized nearly every village and town east and south of the 158th parallel and his days must have been long and full. He made contact with the Alaska Defense Command officials and reported his successes and failures in organizing the ATG. Like Marston, he too, had to practically beg, borrow and steal equipment and supplies from the U.S. Army. His ATG was generally supplied with army leftovers—World War One rifles, uniforms, Tommy-style helmets and canvas leggings.

On November 20, 1942, he made a trip to Kluane Lake and Soldiers Summit, Yukon Territory, with acting Governor Bob Bartlett. The Northwest Service Command was conducting ceremonies formally opening the Alaska Canada Highway at noon that day. Bob Bartlett and Captain Scheibner formally represented the United States Government and the Territory of Alaska. Scheibner also went from Juneau to Skagway by Coast Guard Cutter, then by rail to Whitehorse. He flew to Fairbanks to organize an ATG unit there, then went on to Anchorage via the Alaska Railroad.

The Anchorage ATG unit had 244 enrolled and divided itself into three groups. They attended drills Mondays, Tuesdays and Thursdays where they learned close-order drill. Uniforms were being issued when Scheibner arrived. He checked on 2,000 rifles at Fort Richardson. Marston shipped a thousand of these to Bethel and Nome. Scheibner made the rest available to units in Anchorage, Fairbanks, Seward, Cordova, Valdez and Palmer. He talked to Colonel Ohlson, General Manager of the Alaska Railroad about shipping supplies for the ATG.

The Commander of the Anchorage unit was Major Walter Mickens, a former Marine Sergeant Major who was one tough little guy, according to Robert Atwood, former owner of the *Anchorage Times*. Atwood served as a Lieutenant in the Anchorage unit, along with Lieutenants Smith, Chadwick, Downes and Ness. The units drilled in a hall in Anchorage and went to the field at Fort Richardson. They marched, crawled under live fire, learned to kill a man without making a sound, threw hand grenades, learned how to make Molotov Cocktails and how to blow up bridges. Atwood remembers the Enfield Rifles and the old uniforms, but he also remembers the newer weapons and uniforms the Anchorage unit eventually received. The Anchorage ATG numbered 8 officers and 243 enlisted men— by far the largest unit in the Territory, although Bethel had 174 men, Juneau 112 and Skagway 197.

Palmer had an interesting ATG unit. Captain Harry DeLand, the local postmaster, drilled his men at the Central School near the Matanuska Maid Ice Cream plant and Co-op Trading Post. The Captain had a rather high-pitched voice when giving his preparatory command, so to achieve some measure of authority, his command of execution lowered itself an octive to a deep gutteral sound. The men would hear, "To the rear—Growl!!!"

The rifles were stored in the school and would be checked out for drill. In good weather, drill could be conducted on the school playground where curious townspeople would gather to gossip and make comments on the soldierly attributes of their fellow citizens. This did not happen.often as attendance usually dropped in good weather. Summer was a busy time in the farm community and militiamen often worked long hours in farming, construction or other war related jobs. During the winter, drills were more frequent and were held in the school gym. Rifles were checked back in to the supply sergeant at the end of each session. The Palmer unit numbered in its ranks some interesting people. Colcord (Rusty) Heurlin, the artist who painted the Alaska War Bond Poster, was a member of the Palmer unit for a while. The Swedish-born artist would later teach art at the University of Alaska in Fairbanks and leave a treasure of Alaska paintings for the enjoyment of future generations. The Reverend Bert J. Bingle, the minister-carpenter who had served the Colonists well when they came to settle the valley in 1935, joined the Palmer ATG. Bingle and DeLand also served as officers on the Adjutant General's Staff.

Other prominent men in the Palmer unit were Jan Koslosky, Shorty Kirchner, the La Roses, the McKecknies, the Moffitts, Johnsons, Barrys, Lentz, Linn and a dozen other long-time residents. Leo Lucas remembers the World War One uniforms with the button-up collars and leggings. He also recalls a parade at Elmendorf Field where the ATG was reviewed by the Top Brass. Afterwards, the troops visited the bars on 4th Avenue and stood around in their World-War-One-vintage uniforms. A couple of young GI's in smart new Ike Jackets walked past the ATG men several times and eyed them up and down. They must have thought Alaska had its own version of the Rip Van Winkle tale. One GI gathered up enough courage to say, "We don't want any trouble, but you're about the roughest looking fellows we have seen since we have been in the service."

Captain Scheibner stopped at the Independence Mine near Wasilla and talked to the General Manager about forming a Fish Hook Road unit of miners, but the GM was not sure whether the Bureau of Mines would authorize the continued operation of the mine. From Anchorage, Scheibner flew to Cold Bay and visited Unga, Belkofsky, King Cove and Sand Point. Fort Randall was unable to furnish any more transportation so he returned to Juneau.

J.P. Williams, the Adjutant General, also made extensive inspection tours throughout the war. The Sitka company had numbered as many as 191 members and had received encouragement from the Army and Navy on duty there. Major Winn Goddard had been the commander but was elected mayor in the fall of '42 and was unable to devote additional time to the ATG. Numbers began to dwindle as construction workers drifted in and out of town, so Colonel Williams changed the authorization to 60 permanent members.

Cordova, that stronghold of the World War One Home Guard, had its problems organizing an ATG unit. The Civil Defense unit had not been allowed to become members of the ATG. Mayor Chase felt they could not perform both functions in a time of emergency. Scheibner suggested the men would put up armed resistance to an enemy in any event and should be offered the international protection of soldiers, which was provided members of the ATG. The Cordova Committee, represented by the postmaster, volunteer firemen, the American Legion and organized labor would study the problem after the fishing season was finished. They would offer command to Superintendent of Schools Rollen E. Nipps who was on vacation in the States for the summer. Scheibner held out little hope for a Cordova unit.

With the regular army and the 297th Battalion in Valdez, Captain Thomas J. Selby, ATG, Doctor Armstrong, Mayor, and Margaret Harrias, the U.S. Magistrate, felt it was a hopeless task to try to continue an ATG company, so Captain Selby was instructed to turn in his equipment to Cordova in hopes that unit might become active.

In June of 1943, the Adjutant General made a trip to Fort Mears on the steamer *Yukon* and from there caught another steamer, the *Delarof*, to St. Paul Island. He inspected some of Marston's units and returned to Cold Bay on the Coast Guard Cutter *Clover*. He helped form units at King Salmon, Sanak Island and at Unga where Captain Allan L. Peterson, Deputy U.S. Marshal, was made Company Commander. Egegik also formed a unit under Captain H.M. Evans, a white man who ran a store in the village. Williams recommended no ATG unit for Unalaska as there were only 22 civilians remaining there and they were either court officials or worked for the Army or Navy. Regulars would defend Unalaska.

In November of 1943, Major Scheibner made an inspection of ATG units in Southeastern Alaska. It was a mixed report the Adjutant General received from the man who had worked so hard to form new units. Lieutenant Weltman and Major Hellman from the Army Air Base at Annette Island accompanied Scheibner seven months later on a second inspection trip. Scheibner pointed out that the ATG was an unpaid militia and the regulars could not expect too much from the units in the way of regular army training standards. The Minutemen had to make a living for their families and could not devote the time to drilling regular servicemen could.

The officers picked a bad time to be inspecting. It was summer and most of the ATG men from the villages were out commercial fishing. The army officers were more concerned about use of government property than drilling and each unit they looked at seemed a little more lax in this matter as their trip progressed. At Klawak, there were five rifles missing. The Major made a speech about the penalty of receiving stolen U.S. property. The speech must have been impressive because all five rifles were returned to Captain Frank Peratrovich in short order. He stored the rifles and locked them up. They were to be issued only in case of an attack on the village.

At Craig, there was not much enthusiasm about the ATG. Captain Giffen received very little cooperation from the community, so the rifles were stored. At Hydaburg, Scheibner found nobody willing to take command so Reverend Verne Swanson, the Presbyterian minister, agreed to care for the government property there in case the citizens had to be armed.

At Petersburg, Captain Wilder rented a storeroom for twenty dollars a month for his rifles. He agreed to withdraw his resignation and try again to build up the Petersburg ATG. Petersburg was a fishing town and the men put in long hours at sea to provide for their families.

At Wrangell, Captain Scheibner reported there was not much enthusiasm in the unit as the men were involved in the fishing and processing industry and were just too busy to join the ATG. However, the Wrangell men were constructing a 50-foot indoor shooting gallery for .22-caliber rifle practice during the winter months. They had also built at their own expense, a 500-yard outdoor rifle range and were holding weekly drills in the high school gymnasium. It was felt the ATG would flourish in Wrangell.

Scheibner was able to report the ATG was strong in Skagway, Juneau and Ketchikan. Ketchikan had reorganized under Captain Richard Hogben and the unit was growing. The other bright spot in Southeastern was Metlakatla. Captain Charles Hinde had resigned in 1943 and Captain Charles Buchert took command. He was assisted by Lt. Henry Littlefield and Lt. Raymond Haldone. The unit was drilling twice weekly and was judged by Scheibner as one of the more outstanding units in his area of the ATG. Captain Scheibner recommended Metlakatla and Ketchikan be strengthened. He also felt the Craig, Klawak and Hydaburg units should be disbanded.

The Eastern portion of the ATG, including Southeastern and the larger towns of mainland Alaska and the interior were of vital importance during World War Two. Nearly 50 years later, this part of the Alaska Territorial Guard remains a largely forgotten chapter of an interesting history. These ATG men trained just as hard, dedicated a portion of their lives to the ATG and would have sacrificed their lives as Minutemen, yet are nearly forgotten—like their organizer, Major Carl Scheibner. Why is this so?

The answer may lay in the fact that America discovered the Arctic and the remarkable people that inhabited it during this time. This discovery caught their imagination during World War Two and became a part of the great event of their time along with the likes of Ike, Patton, FDR, Churchill, Guadalcanal, the Bulge, the Blitz and the Bomb. Mention Alaska and mental pictures developed of the desolate Arctic, the Eskimo and man pitted against nature.

Up to this point, Alaska had been a mystic place of adventure reserved for those fortunate enough to experience travel in an era when travel was limited to two classes—the wealthy or the poor seeking work. World War Two changed all of that and the newsreel cameras brought Alaska just a little bit closer to the average citizen. What he saw on those flickering newsreel films was the Arctic and the Eskimo as he had imagined them. It looked like what he had seen of Byrd, Scott, Amundsen and Perry earlier. He did not see small town Alaska, fishing village Alaska or even Anchorage, Alaska but the desolate Aleutians and the Arctic. That Arctic image was advanced by the man who had lived the ultimate adventure and then wrote and lectured on it—Major Marvin "Muktuk" Marston.

Marston spent the war years traveling from village to village organizing, instructing and strengthening his Tundra Army. He seems to have found his natural place in history along the Arctic coast and up the interior rivers of Western Alaska. He learned the way of the land and embraced the rich traditions and customs of the native peoples he made a part of his adventure. They were his equal in every way and he resented those of his own race who took advantage of their open, honest nature. The longer he lived with them, the more he became convinced of their value to America and the need for America to treat them as full citizens.

Marston's personality created two distinct, very different impressions on those who met him. Many saw him in later years as an opportunist, a hard-driving businessman, a windy, boisterous and egotistical figure who could expand a story far beyond its believable boundaries. To them, he was a relic from another time living out a self-created legend. Those who knew him in his own element during the war, cited his accomplishments against overwhelming odds. The natives loved him because he embraced their cause, understood them, and in a very real sense became one of them. He became a controversial giant of Alaskan lore.

Marston's legacy to Alaska was twofold. He expanded the understanding of the native peoples of Alaska and gave them the opportunity (through their membership in the ATG) to become a part of the American system if they wished to do so. They began to understand the power of organization and the use of the legal machinery available to win guaranteed citizen rights. He opened a window to the future and encouraged them to look out at a changing world from a different perspective.

Marston's second contribution became more apparent during the post-war years. His military organization became the basis for a new Alaska National Guard in 1949. The Tundra Army's shape and makeup helped mold the character of the Alaska Army National Guard. Many of the former ATG men joined the new organization, while those who departed left it a military heritage and tradition.

Like any historical figure, Marston the man and Marston the legend became hard to separate with the passing of the years. He did not single-handedly build the legend—he had a great deal of help. Governor Gruening advanced Marston's cause and even argued with General Buckner about a promotion for the Major.

Gruening and Marston formed a strong team in the struggle with army officials for supplies and recognition for the Alaska Militia. They corresponded almost daily and met often to plan for the expansion of the organization. Indeed, Gruening delighted in flying back and forth from Juneau to Anchorage in military aircraft to meet with Marston. The Governor would insist on flying back to Juneau in the worst weather conditions with green Air Corps crews who had never been there before. He would sit up front in the cockpit and tell them "how to get there." His friends were sure he would die in an aircraft mishap before the war ended. He was in a C-54 once which came into Juneau during a driving winter storm and ground looped at the end of the runway.

Marston became a close friend of one of the better-known hunters and dog mushers in the Arctic, Johnny Schaeffer. The two mushed together on several trips to isolated villages on ATG business and travelled uncounted miles crossing the endless snows. Johnny was a good teacher and Marston was a good student. The musher's young son, John W. Schaeffer, would become an Eskimo Scout in the Alaska National Guard in later years and then a Major General at the end of a long and distinguished National Guard career.

During the summer of 1943, the U.S. Army sent an art unit north to make drawings and paintings of the war in Alaska. Lieutenant Henry Varnum Poor was given a tour of the ATG and met Major "Muktuk" Marston. Marston had acquired the nickname as a result of an eating contest in which he outlasted a native headman in devouring raw whale blubber. The artist and the Air Corps Major made a trip up the Arctic coast on the *Ada*, an old boat Marston used to transport ATG weapons and supplies to the villages. Poor wrote a book titled *The Cruise of the Ada* in which he described the dangers of the journey and the fascinating people he met. He pictured Marston's dedication to the ATG and the Eskimos under his command.

The journey took them to Nome, St. Michael, Little Diomede, Shishmaref, Teller, Unalakleet, Golovin, Kotzebue, Point Hope, Wainwright and Barrow. Everywhere they stopped, Marston was greeted as an old friend. Rifles would be distributed, Marston would make his speech and sign up more Eskimos for the ATG.

> "We need you to be the eyes and ears of the army . . . you are fine shots . . . you will stay at home and go about your usual work, but you will be on alert . . . when you get your rifles, you must keep them clean and well oiled . . . be ready at a moment's notice to use them."

Then Marston would tell them the ATG patch was their badge of honor. Poor related how the Eskimos would crowd around the two white men to sign their names on the enlistment papers. He said, "Some told me their names and I took their hands and guided them to form the letters. They were hard, thick, scarred workingmen's hands . . . and these eager faces, so unquestioning and singlehearted and good, and still so gay and lively, touched me deeply. My God, I'm going to fall in love with the Eskimos, like all the explorers do."

The *Ada* went on to Barrow where Marston and Poor met Frederick G. Klarekoper, the local minister and ATG Captain. Captain Steinfield, a New York doctor from the government hospital, was also a member of the Barrow ATG. The parson had signed up Fred Ipalook, Lee Suula, David Brower and Ned Nusunginya as Lieutenants in America's farthest north military unit. Governor Gruening had met Klarekoper and his wife earlier and had offered to evacuate the minister and his family. The Klarekopers were devoted to the Eskimos and chose to remain in Barrow to do God's work and the ATG's work at the top of the world.

The Barrow unit was strong throughout the war and the minister who was also a captain dedicated himself to taking care of the spiritual and physical needs of his tundra soldiers. He was an avid photographer and left a remarkable collection of pictures which documented the life of the Barrow ATG men.

One of the interesting characters in the Arctic Army was Captain George Goshaw, Commanding Officer of the Shishmaref ATG. This was the same

Henry Varnum Poor's painting, "Eskimo Guerillas," was done during his trip up the Arctic coast with Major Marston. U.S. ARMY ART COLLECTION. WASHINGTON D.C.

Henry Varnum Poor depicts an Eskimo Scout patrol leaving its home village for duty with the ATG.
U.S. ARMY ART COLLECTION. WASHINGTON D.C.

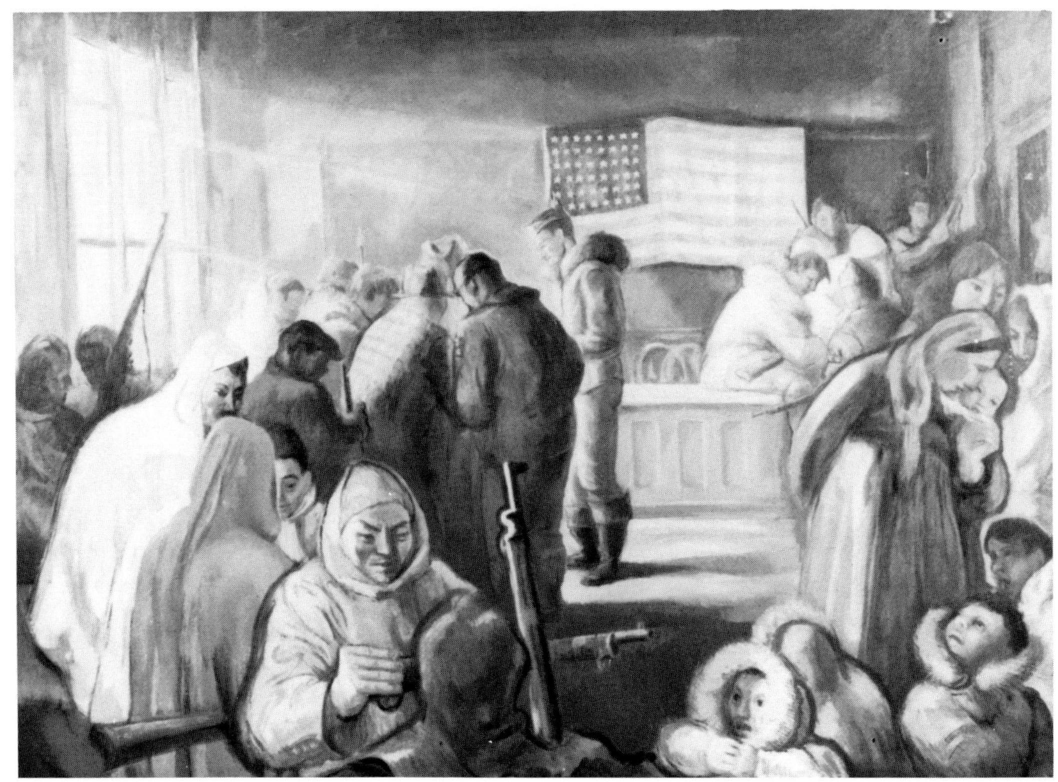

Artist Henry Varnum Poor accompanied Muktuk Marston up the Arctic coast to deliver supplies to
ATG units. Here he shows Marston signing up Eskimos in the village school house.
U.S. ARMY ART COLLECTION, WASHINGTON D.C.

The U.S. Army sent artists to Alaska during World War Two. Here, artist Joe Jones depicts Major
Marston signing up Eskimos for the Alaska Territorial Guard. U.S. ARMY ART COLLECTION, WASHINGTON D.C.

George Goshaw who had served in the Home Guard of 1917 and in the First World War. The years since his letters to Governor Strong volunteering his services back in 1917 had not dampened his enthusiasm for serving his country. The length of the letters had increased since 1917.

He wrote a long rambling letter to Governor Gruening shortly after Pearl Harbor. He predicted a National Guard and Statehood for Alaska following the war. He told the Governor there was a lot of oil in the Arctic and that someday a pipeline would be needed to transport the oil south. He said another pipeline could be built across the Bering Strait to tap the natural gas in Siberia. The visions from Shishmaref were vivid. His letter ended with the revelation that he had discovered a cure for the crabs—those microscopic body lice which had accompanied soldiers into war for at least a thousand years. He assured the Governor this information was vital to the war effort and that he was willing to serve his country once more. The Governor made him a Captain.

Goshaw made a good Captain and continued to write epic-length letters throughout the war. The only short letter he ever wrote was one of anger he dashed off to ATG Headquarters in Nome when a supply of ammunition did not show up during the *Ada*'s annual trip.

> Dear Major,
>
> Let me know by wire if there will be any 22 cal. ammunition issued to the ATG unit at Shishmaref for target practice during the coming winter. If none is to be issued, then I suggest the ATG Companies be turned into Girl Scout organizations.
>
> Yours respectfully,
> George R. Goshaw
> Captain, ATG

Marston was able to recruit a remarkable man to serve as Quartermaster of the ATG, Otto William Geist. He was born in 1888 in Eiselfing, Bavaria, Germany, and was to become a world-famous archaeologist, naturalist and paleontologist. Geist had served a stint in the Imperial German Army before immigrating to the United States in the early 1900s. He would also serve in three wars for his adopted country.

Geist joined the U.S. Army and was sent to the Mexican border. He learned about logistics and transportation while serving under General John J. Pershing. He went to France with the army during the First World War. He was a Sergeant Chaffeur assigned to the American delegation during the

Otto Geist in dress uniform in 1919. Geist served as a driver during the Peace Conference at Versailles, France. OTTO GEIST COLLECTION, UNIVERSITY OF ALASKA, FAIRBANKS

Otto Geist, the little Quartermaster of the Alaska Territorial Guard. OTTO GEIST COLLECTION, UNIVERSITY OF ALASKA, FAIRBANKS

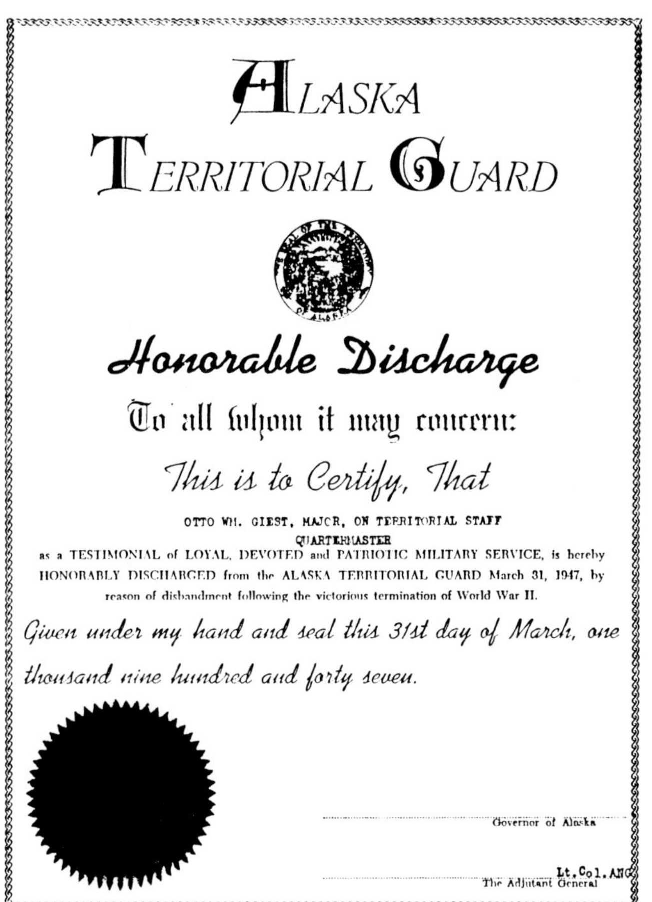

peace talks following the Armistice. While he was stationed in Paris, he had the unique opportunity to drive some of the more famous people of the time. He drove David Lloyd George, Clemenceau, President Wilson's daughter, General Bliss, Alexander Kerensky and a variety of French generals and government officials. He became a self-taught scientist after the war and found his way north to the college near Fairbanks, Alaska.

Geist was appointed Chief Quartermaster of the Alaska Territorial Guard by Governor Gruening after Marston convinced him he was needed to organize the logistics nightmare centered at Nome. He proved to be a good choice for a difficult job. His years of work in the Far North for the University of Alaska and his experience with the U.S. Army in France more than qualified Geist for the job. He set up an office in Nome and travelled through the Eskimo villages helping to organize the famous Scouts. He administered the supply system, got the paperwork flowing and was able to outfit the units throughout the Arctic.

The little Quartermaster was always on the go. He procured needed equipment from the army, unsnarled logistic problems and sometimes acted as mediator when things didn't go right for the ATG. He was tough and demanded proper procedures when it came to paperwork—even from Major Mars-

ton. His value to the Guard was recognized by Adjutant General Jason Williams who said, "Colonel Marston was fortunate in having the assistance of Major Otto Geist who was Chief Quartermaster. Major Geist is a high ranking scientist along the lines of anthropology and ethnology pertinent to Alaska. His extensive knowledge and acquaintance with the Eskimo people, their habits and way of life, enable him to accomplish what few other men could have done. The man and his work will always rank high in my esteem."

Official correspondence between Geist, Marston and the Governor charted the ups and downs of the Territorial Guard during the war years. Serious issues, such as shortages of supplies for the scattered units, forced the Quartermaster to travel to the villages to straighten out problems. Geist kept notes in pocket tablets and his long years of field work in science and his habit of jotting down bits of information left a sort of history for an organization that had no historian. He kept track of expenses and accounted for all funds paid out by his office. If he hired Billy Beans to haul supplies to Mountain Village or Jack Kernak to mush from Napakiak to Bethel, the amount paid by the ATG always appeared in the little notebooks.

Otto Geist spent long hours in his Nome office and distributed supplies all over Western Alaska from his warehouses. He hired Fritz Kineoak and Moses Buzz for 75 cents per hour to work in the warehouse. Geist became a well-known figure in Nome during the latter part of the war. When the right supplies did not arrive at the right place, he became the target of ungrateful letters from unit commanders. Many of the uniform clothing items sent out by the army were manufactured for average size or larger American soldiers. They were miles too large for the Eskimo Scouts. This was often the case for footwear and the native ATG men would go back to wearing hand made mukluks, a superior product to begin with. When Geist received letters of complaint, he would patiently explain why there were delays. He sometimes questioned whether he should continue his work or turn it over to another person, but he stuck with it and did a superb job for the Alaska militia.

One day, a native boy ran into the ATG Headquarters shouting the roof was on fire. Geist had been burning a lot of waste paper in the wood stove. He called the Nome Fire Department and the firemen, with the help of bystanders on Front Street, soaked down the roof of the ATG Headquarters. Geist had to make out an accident report and wrote the Governor the next day. He requested a tall ladder for future such emergencies.

Geist travelled a great deal during the war. He

A unit of Marston's **Tundra Army** awaits inspection. The Eskimo Scouts were experts in spotting anything unusual in the Arctic and kept the U.S. Army informed. ALASKA NATIONAL GUARD

walked, mushed, went by boat and flew on any military aircraft available in the area. He continued his interest in scientific matters. If ancient bones showed up in a stream bed, Geist was there to make scientific notes. He experimented and found that vitamin B seemed to work against the clouds of mosquitos that dominated the low wet lands of Western Alaska. He also tried thiamin chloride: "Four to eight milligram size tablets a day for five days, then two tablets a day."

On March 19, 1945, Major Geist flew to Nunapitchuk when two native ATG men, Sergeant George Keene and Sergeant Oscar Beaver, found a piece of iron which probably belonged to a Japanese incendiary balloon. The three men walked two miles over the tundra, secured the part and flew it to Bethel the next day. The Japanese began launching the balloons from the Home Islands late in the war. Several of the balloons were found along the coast of Alaska and some floated aloft all the way to the West Coast of the United States.

Geist had a particular interest in the balloon project. Whenever an explosive-laden balloon was reported, he would personally go to retrive what he could find and send it off to the army for analysis. The government did not tell the general public much about the Japanese effort. Fears of germ warfare could have caused widespread panic. The ATG investigated and located many of the balloons. It was just another mission the ATG carried out successfully during World War Two.

As the war moved out of the Aleutians and on across the Pacific towards its end, there developed an unusual attitude towards the Alaska Territorial Guard. The army officials acknowledged the ATG had been effective and had carried out its mission, but certain officials began to question the need to continue the force.

The ATG men had come from all walks of life. They were businessmen, teachers, fishermen, trappers, doctors, lawyers and laboring men. There were tiny units of the ATG which were formed in almost unknown villages of Alaska from Ketchikan to Barrow. Some units were small local branches of larger units. There was even a Glacier Highway Company outside of Juneau. Curtis Sherwood, a dairyman who supplied Juneau with fresh milk, served as a corporal in the unit. If a unit lost members to the draft or through the movement of people—like the small unit at Wasilla—it would be disbanded and the remaining members would transfer to an existing unit nearby.

Over 6,000 people served in the ATG during the war in the 110 or so units that were formed. Many would become prominent people during the postwar years. The Tundra Army alone in 65 villages across Western Alaska produced about 3,000 trained and armed natives. With its auxiliaries—women and children who rendered all kinds of services—such as quartermaster duties, food services, transportation, communications, etc., the ATG numbered perhaps 20,000 people. There were women ATG members like Laura Wright, who could hit 49 of 50 targets in practice and a letter from the Commander in Kotzebue reported he had signed up 30 women and needed guns for them. The women were not officially members of the ATG, but they served anyway.

The thought of an organized force of armed natives who were now becoming aware of their rights as citizens must have been alarming to the exploiters who had made a living off the natives for years. They began to eye the ATG as a threat and watched Marston carefully. They vocalized any infraction and worked hard to discredit the Tundra Army. It was an inglorious end to an American miracle.

As early as mid-1944, army inspectors began to find fault with the ATG. The loose nature of the ATG organization, its ability to act independently and its lack of formal training did not set well with army officials. Some of the shortcomings noticed by the inspectors were valid. Even Marston realized leadership was lacking in some units. He requested that ten Alaskan Scouts from "Castner's Cutthroats" be assigned as instructors to the ATG.

Marston himself became a target of those who did not support the ATG. He had not been popular with General Buckner from the beginning and now, Buckner's successor, Lt. General Delos Emmons seemed to regard Marston as a liability. Marston was turned down for promotion time and again and

Even the smallest villages formed scout units for the ATG. The men took great pride in being "Uncle Sam's Men." OTTO GEIST COLLECTION, UNIVERSITY OF ALASKA, FAIRBANKS

Nearly every village had an Eskimo Scout unit of the ATG. They were America's major defense effort along the coastline of the Bering Sea and the Arctic Ocean. OTTO GEIST COLLECTION, UNIVERSITY OF ALASKA, FAIRBANKS

The ATG scout units became the "eyes and ears" of the arctic. The patriot army served without pay.

began to talk of leaving the ATG late in 1945. He had been criticized for his participation in a Jade Mountain Syndicate. With native help, he had found a mountain of jade during the war and had formed a partnership to mine the precious stone. He felt the jade could be made into jewelry by natives and could become a source of income for the people in the villages. When his motives were questioned by army officials, Marston withdrew from the syndicate.

Marston kicked off a furor when he publicized acts of discrimination against natives by the owner of the Dream Theater in Nome. One of the local native girls had dated a GI. When the couple showed up at the theater, the girl was asked to sit on the "native" side of the aisle. Major Marston became angry over the incident and proposed the natives run and manage their own theater in competition with the Dream Theater. He had picked up this idea from Major Geist. He was accused of using his military position to meddle in civilian affairs.

During the course of the war, Marston had taken motion pictures of his Tundra Army. Some officials thought he might use these movies to advance his own interests, so Marston once more became the target of an official investigation.

On October 5, 1945, the Chief of Staff for the Alaska Department sent a memo to General Emmons: "Subject to your approval, I propose to: (1) Relieve Marston and Scheibner at earliest practicable date, obtaining concurrence of governor. (2) Cancel Marston's orders for TDY at Rochester (Kodak Company) (I don't know how he got these.) (3) Check as to whether the films are personal or government property." Marston was on his way out, but he was not finished. He would continue to be an important influence on Alaska's Minutemen for many years to come.

Although the Second World War had ended in August of 1945, the Territorial Guard would continue for almost two more years. The man who would stay on, fight for the existence of the ATG as a foundation for a National Guard and eventually oversee its dismemberment was the Quartermaster, Major Otto Geist. He put off his post-war career and risked losing his beloved homestead near Fairbanks to assure that the Soldiers of the Mists would not disappear again from the Alaska scene.

And where did Muktuk Marston go? He remained a major figure in Alaskan affairs, made a fortune in Anchorage real estate and continued to champion the native cause as long as he lived. The State of Alaska would make him a Brigadier General in 1973 and he would live until 1980. He had walked a 91-year trail and had left a lasting imprint on the pages of Alaska's history.

Perhaps the greatest tribute ever paid to Muktuk Marston was that given in a letter from ATG Headquarters in Nome dated December 28, 1945. It was written by the little Quartermaster from the University of Alaska:

"When a book will be published on the Alaska Territorial Guard, I feel certain that your name will be emblazoned as the one who really organized it and together with Governor Gruening will reap a well earned acknowledgment to this fact.

Way down in my heart I assure you that I shall look upon you as a sort of apostle to the Eskimos who although American citizens, have never before received such an appreciative idea of what they may mean to the American government in general. You have been unselfish in every respect in order to do that what was right with these people and all those you have contacted during your many years among them would feel rather "lost" if they would know that you have not only left the service with the US Army but have left these people as well. I cannot help but think that even if you were out of the Army that you would continue to be of aid to these people in various ways once they had accepted you as the man who was able to put them closest in contact with our American Government. You and Governor Gruening I assure you (from my correspondence) are the two persons who really did most for these long neglected aborigines. Please keep on boosting for them and I assure you of a most thankful population which is just about one-half of the entire population of Alaska. For what you did and what you may do, I admire you and my deepest respects and gratitude are yours."

One hundred years after the last ATG soldier has disappeared into the mists of time, a historian researching the story of Alaska's World War Two Militia might wish to engage an artist to illustrate his work. Would he paint a lonely figure on a sled mushing across the blinding white silence of an Arctic landscape, or would it be of soldiers drilling in a city or in the rain of a Southeastern Alaska fishing village? Perhaps he would create a composite of a thousand faces or strive for the simplicity of Rusty Heurlin's painting of three figures, "On Guard from Metlakatla to Barrow." Whatever his choice of presentation, the artist would have to use one common denominator for all his figures. That would be the cobalt blue patch with the golden stars and the large white letters that proudly proclaimed, "I'm a member of the Alaska Territorial Guard."

The ATG parades on Sitka's main street during the war. There were ATG units in southeastern Alaska, the Interior and in the Territory's larger cities and towns as well as in the Arctic. HANNA-CALL COLLECTION
UNIVERSITY OF ALASKA, FAIRBANKS

THE NATIONAL GUARD COMES HOME

THE ALASKA TERRITORIAL Guard had compiled a remarkable record of service to the Territory and the Nation by the time the Second World War ended in August of 1945. Leaders within the ATG, and the Governor, began to formulate plans to continue the Militia and use it as a basis for building a strong National Guard program. It was "assumed" the Alaska National Guard's four infantry companies which had been federalized in September of 1941 would be allocated back to the Territory at the end of the war. The National Guard did come home to virtually all the States and Territories by 1946, but it did not happen in Alaska.

The ATG had not fired a shot in anger at any enemy, but it had done a job the Army could not afford to do while the war was in progress. The ATG's Eskimo Scouts had caught the imagination of the public. The concept of intelligence gathering and surveillance while making a living in the harsh and isolated Arctic held a certain appeal for some military planners. It threw a new wrinkle into the military organizational plans for post-war Alaska at the National Guard Bureau level. The planners in Washington D.C. viewed the post-war National Guard along traditional U.S. Army lines, while Governor Gruening and the Alaskans recognized the value of the small unit scout organization which had proven so successful during the war. Therein lay the fight between Gruening and the military.

When Ernest Gruening took office late in 1939, he asked the War Department for a 5th National Guard Company to be located in Nome, Alaska. He did not get the Nome unit but ironically, Nome became the center for the ATG Eskimo Scouts. It was here, in the middle of the war, that plans began to develop for the conversion of the ATG into an Alaska National Guard. The man who pushed for the idea was the little Quartermaster, Major Otto Geist.

As early as 1944, Otto Geist began to write the Governor concerning the future role of the ATG as the war moved towards its end. He took note of how the ATG membership had given natives a new-found pride in citizenship. Geist felt the natives would continue their interest in military matters and would transfer over to National Guard units as they were established. Other natives had served in the regular military. These veterans would also be interested in serving in the National Guard. Muktuk Marston added weight to the argument that the ATG should continue serving Alaska until a National Guard could be established. He pointed out a new reason for maintaining a Tundra Army:

"The Eskimo is a nomad and travels from hunting camp to fishing camp to his village and back—all within a radius of 100 miles. Such nomadic life makes it difficult to comply with regulations such as in a traditional National Guard, or other regulations established military organizations require. He is practically the only inhabitant along the 5,000-mile coast line which faces two foreign countries, Russia and Japan. The migration from Siberia across to the mainland of Alaska is still going on. I have seen as many as 40 arrive from Siberia on fishing, hunting and trading trips. Our Eskimos go to Siberia also on these same missions. I am convinced, from knowledge gained through our Eskimos who visit Siberia, that Russia has a definite (military) program with the Eskimos in Siberia. If the Army elects to take the guns, helmets, parkas and the ATG shoulder patches away from the Eskimos here, it will undo a lot of the good work done in causing the Eskimo to be proud of his citizenship."

Marston realized the Western World had its eye on the development of the Cold War in Eastern and Central Europe, but had failed to note that the Cold War was also coming to Siberia. The Ice Curtain was developing along the far eastern fringe of the Soviet Union to match the Iron Curtain along the western buffer zone of the USSR. There was still a need for the ATG.

The ATG had many powerful enemies who hoped to disband the militia. Among these were anti-native forces, Marston's personal enemies, some professional military officers, politicians, some labor union people and others who wanted a return to the old Alaska. Marston was a little more blunt: "The opposition to the Tundra Army comes from the exploiters of the natives. These exploiters are the traders, local shippers, and liquor men, principally located in Nome. These interests do not want the natives organized even in a military way for fear the natives through the military organizations will learn to organize in an economical way and ask for some of the blessings of a democracy."

On January 9, 1945, seven months before the war in the Pacific would end, the Alaska Congressional Delegate, Bob Bartlett, introduced House Resolution 1271 to the First Session of the 79th Congress. HR 1271 was to amend Section 7 of the 1941 Alaska Military Code. It would read, "During such time as the Alaska National Guard, or any part thereof, is in active Federal Service, and at such other times the organization and maintenance of the Alaska National Guard in the sparsely settled communities of Alaska is determined by the Governor of Alaska to be not feasible, the Governor of Alaska through voluntary enlistments, may organize a Territorial Guard or continue the Alaska Territorial Guard as now organized under such regulations as to discipline in training as the Secretary of War may prescribe." One way or another, Gruening would have his Soldiers of the Mists. The ATG would be around until March, 1947, and the Alaska National Guard would come home eventually.

Major Geist longed to return to his career at the University in Fairbanks, but continued his work in Nome as Quartermaster of a shrinking army. He sought support for the continuation of the Alaska Territorial Guard. Although the war was finished, there was much to be accomplished by the ATG. The Militia was called upon to fight fires, for flood relief and search and rescue missions. It continued to patrol, work on trails, maintain a series of ATG cabins, and always, observed and reported unusual happenings in an area nearly as big as the States east of the Mississippi River. As the Cold War developed, the surveillance and intelligence portion of the mission took on a new importance.

The struggle to maintain a militia was not limited to distant officialdom along the banks of the Potomac, but pressure grew within the Territory as well. Major Geist wrote a letter from Nome to E.L. "Bob" Bartlett, in Washington D.C., on November 29, 1945:

"Concerning the conversion of the ATG to the National Guard. If we do not do this, the Legislators at Juneau will cut off appropriations and let the ATG disband. In light of the present international situation, we must continue. Most Legislators I know are unwilling to listen or spend money, now that the war is over. Personally, I can see the value of a National Guard for Alaska."

The ATG Quartermaster lead a busy life keeping the Militia supplied. He negotiated to purchase and transport army surplus buildings to be used as village armories. The armories would serve as drill halls, storage areas and community centers. He called it his "Kashim-Armory Project." He wanted to buy surplus weasels and snow jeeps for search and rescue work. He made contact with officials at Elmendorf Air Base and hoped to set up a cooperative agreement with the Air Corps' 10th Rescue Group. He thought the ATG-10th Rescue combination would be a natural for his Eskimo Scouts and would strengthen the argument for continuing the Territorial Guard. The strong part of the ATG in 1946, was Marston's old area of command.

Yet, the Militia fought a losing battle. The units in the larger cities of Southeastern, Southcentral and Interior Alaska lost members almost from the day the war ended. Captain Forbes Baker of the Fairbanks ATG reported on June 9, 1946, that, "The members desire deactivation of this unit and wish to turn in their equipment." Two days later, Major Walter Mickens deactivated the Anchorage unit. On July 19, Captain Harry Edward deactivated the Bethel ATG.

Geist, to say the least, was disappointed. He wrote to J.P. Williams, the Adjutant General, on August 8, 1946. "We have had bad luck with the Bethel unit and nothing we can do will straighten out this unit because it is a sad mixture of whites who want to hold all the offices, but do nothing and natives who, as far as I can see, were the only ones willing and eager to drill. We have a similar case with the Nome unit and I have an idea that sooner or later, something will have to be changed here, too. I wish to close down my office in Nome and return to Fairbanks. If no money is forthcoming to close down, I would be willing to carry on the work for no fee for a limited time. I have just applied for my papers on the homestead I nearly lost near Fairbanks and hope to have better luck this time in doing the required work. If I leave this office around the 1st of October, I can comply with my residence requirements by May 1st. I can move on and be doing something useful as well as be happy, because I never intend to become a burden to other people as I grow older, but could make a decent living off a homestead when I should fail in other work. I am now 57 years old."

Otto Geist, loyal and duty-bound to the end. Soldier, scientist, adopted brother of the Eskimo and immigrant American—perhaps the best kind of American of all. He did one other thing before he returned to the University. He fought for and received permission from the army to distribute the ATG rifles and uniform clothing to the members who had served so faithfully for so long—small payment for this remarkable unpaid army. Even this small victory was bittersweet. Muktuk Marston had to convince army officials at Fort Richardson that the turned in clothing might contain "Eskimo Germs" that would prove fatal to white soldiers if the clothing was reissued? Only then would the army agree to give away the nearly worn out government issue items.

Muktuk Marston and Major Scheibner were replaced in 1945. General Emmons, however, continued to show interest in the ATG and replaced the two original organizers with Captain Geoffrey H. Goss and Lieutenant Neal. The two regular army men were good choices. Both had spent time in the Territory and both became avid supporters of the ATG.

In March of 1946, Geist wrote Governor Gruening that "this would be very detrimental to the Territory to lose the Guard at this time. I should venture to guess that more than three-fourths of the people living in Alaska think that since the war is over now, things are just "rosy" and never even give it a thought that something may happen overnight." He was concerned about a Territorial bill designed to destroy the ATG. Senator Frank Whaley from the Nome area had been a strong supporter of the bill. Governor Gruening was pleased to write back on May 17 that the bill had been defeated and Senator Whaley had been beaten in the primary election.

On March 15, 1946, the *Daily Alaska Empire* in Juneau ran an editorial supporting education for veterans. However, the article noted that the University of Alaska was short of housing for veteran students. The newspaper supported a bill by Senator Edward Coffey that would cover back into the general fund any money still in the hands of the Territorial Guard. The fund could be used for student housing. The strange things going on across the Bering Strait on the Russian side seemed more serious from where Geist and his Scouts sat in Nome than from an editor's desk in Juneau.

On August 27, 1946, Geist sent a report to the Commanding General at Fort Richardson concerning the activities of the Soviet garrison on Big Diomede Island. The Eskimo Scouts were still carrying out their mission of surveillance. The Russians observed weather, patrolled the island, acted as frontier guards and operated a radio and weather station on the back side of the island just six miles from America's Little Diomede Island. He said, "The Russians have forbidden American Eskimos to hunt across the international border and have become more strict on trade between American and Siberian Eskimos. They arrested and held a native of Little Diomede who was hunting. He was blindfolded— taken to the Russian garrison and questioned before being released.

Governor Gruening used the menace of the growing Cold War to advance his case in Washington D.C. that a Guard or Militia for Alaska deserved national support. At the beginning of his battle, he stated, "The perpetuation of the Territorial Guard is, in my judgment, a matter of prime importance— far more important than the reestablishment of the four National Guard companies that we had before the war. Frankly, those four companies have no great value, although I would naturally be for their reestablishment. In the Eskimo country the Territorial Guard means a great deal and I feel it has a definite and great military value. Those 2,500 Eskimo Guardsmen are far more valuable than regular soldiers. For Uncle Sam to maintain that kind of establishment with housing, commissary, pay, etc., would run into millions of dollars every year and even then the type of service would not be equal to that which is rendered by the Eskimo who is thoroughly acclimated, familiar with the terrain and in a better position to see and hear anything unusual. To sum up: The perpetuation of the Territorial Guard means that Uncle Sam will always have an alert, vigilant force scattered from Bristol Bay to Barrow at virtually no cost."

The best of both worlds would be a combination of a regular National Guard for the populated centers and the small scout units along the Arctic frontier. This is what Gruening would fight for and eventually win for the people of Alaska. There would not be another National Guard anywhere in America organized in this fashion.

The Governor met with Otto Geist in Nome, late in 1946 to discuss the reorganization of the ATG into an Army National Guard organization. They reviewed an excellent plan which outlined both the traditional Guard companies the National Guard Bureau insisted upon and the small scout units in Western Alaska the Governor favored. The value of having scout units scattered in small villages for search and rescue purposes was an added feature of the plan. The Bureau's worry over training schedules, especially during the traditional hunting and fishing seasons, would have to be worked out. Captain Goss had devised the plan and he would be sent East with the Governor's blessing to sell the plan to the Bureau.

Although much of the ATG outside of Arctic Western Alaska had disappeared by 1946, there were a few bright spots left. Juneau and Ketchikan still had volunteers who continued to drill. There were inquiries from members of the Reserve Officers Association seeking information about the return of a National Guard. Interest sometimes came from long distances. The Governor received a letter from the Veterans Alaska Co-Operative Company of Washington D.C.

Fort William Seward had been established at

Haines, Alaska in 1903. The Third U.S. Infantry and elements of the Tenth Infantry had served there during the early 1900s. The post was renamed Chilkoot Barracks in 1922 and it had served as home to troops from the Fourth U.S. Infantry. In 1941, part of the Alaska National Guard's 297th Infantry moved into Chilkoot Barracks. The post was declared surplus property in July of 1944 and sold to the Veterans Alaska Company. Some young World War Two veterans who had pooled their resources to buy the post had dreams of establishing a settlement of former servicemen in the Far North.

The driving force behind the settlement program was Carl W. Heinmiller, a retired Major of Infantry. He hoped to have 600 to 1,000 ex-servicemen and their families at Haines by the spring of 1947. Heinmiller contacted the Governor and proposed forming a scout and reconnaissance company for the National Guard. The veterans planned to go into small businesses and industries and felt Haines would be an ideal place to raise their children. The Port Chilkoot Company had hoped to open up the land around the base in 5-acre homesites and with the help of G.I. loans, build a thriving community. The Veterans would be ideal candidates for a National Guard unit.

Heinmiller would have been an ideal Commander. He had organized the Fiji Commandos and the South Pacific Scout Company during the war. He had won a Legion of Merit with Valor Citation (VC), a Bronze Star with VC, a Combat Infantry Badge and a Purple Heart. He had served in New Georgia, Hendova, Guadalcanal and Fiji and had lost an eye and part of a hand from a booby trap explosion during the war. He would later become a U.S. Magistrate, friend of the natives and a genuine Alaska character. Unfortunately, the settlement and the National Guard unit did not develop as anticipated at Haines.

On November 21, 1946, Gruening wrote to Secretary of War, Robert Patterson. He said, "In view of the international situation and the paramount strategic importance of Alaska, I believe it wise to proceed as rapidly as possible with the reconstitution of the Alaska National Guard." He needed an answer before the biennial meeting of the Territorial Legislature which would begin on January 27, 1947. He was beginning to pick up support at the Bureau level. He had even convinced Major General Butler B. Miltonberger, Chief of the National Guard Bureau, that Alaska needed its National Guard back. Gruening's battle would now be with his own Legislature in Juneau.

The Governor did not have a great deal of help in his fight to bring the National Guard back home. His own job was on the line and in 1947, Cap Lathrop, an old time Alaskan who had made a fortune in mining, testified in Washington D.C. against Gruening being reconfirmed for the Governorship. A former Territorial representative from Fairbanks, Frank Angerman, said Gruening pressured him in favor of reestablishing the National Guard. He represented the labor unions and was opposed to bringing the Guard back to Alaska. In answering the charges, Gruening said, "I told the U.S. Senate, anyone who knows Alaskans would know that nobody can tell them what to do." The Governor had no problem being confirmed by the Senate.

Gruening had to battle outside interests as well as those within the Territory who were anti-National Guard. Businessmen in Seattle who had controlled Alaska's destiny for decades fought Gruening's programs for the Territory. The Chamber of Commerce of Seattle endorsed statehood for Hawaii but never for Alaska.

Gruening found a friend in Air Force General Nathan Twining, Commander in Alaska. The Governor had asked for an Air National Guard Squadron in his National Guard organizational plans. General Twining, in a letter to the Chief of Staff, United States Air Force, dated December 3, 1947, stated: "This Headquarters is vitally interested in establishing an Air National Guard in Alaska. It is felt that such an organization will furnish a medium whereby the knowledge and skills of civilian airmen in the Territory can be translated into effort that will be of value to this command."

The Alaska Territorial Guard was officially disbanded by the Territorial Legislature on March 31, 1947. Some of the units continued to meet and drill. In September, the Governor had to tell Captain Cahill of the Douglas ATG that the Legislature had voted down funds to keep the ATG going. He thanked the Guardsmen for their long years of service and dedication and noted that the ATG soldiers had always given freely of their time and energy. He felt the Militia would appear again in some far distant crisis if called upon. They always had—for hundreds of years in the Great Land's written history and perhaps for thousands of years in its spoken history. The Alaska Territorial Guard was no more. The National Guard would now be the target of the shortsighted.

On October 19, 1947, the *Chicago Tribune* ran a story under the heading: F.D.R. Appointee Found Delaying Alaska's Guard (Chicago Tribune Press Service)

Washington, Oct 18—Alaska is the only portion of the United States not protected by a National Guard unit of citizen soldiers, the army disclosed today.

Organization of a Federally recognized guard unit in the strategic Northwestern outpost has been delayed for nearly a year by demands of Governor Ernest Gruening of Alaska for recognition of his own type of Militia, it was learned.

Gruening, appointed by the late President Roosevelt, has rejected army proposals for a standard National Guard organization, army officials said. He has demanded instead a "scout" organization scattered thru the tiny villages of Alaska. The army contended that a well organized militia along traditional patterns was the only reliable type of defense organization. It suggested a guard regiment of three battalions. After months of negotiations, the army retreated and agreed to accept Gruening's scheme—two scout battalions totaling 43 officers and 885 men.

Army sources said National Guard units have developed without obstructions from local officials in all 48 States, the District of Columbia, Hawaii, and Puerto Rico.

The boys from Lake Michigan did get one thing right in their article. The army had accepted, in theory, the Eskimo Scout concept. The Bureau was now ready to go to work to build a National Guard in Alaska.

The old war horse, Lt. Colonel J.P. Williams, Adjutant General of Alaska from 1942 to 1947, left during the summer. He was 70 years old and his wife was not in the best of health. The couple moved to Eugene, Oregon, to enjoy a few well-deserved years of retirement. The Governor did not appoint a replacement for the old Alaskan, pending the outcome of the Guard Bureau's efforts to establish a National Guard unit for the Territory. The Bureau would assign an advisor to help the Governor build his army.

Hal D. Steward & Associates of Washington D.C. sent a report to the Director, Plans and Training Division, Department of the Army. They had completed a study on the organization of an Alaska National Guard. The report recommended the National Guard create and maintain "Alaska Scouts" as a measure for the defense of the Far North Territory. Colonel Steward stated, "This recommendation is prompted not only by my own study and tour of Alaska, but by the opinions of Arctic explorer, Vilhjalhmur Stefansson, who recently stated that strategically, the Arctic Sea is the most important body of water on earth. He further stated that the Russians are giving their Far Northern defenses a broad base through intensive colonization. The United States and Canada are failing to do so."

"From the Old to the New—Klondike Kate to the Cold War and Atomic Age in One Lifetime!" Both articles were in the Juneau newspaper during March 1948.

Daily Alaska.
Juneau, March 29, 1948.

VOL. LXVII., NO. 10,848

BIG AIR BASE IDENTIFIED AS EIELSON FIELD

Is Reported Equipped to Accommodate Army's Giant B-36 Bomber

DENVER, March 29.—(AP)—An Alaskan air base now is equipped to accommodate the Army Air Forces' Giant B-36 bomber, the Denver Post said in a story published last night.

The hitherto highly-secret base, once known as "Mile 26," has been named Eielson Field, and is, according to the Post, so located as to serve for launching air attacks on any spot in the Northern Hemisphere.

Only three fields in continental United States, aside from Eielson, have been previously announced as capable of handling flights of B-36's on a regular basis. These are located at Fort Worth, Tex., Elgin Field, Fla., and Wright Field, Ohio.

The story said announcement of Eielson Field's existence was approved only today by proper official sources. Prior to this time, its existence had been screened behind a cloak of official silence, and even now its exact location—other than that it is about 26 miles southeast of Fairbanks is guarded information.

Significance of the announcement was added to the statement earlier this week by Air Secretary Stuart Symington in Washington that our B-29's based in Alaska and Labrador, could make bomb runs over any portion of the Soviet Union.

The Air Forces have announced that the B-36 could carry an atomic bomb to any inhabited region in the world and return home without refueling.

The plane is designed for a normal range of 10,000 miles with 10,000 pounds, without extra fuel tanks. The Air Forces have 100 of the giant six-engined bombers on order.

KLONDIKE KATE WILL WED AGAIN

Former Belle of Yukon to Take Second Mate at Vancouver Thursday

BEND, Ore., March 31.—(AP)—Klondike Kate, once the belle of the Yukon, will take a second husband at Vancouver, Wash., Thursday.

Now 68 and known as Mrs. Kate Rockwell Matson, the one-time beauty of the Northlands will be married to W. L. Van Duren, Bend accountant, whom she has known for 18 years.

Her first husband—she did not marry, until she was 58—died a year and a half ago on a frozen Yukon trail. He was John Matson, a miner who had carried his love for her 33 years before he worked up the nerve to ask her hand.

After her days as queen of the dance-hall girls in the Alaskan gold rush, Kate homesteaded on dry farmland east of here. She first met Van Duren when he entered a convalescent home she started here later.

The couple will leave for Portland tomorrow. After the wedding Thursday, they plan a short honeymoon trip, probably to California.

It will be Kate's first real experience as a housewife.

After her marriage to Matson, she came back to Bend, and he went to his diggings in Alaska. They met only occasionally through the years, generally when Kate made a trip to Dawson.

Matson, then 83, died after a heart attack while hiking out from the Yukon to meet Kate in October, 1946.

— March 31, 1948.

FIRST STEPS TO FORM AN ALASKA NATIONAL GUARD

The first steps toward the reorganizing the Alaska National Guard were taken today by the Governor's office. It issued a call for all former Army officers who are interested in such an organization. These men are requested to submit a brief letter to the Governor's office, outlining their military and civilian experience.

This should be done, said the announcement, as soon as possible, if interested in organizing a Territorial National Guard.

The information received will be compiled by the Governor's office so that when both Territorial and Federal funds are available, immediate steps can be taken.

Further details concerning National Guard plans were not released at this time. The 297th Infantry Battalion, former Territorial National Guard organization, was demobilized following the conclusion of World War II.

Daily Empire
March 27, 1948.

NATIVES CONDEMN NATIONAL GUARD

The Alaska Native Brotherhood and Alaska Native Sisterhood camps of Juneau wrote a letter to the House of Representatives today, urging the National Guard be not established in Alaska.

The communication said: "Too often the National Guard has been used to abridge the rights of American citizens."

Today's News Today.—Empire.

ALASKA HEARINGS ON NOMINATION OF GRUENING POSSIBLE

The Republican Central Committee has been informed that the protests filed with Senate Committees against confirmation of Democratic appointments in Alaska have been given consideration and therefor confirmation prior to the Presidential elections is not anticipated.

The nomination of Gov. Gruening for a third term has been referred to a sub-committee headed by Senator Cordon of Oregon and it is expected that hearings will be held in Alaska on this nomination before confirmation.

FAIRBANKS POST ASKS NATL. GUARD

A communication from the Fairbanks American Legionnaires added fuel today to the Legion fight for a National Guard unit in Alaska.

The Golden Heart city group also urged such a unit, adding their plea to a number of other Legion post requests.

The Colonel felt that if war ever came to the Far North, the people in such cities as Nome, Fairbanks, Anchorage, etc., would be right on top of the front lines. The experience and "know-how" of the Alaskans could be of the highest value to the U.S. military forces. A copy of the report was sent to the Chief of the National Guard Bureau.

In June of 1948, Major General Kenneth F. Cramer, Chief, National Guard Bureau, appointed Lt. Colonel Joseph D. Alexander as Officer in Charge of National Guard Affairs, Alaska. The highly decorated Chicagoan had graduated from Infantry School in 1929 and had seen 16 months of combat service during World War Two. Colonel Alexander came to Alaska in August with three officers

Colonel Joseph Alexander became senior Army advisor to the Alaska National Guard. He and Governor Gruening established the new Alaska National Guard in 1949. Colonel Alexander served as acting Adjutant General during the formative years of the Alaska Guard. ALASKA NATIONAL GUARD

from the Guard Bureau. They toured the Territory, met with army officials at Fort Richardson and with the Governor in Juneau. They submitted a report to General Cramer.

The General reviewed the report and said, "I am impressed with the enthusiasm for the establishment of an Alaska National Guard which was evidenced in all quarters visited by the National Guard representatives. I realize that many obstacles will have to be overcome and many problems solved before an Alaska National Guard can become a reality. You can expect my fullest cooperation in assisting in the implementation of present plans for the establishment of an Alaska National Guard, and any changes in these plans developed by you and the Commanding General, U.S. Army, Alaska which are approved." Gruening had his green light to go and had won his battle for the type of National Guard he felt would best serve Alaska and the Nation.

Now, the Governor wished to have a personal hand in organizing the National Guard. He needed to travel throughout the vast Territory to talk up the Guard. He had submitted his budget for the Gover-

nor's Office but Congress had cut out $6,215. The Governor fired off a letter to Congressman Ben Jensen who controlled the purse strings and admitted that the $1,800 he had requested for the painting of the Governor's House (last painted in 1940) could be dropped, but he requested the money should be used for expanded travel due to the organization of a National Guard in Alaska:

"We are about to organize a National Guard in Alaska on a special formula approved by the War Department. It will include units scattered widely throughout small communities along the Bering and Arctic Seas. The importance of these units for scouting and patrolling and for apprehending any espionage from the other side of the Bering Sea, cannot be overestimated. There has been a very unfortunate delay in the organization of the Guard owing to the fact that from the time I urged it immediately after the cessation of hostilities in 1945, the War Department had no funds for this purpose. . . . It is, therefore, of the highest importance that either I, or someone from my office spend time in the immediate future organizing these units." The Governor already had a person in mind to help Colonel Alexander organize the Guard. He came from the past and his name was Marston.

Muktuk Marston had been out of the picture for over three years, but he kept an eye on the Alaska Guard scene. He wrote to Gruening on March 16, 1948, from Long Beach, California. "At the time the OSS in Washington D.C. was dissolved, plans were well underway for the maintenance of some such undercover intelligence service along these shores.

Colonel Joseph Alexander and staff at Juneau. Members of the Instructor Detachment were sent all over the territory to teach and organize the new Alaska National Guard. NATIONAL GUARD PHOTO

They provided for the assignment of a regular officer for year round-duty along the Bering Sea and the Arctic Ocean. I am sure it is high time a watch be established without further delay, and I also believe that I am peculiarly qualified for this very job. I know no one else with the knowledge and experience necessary to do this job without loss of time in training for it. Hence, I am now willing to undertake the job." Gruening recommended Marston to General Twining and Muktuk was given the opportunity to create a little more Alaska history.

All that was left now was the approval and an appropriation of $100,000 from the Territorial Legislature. The National Guard Bill would be debated in Juneau for several months and supporters for and against the bill began to line up. The *Anchorage Daily News* kicked off the debate with an editorial by Norman C. Brown on February 21, 1949.

EXPENSIVE LUXURY

A Territorial National Guárd in Alaska would be a luxury that Alaska can ill afford at this time, or for many years to come, for that matter. We were surprised at some of the infantile arguments used in the House Saturday by proponents of the bill, which provides for the setting up of a National Guard on a State-side basis, and appropriates $100,000 as a starter. In pushing for the bill, advocates brought up the wearisome and hackneyed "Joe Stalin" bugaboo—an argument so silly as to be without weight whatsoever.

Equally far-fetched are the arguments of some opponents who dangle labor before the issue. It is folly to think that a Territorial National Guard would forestall an attack on Alaska from Russia, and it is equal folly to fear that the National Guard would be called to use its force against Alaska workingmen who are arguing the cause of better wages or better conditions through strike.

The issue is clearly whether or not the Territory can afford to go into the National Guard business—whether during this time of conjuring up every possible kind of tax to meet costs of government, we should indulge in a luxury that is sure to cost hundreds of thousands of dollars a year more.

Under the National Guard plans, it is incumbent upon the Territory to furnish armories to house equipment and provide places for drill. Admittedly, the units at first would be small. In some of the outlying communities, twenty-five or thirty men would likely be the entire strength of the unit, and a drill place would not be too much of a problem. In larger communities, such as Anchorage, it would not be difficult to recruit, 200 to 300 men, and indoor drilling would immediately become a major problem.

Four years ago when the National Guard Bill was up for consideration in the Legislature, it was estimated that four armories in the principal cities of Alaska would cost $250,000 each. It would be entirely safe to say that construction costs have risen 50 per cent since then.

Under the army-civilian cooperative plan for establishing a militia, the Federal Government would supply arms and equipment and uniforms. The government might even go so far as to supply surplus buildings for armories, but it would fall to the Territory to move, install and equip such buildings. Past experiences with this type of equipment have shown that very little is saved over new construction.

The Territory on the other hand, must pay an Adjutant $7,500 yearly, an assistant $6,500 yearly and be constantly harassed by building and maintaining armories. We can see where the $100,000 appropriation the bill now before the Senate calls for would be only a drop in the bucket in perpetuating the Guard in Alaska.

It is to be hoped the senators, all practical businessmen, will look upon the National Guard Bill as one of the luxuries the Territory cannot afford at this time, and kill it.

The Governor got his Enabling Act passed by a narrow margin. The Legislature appropriated $75,000 for the bienium and a survey of potential units was made. By the end of 1949, seven units, principally in the Scout Battalions had been organized and Federally recognized. As of December 31, 1949, the Alaska National Guard had 25 officers and 292 enlisted men.

Colonel Alexander was assigned regular army advisors who were sent to the various units. They acted as instructors and gave the Guard the professional push it needed to get started. Muktuk Marston became Assistant Adjutant General and was promoted to Lieutenant Colonel. He was not a "paper man," so he travelled and organized in the villages in which he had been a familiar figure during the war. In most cases, the building of units was merely a matter of the old ATG Eskimo Scouts changing over to the new Alaska National Guard. Love of military became part of the passage to manhood for the young natives of the Arctic. Father to son to grandson became a tradition in the Guard

Governor Gruening took a personal interest in the development of the Guard. On Governor's Day he congratulates the top scorer of one of the scout units. ALASKA NATIONAL GUARD

The Cold War created the Ice Curtain as well as the Iron Curtain. Here, Gruening, Bartlett and Rivers (R-L) point out the need to reestablish the Alaska National Guard. The three leaders would become Alaska's first Congressional delegation following statehood in 1959. ALASKA STATE LIBRARY, JUNEAU

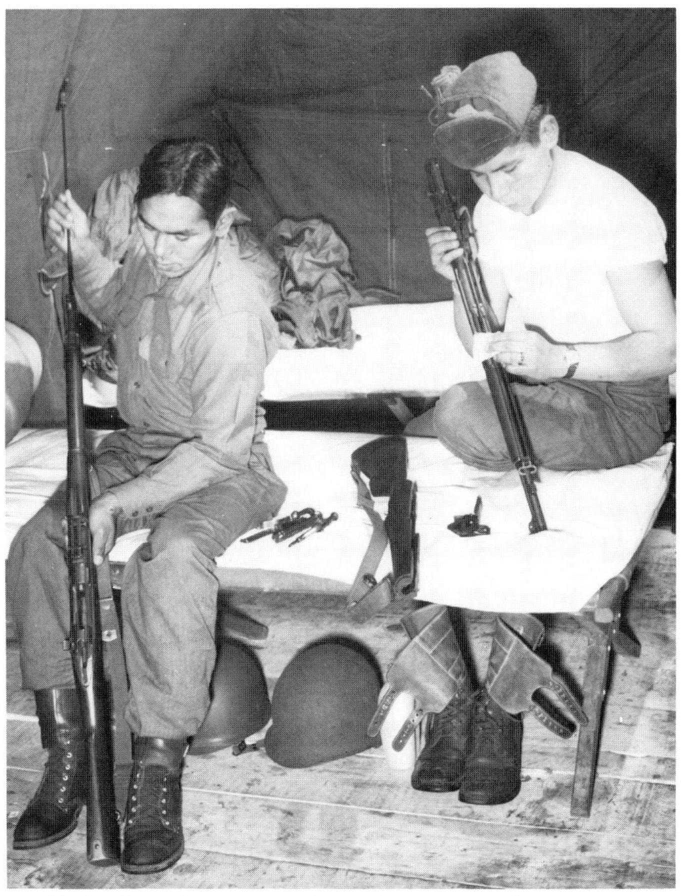

Early Guardsmen were issued two types of weapons. Sgt. Nathan Awawrok of Unalakleet cleans his model 1903 rifle while Sgt. Frank Paul, Jr. of Sitka (in white shirt) works on his more modern M-1 Garand during 1951 annual training near Juneau. U.S. ARMY PHOTO

Alaska Guard's 208th Infantry advances across frozen lake at the base of Mendenhall Glacier during war games in 1951. U.S. ARMY PHOTO

A new generation of Eskimo Scouts join their fathers in the 1950s to carry on a proud tradition. ALASKA NATIONAL GUARD

Four members of the 208th Infantry Battalion (separate) pause on a lonely patrol across a frozen lake during encampment of the Alaska National Guard near Juneau. In the background is world-famous Mendenhall Glacier. U.S. ARMY PHOTO

and rosters of ATG men in 1943 match last names with rosters of Guardsmen in 1991.

By 1950, seven more units had been added to the Alaska National Guard. The units stretched from Ketchikan to Barrow in approximately 50 villages and towns and numbered 57 officers, 3 warrant officers and 1168 enlisted men.

After two years of operation, the Guard had nearly 75 percent of its authorized units organized and had a Federal civilian employee force and full time active duty personnel in Sitka, Fairbanks, Anchorage, Nome, Juneau and Bethel. Besides the two scout battalions in Northern and Western Alaska, the Guard had two battalions of Infantry, the 207th and the 208th. The pre-war 297th Infantry came back to Juneau during the summer of 1950.

At the very time the Alaska National Guard was being formed, Communism seemed to be spreading in nearly every quarter of the world. Eastern and Central Europe had been isolated behind the Iron Curtain. Communism had taken China, North Korea and minor revolutions were breaking out in Africa, Southern Asia and in other places. The West did not take a real stand until the Berlin Crisis of 1948–49. With that event came the formation of NATO and a deepening of the Cold War.

The Alaska National Guard was authorized an additional 2,000 men. The outbreak of the war in Korea in 1950 hastened the necessity to fill the ranks with Guardsmen. Secretary of the Army Frank Pace wrote Governor Gruening in August 1950 urging him to step up recruiting efforts. Only 652 of the 2,000 personnel authorized for fiscal year 50/51 had been added to the Alaska Guard.

The Governor sent a letter to Colonel Alexander in which he pointed out, "I was very much shocked upon learning that we only had 650 enrollees. The Guard has been authorized for nearly a year and a half. I see little justification for the long delay in getting going. I desire to have you clear the way immediately so that Marston may go out and organize the balance of our Table of Allowance of 1300 men. I desire to have this accomplished by October 1st. At that time I want these men enrolled, in receipt of equipment and weapons and on the payroll. A year and a half is much too long a time for the enrolling of only about 700 men." Gruening was beginning to sound like a real Commander-In-Chief and things would roll in the Arctic.

The Guard began to grow that winter. By March 31, 1951, Alexander was able to report, "The Guard came into being on 22 March 1949, at which time there were no personnel enrolled, no armories and no storage buildings. As of 17 March of this year, the strength of the Alaska National Guard was 1302

Three ATG veterans of World War Two joined the Eskimo Scouts of the new Alaska National Guard. Shown here at Bethel Armory are James Lott, fisherman and trapper; Peter Lott, storekeeper, both of Tuluksak; and Carl Kawagley of Aniak (l to r). COURTESY *THE TUNDRA TIMES*

or 1 percent of Alaska's population. This percentage is without precedent anywhere. The Alaskan percentage is four times greater than that of the U.S.

We were at the very end of the supply line, had a small population, and the non-existence of armories and warehouses. As contrasted with the U.S. proper, some states have organizations dating back to the pre-Revolutionary War times. Every other state has had a Guard organization not less than 25 years. Moreover, the states' own armories valued in excess of 500 million dollars and are close to all supply sources. Alaska can well be proud of its two year record."

Colonel Alexander was right. Armories had been built on a 75-25 Federal-Local cost plan in the larger towns and army surplus buildings had been transported to the bush at little or no cost to the Territory. Several buildings which had been used by the Territorial Guard had been remodeled for the National Guard. Much of the work in moving or constructing small armories in the bush had been performed by natives donating their labor.

The Army Instructor Detachment sent members to the villages to train the scouts and the army furnished two airplanes to fly the instructors to the units needing training. A supply system had been established, warehouses set up and the Guard's first Property and Finance Officer, Major Meredith "Mickey" Jelsma headed up a staff of 21 employees in Anchorage by 1951. The Anchorage Chamber of Commerce put pressure on Colonel Alexander to move the National Guard headquarters out of Juneau. That would not come about for many years.

Colonel Alexander had taken an authorization order and had built an army from the ground up. His tour of duty as acting Adjutant General ended during the Spring of 1951. Now an Alaska National Guard existed and the search began for the first official Adjutant General.

The five years following World War Two had shaped a new world which was divided into three parts—the Western World of democracy, the Communist World of hopelessness and a Third World of have-nots who would get caught up in the struggle between East and West. The time had spawned a Cold War which would effect a good part of the world's peoples for the next four decades. It was an insecure world in which governments came to rely on ever increasing military commitments.

America's Last Frontier, struggling to be chosen as an equal partner in the Great Republic, was caught up in this strange new world. It would emerge at the half-century mark stronger and clearer in purpose and the National Guard would be a factor. The men who shaped Alaska's destiny are still controversial today. However, those critics who disliked the giants of the land—Gruening and Marston—had to admit, the Territory had come a long way during this speck of time.

The second tier of giants—J.P. Williams and Otto Geist—had performed their work extremely well, yet would be nearly forgotten by future generations of Alaskans. There would be new leaders to carry on and they could be guaranteed some measure of security. There would always be that line of faceless figures stretching across the years of time. They would wait in the mists to come forth as soldiers if the clouds of war approached the land again.

These ATG Eskimo Scouts, who served with Muktuk Marston, joined the new National Guard.
THE *TUNDRA TIMES*

BUILDING THE FORCE

THE GENERATION THAT provided the Allied victory in 1945 had no grace period to adjust to a wartorn world or to mend disrupted lives as had happened following World War One. Political considerations had halted the race for Berlin and the prize was left for the Soviets who began consolidating gains for Communism before the angry sounds of war had ceased. The quick dismantling of America's war machine was followed by a military rebuilding program, massive foreign aid expenditures and a soaring national debt. The West struggled to meet the challenges of the loss of Eastern and Central Europe, the First Berlin Crisis, the rise of the Warsaw Pact, the Korean War and a series of Communist-backed revolutions in many quarters of the globe.

The Polar Projection view of the earth with its accompanying emphasis on Great Circle Route flight patterns placed Alaska where Billy Mitchell had said it was in the 1920s. As the Cold War ebbed and flowed, so did the military population in the Territory. Alaska's strategic position became a given factor as the Cold War intensified in the 1950s and '60s.

The magic land attracted thousands of young Americans who saw opportunities that did not always exist in middle-aged America. There was a sense of being part of something big and historic. That frontier spirit truly existed—perhaps for the last time ever—and these modern pioneers, like generations of frontier people who had preceded them for two hundred years, were pushing to the very limits of America. That sense of unbounded, unrestricted freedom and the desire for an uncluttered life drew people to the Last Frontier and away from the crowded former frontiers.

There was the land itself—big, bold and challenging. It was exacting and demanded the best of people. Yet, it rewarded as well as demanded. It shaped an independent, self-reliant attitude that was not evident in any other section of America. The setting was overwhelming. The mountains, rivers, glaciers and wildlife could not be matched and the land was colored by the Midnight Sun in summer and by the Northern Lights in winter. Newcomers could only reason that God must have saved his best work for the last.

The Alaska National Guard was organized and directed by veterans of the Second World War during its formative years. The winds of fate lofted talent from all corners of the Big War and directed this talent towards the Great Land. The future leaders brought a wealth of wartime military experiences, which helped them develop one of the finest National Guard organizations in the nation. Most did not know they would fulfill their destinies in the Far North.

While Colonel Joseph Alexander was serving as a young infantry officer in Europe, future Brigadier General Charles Casper was going through the Battle of the Bulge experience nearby. Not far away, Lieutenant Thomas Patrick Carroll was earning a Silver Star, two Bronze Stars for Valor and two Purple Hearts as a member of the 315th Infantry of the 79th Division. He was recommended for the Congressional Medal of Honor and would become a Major General in the Alaska National Guard. Cadet Bruce I. Staser, an Alaskan and a member of the Class of 1943, was boxing at West Point and completing an education that would make him a competent army career officer. He, too, would become an Adjutant General of Alaska.

From the very beginning of the war—Pearl Harbor Day—future Alaskan leaders were being tested in battle. America's first air heroes, Lieutenants George Welch and Ken Taylor were up in P-40s destroying enemy aircraft over Hawaii. Lieutenant Taylor would wear a star as Assistant Adjutant General of Alaska.

Coming into Hickam Field near Honolulu on December 7, 1941, was a flight of unarmed B-17 bombers from Hamilton Field, California. It had been a long uneventful flight, but weary crew members were unknowingly flying into a war. The airfields on Oahu were under attack and the heavy bombers had to put down wherever they could. One fuel-starved Flying Fortress bellied in on a golf course. The crew survived the rough landing and walked away from the disabled aircraft. The unit had aborted a couple of aircraft at the beginning of the flight just off the coast of California and had several more aircraft damaged on the Hawaiian end of the mission. A few weeks later, new airplanes were picked up at the Boeing plant in Seattle and Major Conrad F. Necrason led them back through Hawaii, on to the Philippines and then to Southwest Asia where he would command the famed 7th Bombardment Group in the China-Burma-India Theater. Following the war, he would serve as Adjutant

Col. John R. Noyes on the beaches of Italy during World War Two. General Noyes died as a result of an aircraft crash near Nome in 1956.

had first come to Alaska during the 1930s. He fished in Bristol Bay and worked as a miner at the Independence Gold Mine near Willow. He received a commission and was sent to the Aleutian Islands as an engineering officer to lay out airfields. He saw the first American warplane shot down by a Japanese pilot in the Aleutian Campaign while working on one of the airfield sites. His heart was in flying and eventually, he attended flight school, went off to war and was highly decorated for combat action in the South Pacific.

Rare photo of Alaska's first adjutant general. Major Lars Johnson and his A-20 *King of the Tundra* in Mindoru, Philippine Islands, 1944.

General of Alaska for many years.

Colonel John R. Noyes, West Point Class of 1923, was busy on the beaches of Italy and in Western Europe during the war, while Private First Class Edward G. Pagano saw action as a rifleman during the invasion of Okinawa. Both would become Commanding Generals of the Alaska National Guard. PFC Pagano had no way of knowing that one of the B-24 Liberators flying from the raw airstrip on Okinawa to hit targets in Japan was being piloted by First Lieutenant William S. Elmore.

"Pappy" Elmore would become a Major General and serve two separate tours of duty as Adjutant General of the Alaska National Guard.

Alaska's first Adjutant General following the re-establishment of the National Guard in 1949, was a fighter pilot in the Philippines during the war. He had an Arctic wolf and a golden North Star painted on the nose of his A-20 and named the airplane the *King of the Tundra*. His pride in his adopted homeland streaked across the South Pacific skies in pursuit of Japanese targets. Larry Lars Johnson would play a significant part in the development of America's farthest north National Guard.

Governor Gruening considered several candidates for the position of Adjutant General following Colonel Alexander's departure for an assignment at the National Guard Bureau in Washington. Larry Lars Johnson applied for the job early in 1951. He

Some of Governor Gruening's associates pointed out that Colonel Johnson, if appointed, would be the youngest Adjutant General in the country. Johnson himself was aware of this and wrote the Governor on July 18, 1951. "I would like to repeat that I feel qualified to handle this (position) and believe that my record will stand up with any Alaskan's. I would not want my age to be considered a detriment as I believe my experience in making decisions which affected many lives and the responsibilities therewith connected should off-set what might be thought of as immaturity due to insufficient age."

Lars Johnson was appointed Adjutant General on August 1, 1951. The young flyer's ability to command became apparent almost from the beginning. What many who questioned his young age failed to realize was that Lars Johnson possessed the courage which is the hallmark of the fighter pilot. He had seen friends die in the South Pacific and had taken on ever-increasing responsibilities until at last, he became one of the youngest Air Corps Commanders in the Pacific while still in his twenties. Within six months after taking command of the

Gov. Ernest Gruening and Col. Lars Johnson, Adjutant General, dine in the field with the 208th Infantry Battalion during the Alaska Guard's first encampment on Nov. 29, 1951. U.S. ARMY PHOTO

Col. Lars Johnson, left, founder of the Alaska Air National Guard and first Adjutant General of Alaska with Brig. Gen. John R. Noyes, Alaska's second Adjutant General. Both men were veterans of World War Two. GORDON HOMME COLLECTION

Alaska National Guard, the new Adjutant General was able to report that the medical detachment in Sitka and Company D, 1st Scout Battalion in Barrow had been added to the 15 existing units of the Alaska National Guard.

Most of the units had conducted armory training during their three-year existence, but Colonel Johnson realized their federal recognition was in jeopardy because field training had not been accomplished. Within a month Johnson ordered field training exercises. The first was held for men from Nome's 1st Scout Battalion. A two-week river reconnaissance on the Kobuk and Noatak Rivers took place during September 1951. The men were flown to the upper waters of the two rivers and travelled on rubber rafts to Kotzebue.

The 207th Infantry Battalion attended its first field training at Fort Richardson in October. The 208th Battalion trained for 15 days near Juneau in November and the Scout Battalions spent 15 days at Fort Richardson in January 1952. Many of the Eskimo Scouts had never been to Anchorage and some came to their pickup points in the bush by dog team in the dead of winter to catch the flight to the city. The airplane flight itself was a first-time experience for many of the Eskimo Scouts. Several small field problems were also conducted locally in which men of one village would raid another village. These exercises were conducted with dog teams and travel was done under cover of the dark winter nights.

Colonel Johnson organized a non-commissioned officer school in Nome and sent many officers and men to army service schools in the United States. He supported the construction of indoor rifle ranges and an expanded armory program. The National Guard was moving forward, but was not without its problems. The U.S. Army in Alaska sometimes looked upon the Guard as a necessary evil and the old logistical support problems continued. Hand-me-down equipment continued to be pushed off on the Guard until it could prove itself and be integrated into the system. Confidence continued to grow in the ability of Alaska's young Adjutant General.

Victor Rivers, a politically powerful Alaskan, wrote a letter to Governor Gruening in which he stated: "I understand from officers of the regular army, that the first encampment was carried off successfully and a credit to our National Guard. Major Kunkle advised me that he was much pleased with the attitude and general competence of Colonel Larry Johnson. He stated that he believed that Colonel Johnson was a first class officer and was going to be wholly successful in the position of Adjutant General. I feel very kindly towards Larry and also because, in view of his relative youth, that I was somewhat dubious as to his ability to hold his own with older officers and Staff and Command groups. It is very gratifying to me that he is doing the job well."

The Governor replied, "I am glad that those who reported to you on the subject share that view. It has the further advantage that Larry is genuinely interested, that he is thoroughly Alaskan and has no desire to spend his life anywhere but in the Territory.

Pvt. Bill Cook of Hoonah lends a hand to Pfc. Charles Martin, Hoonah fisherman. The National Guardsmen negotiate the face of Mendenhall Glacier near Juneau during the first encampment in 1951. U.S. ARMY PHOTO BY CPL. JOHN MANN

Youth, when it is accompanied by competence, is not only no disadvantage but, in my judgment, a definite advantage."

Field training was planned for November 1952 at Fort Richardson. It was estimated that nearly a thousand Guardsmen would assemble for the camp. Colonel Johnson sent his assistant, Captain Lee Lucas to make arrangements with the army. The Guardsman was given the cold shoulder by the regular army one-star he was dealing with. Out of frustration, Lucas asked to use the General's phone. He called Governor Gruening in Juneau and explained the situation. Governor Gruening replied, "Stay right where you are and give me ten minutes." The two officers eyed each other in silence. Ten minutes later, the phone rang and the General listened. He visibly turned white, strung out about ten "Yes Sirs," hung up the phone and said, "Captain, you can schedule the use of Fort Richardson any time you like." Gruening later confided he had called the White House and Major General Harry Vaughn, President Truman's Military Aide took the call. General Vaughn had the Chief of Staff of the U.S. Army personally call the one-star at Fort Richardson to explain the facts of life to him. The

Alaska National Guard had very few problems with the regular army while Lars Johnson was Adjutant General.

Colonel Johnson's major contribution was in gaining an Air National Guard unit for Alaska against overwhelming odds. Again, his right-hand man was his assistant, Lee Lucas. The two men became fast friends and did a tremendous amount of work to establish an Air National Guard unit in Anchorage. It was only fitting that the State Legislature bestowed the state rank of Major General upon Larry Lars Johnson in 1989 and Brigadier General upon his assistant, Lee Lucas in 1990. The two pioneer Alaskans were giants in a giant land.

In September of 1953, the new Governor of Alaska, B. Frank Heintzleman appointed Brigadier General John Rutherford Noyes to the position of Adjutant General of Alaska. Governor Heintzleman had been appointed to his position by President Eisenhower on April 10, 1953. The Republican Governor had spent many years in Alaska with the Forest Service.

John R. Noyes had been a career soldier. The West Point Class of 1923 graduate had served as head of the District Corps of Engineers before the war and had seen much of Alaska while supervising the building of many roads in the Territory. He was from a prominent New York family and was the son of a West Point career soldier. His grandfather had been a founder of the Oneida Community experiment in New York—the silverware people. General Noyes was a no-nonsense, serious soldier whom West Point classmates had dubbed "the judge." Underneath that cool exterior lay a tender-hearted family man, a scholar and poet and an efficient officer.

John R. Noyes, through his army connections, moved the Guard closer to a partnership in arms with the regular army. The Guard expanded and made plans for joint winter exercises. The armory program became a priority and General Noyes travelled throughout the Territory inspecting facilities in anticipation of a new role for the Alaska National Guard. His work was cut short by a tragic aircraft accident on January 27, 1956. General Noyes and three companions had been on an inspection trip to Shishmaref, located on the Arctic Ocean on the north side of the Seward Peninsula. They were returning to Nome when the L-20 Beaver aircraft ran into a blizzard just 20 miles from Nome. The pilot frantically radioed the Nome airport but was unsuccessful in gaining directions. A white-out condition hid the low mountains in the area. The plane hit a ridge and slid downhill about 300-feet before coming to a stop. Major Siegwart, Commander of the Nome National Guard unit, was

Drill night during the 1950s. Armories were typically World War Two Quonset huts, which were small and overcrowded.
ALASKA NATIONAL GUARD

Typical small armory drill during the 1950s. Ike jackets and M-1 rifles were still the style and NCO's were generally World War Two veterans.
ALASKA NATIONAL GUARD

thrown out of the plane. Major Kolb, the pilot, was injured severely. Sergeant August, the aircraft mechanic, broke some ribs but was conscious. Siegwart and August managed to get the moaning pilot into a sleeping bag to keep him from freezing to death. The General was pinned in the wreckage. "We believed the general was dead as we could detect no pulse and being too exhausted to do anything further, lay down to wait until the storm abated, which was not until about five o'clock Saturday morning," related Major Siegwart.

Sergeant August later climbed to the top of the flat mountain but could not see where they were as a heavy fog lay over the valley below. The two men returned to the mountaintop again when they heard aircraft overhead and burned a parachute, but were not seen by the men searching for the missing aircraft. They checked General Noyes once more and

this time discovered a faint pulse. The men remained in the wrecked aircraft throughout the four-day ordeal in sub-zero weather and were finally spotted about noon on Monday, January 30, by flying missionary Donald Bruckner and his observer, Jim Walsh. The missing aircraft was near Engstrom's Camp on Basin Creek.

The search had been one of the largest ever organized in the Arctic. The Air National Guard sent a C-47 from Anchorage, while the 71st and 74th Search and Rescue Squadrons from Elmendorf Air Force Base in Anchorage and Ladd Field in Fairbanks sent C-54's. Wien Alaska Airline pilots, the Civil Air Patrol and local bush pilots flew many volunteer hours searching for Alaska's Adjutant General. Bush pilots Martin Olson, Philip Lancaster and veteran pilot Bob Munz landed on the flat mountaintop and brought the injured men into

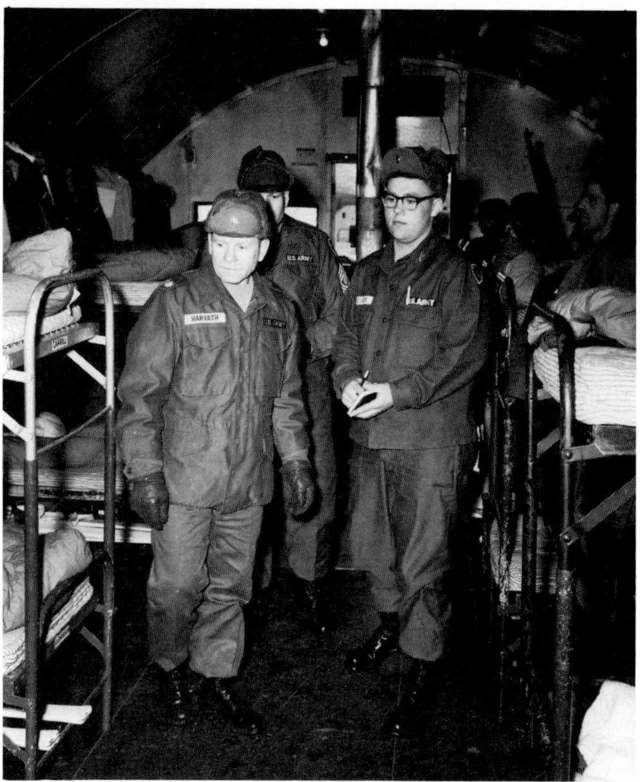

Living conditions were crowded in the 1950s and the pay was low but men continued to soldier for the Alaska National Guard. ALASKA NATIONAL GUARD

Nome. General Noyes had survived the crash and the wait only to die in the Nome hospital a few hours after being rescued.

The General's bride of one year had no way of knowing she would not see her husband again that morning she cheerfully said good-bye to him at the Juneau airport. She had a secret to share with him upon his return to Juneau, but was never able to tell him she was expecting their first child. The son who was born some seven months later would never know his father.

The Oneida, New York, area is a beautiful rolling countryside which disproves many Westerner's concept of New York as a congested mass of humanity barely surviving the Eastern Seaboard megalopolis. Behind the ancestral mansion of the Noyes family in a tiny country cemetery rests a bit of Alaska's history forever—far from the rugged Great Land and its harsh weather that can take a human life in a heartbeat. The headstone in Sherrill, New York, proclaims proudly that this quiet spot is the final resting place of Brigadier General John R. Noyes— the Adjutant General of Alaska. The native son had come home.

Governor Heintzleman appointed Major Elvis M. Farmer as acting Adjutant General. The young Major had come to Alaska in 1952 from the National Guard Bureau as an administrative officer. The 26-year-old officer was a World War Two veteran from Berryville, Arkansas. He had become Assistant Adjutant General in 1954. When he was promoted to full Colonel and made acting Adjutant General in 1956 at the age of 29, some felt he was too young for the position. He was to serve as acting AG for only 19 months. He travelled throughout the Territory, developed a plan for expanding the armory program and represented Alaska at the Pentagon when the regular army announced a plan that required all new Guardsmen to spend six months on active duty before reporting to their home unit. Colonel Farmer felt this policy was hurting the recruiting program at a time the Alaska National Guard needed growth.

A group of 72 Eskimo Guardsmen volunteered to train for six months with the regular army at Fort Ord, California. Colonel Farmer and Major William Crawford, Commander of the First Scouts in Nome, flew to Fort Ord and met the Alaskans upon their arrival. The Eskimo Scouts were judged outstanding by the army personnel in California. The change of climate and scenery was quite an adventure for the Alaskans from the Bering Sea coast.

In March of 1957, elements of the 207th Infantry Battalion trained in Fairbanks. A group of 20 Eskimo and Indian Guardsmen attended the Yukon Command NCO School at Eielson Air Force Base near Fairbanks. They went on to Camp Denali on Fort Richardson in April to become leaders at annual training. The National Guard was beginning to utilize the talents of its native soldiers.

In November of 1956, President Eisenhower was elected to a second term as President of the United States. In January, 1957, Governor Heintzleman left his position in Juneau and Waino Hendrickson became acting Governor of Alaska until the President could appoint a new Governor. Mike Stepovich, 38-year-old Republican lawyer and homesteader from Fairbanks was selected to become the 15th Governor of Alaska. He arrived in Juneau on the warmest June 6th ever recorded with his wife and seven children. The Guard was there to greet him and Colonel Elvis Farmer remained as acting Adjutant General.

The Cold War was never far away. On July 13, 1957, Sergeant Max Wright of the Alaska National Guard and a fellow workman were in a boat near Dutch Harbor when they spotted a mysterious submarine. They reported their sighting and the Navy admitted there were no U.S. submarines in the area. They watched the submarine set a course towards the northwest and Soviet Siberia.

Governor Mike Stepovich inspects an honor guard of the 1st Scout Battalion who were flown to Juneau to participate in the inauguration of the new Governor in June 1957.

Bureau of Land Management crew unloads an Air Guard C-123J at Flat, Alaska, during the fire season in the 1960s. The National Guard transported people and equipment to remote areas of the state for a variety of emergencies.

Home on the range. A young buffalo finds a new home near Delta, Alaska, after being transported by an Air Guard C-123J. The Guard worked with Fish and Wildlife on the successful experiment.

Colonel Farmer's short tenure as acting AG was marked by several significant events. The Seward Armory, the first of many new armories, was dedicated by Governor Stepovich and the acting AG on September 21, 1957. The Air National Guard changed missions while Colonel Farmer was in charge. The 144th Fighter-Interceptor Squadron traded in its F-86 jets and became the 144th Air Transport Squadron and began flying C-47 transport planes. Colonel Farmer changed the look of the Army Guard uniforms by introducing the Big Dip-

per shoulder patch to replace the familiar U.S. Army Alaska Polar Bear patch. The Big Dipper has continued to be worn by Alaska Army Guardsmen to the present day.

In August of 1957, Colonel Farmer announced he would step down at the end of October, setting off speculation as to who would lead Alaska's Minutemen. The Alaska National Guard Officers Association endorsed two candidates—Major Thomas P. Carroll from Anchorage and Major William Crawford, Commander at Nome. It was rumored that

Republican Central Committee Chairman, Robert Groseclose of Fairbanks, was pushing for retired army Colonel Edward B. Millett of Cordova.

The *Anchorage Times* reported on August 9, 1957, that former acting Adjutant General, Colonel Joseph Alexander, had applied for the position. Alexander had originally organized the Alaska National Guard while serving as Senior Army Advisor to Governor Gruening. He had served as Senior Army Advisor to the Puerto Rican National Guard after leaving Alaska. Governor Stepovich announced on October 23, 1957, that he had chosen Major Thomas P. Carroll as Alaska's new Adjutant General.

Thomas Patrick Carroll was born in Edgemont, South Dakota, in 1916. He began his military career as a Private in the South Dakota National Guard in 1937. He was called to active duty with the 34th Infantry Division when it was sent to Northern Ireland in February, 1941. He would do his fighting during the war in Western Europe. He won his Silver Star by averting an ambush of his company by German soldiers, 18 of whom he either killed or wounded. During the war, he served as a Rifle Platoon Leader, Company Commander and a Battalion Staff Officer.

Carroll came to Alaska following his discharge from the army. He joined that throng of restless young veterans who were not satisfied to return to dull, small-town America. The Big One had given them a taste of danger, adventure and foreign travel. The plains of South Dakota held little appeal compared to the land of towering mountains, high adventure and unlimited opportunity. Jack London, Robert Service and Company could still light fires a half century after the fact.

Tom Carroll was an accountant for the Alaska Railroad from 1946 to 1950 when he joined the maintenance division of Reeve Aleutian Airways. Bob Reeve, the famous Alaskan bush pilot, probably "Alaskanized" the former Dakota soldier as was his habit with new employees. In that same year, Tom Carroll committed his life to Alaska by joining the newly organized National Guard as Commander of Headquarters and Services Company of the 207th Infantry Battalion in Anchorage. During his tenure as Adjutant General, the Alaska National Guard expanded and a vigorous program of armory construction began. His wartime service in Europe had made him aware of the value of air support and he fostered the growth of the Air National Guard. More funds were put into the air service and newer, larger aircraft were acquired for both the Army and the Air National Guard. The Air National Guard expanded quickly and missions were extended within Alaska and to areas outside the Territory. The Army and Air National Guard became major players in the winter war exercises conducted by the Army and

Air Force in Alaska. General Carroll became known throughout the Alaska National Guard as an inspirational leader, organizer and a soldier's soldier.

The Territory of Alaska came of age during the Carroll years. The question of statehood was an old issue that had been advanced without success since the early 1900s. There had been promises made and promises broken, but the late 1950s brought renewed interest in the issue. There was a concerted effort by those who advocated statehood. To overcome opposition to the plan, pro-statehood groups planned strategy based on other State's experiences of gaining membership in the Union. State constitutions were studied and Ernest Gruening, who had left the Governor's Mansion a few years earlier, continued his battle for statehood. He wrote numerous articles for national magazines and a book, *The State of Alaska*, to sell the plan nationwide. Congress had to be prodded into considering the Alaska statehood issue. Much of the opposition came from the southern block in Congress and from some eastern states that could see political clout dissolving and immigrating to the West Coast. The shopworn argument of Alaska and Hawaii not being contiguous with the older 48 States was polished up for use while the real political issues were deemphasized as battle lines were established in Congress.

The Alaskans studied the Tennessee Plan, which had been used by that state many years earlier when it sought admittance to the Union. It called for a Statehood Convention, the writing of a constitution, the election of a Congressional delegation and the presentation of a ready-made state to the Congress.

Fifty-five delegates were chosen—not unlike the Philadelphia Convention—to become the Founding Fathers (and Mothers) of Alaska Statehood. They met on the campus of the University of Alaska in Fairbanks on November 9, 1955. Some who attended were aware of this linkage with America's Constitutional Convention. Here was raw democracy at work on America's Last Frontier. The delegates would become powerful figures on the Alaska political scene. In an almost religious setting, the delegates met, debated, studied and hammered out a state constitution modeled somewhat on that of New York State. Where they met became known as Signer's Hall, which is a hushed place of great dignity and a "must" on the tourist route around the city of Fairbanks.

The Convention elected William Egan of Valdez as President of the historic meeting. One of the delegates, Ralph Rivers, would become Alaska's first elected Representative to the U.S. House of Representatives while William Egan would become Gover-

William Egan, Alaska's first elected governor following statehood, supported the expansion of the National Guard. He used the Guard extensively during the great earthquake of 1964.
ALASKA STATE LIBRARY, JUNEAU

General Carroll and Governor Egan review the troops at Camp Denali shortly before the '64 earthquake. The General was killed in an aircraft accident at Valdez. A portion of the base was named Camp Carroll in 1967. U.S. ARMY

nor of Alaska. The keynote speaker was Ernest Gruening; who would become Alaska's first junior United States Senator. Bob Bartlett, Gruening's friend and helper for so many years in Juneau and Alaska's Congressional Delegate would become senior United States Senator. Following the convention, Gruening set up an office in Washington D.C. to lobby for statehood.

Alaska became the 49th State in 1959. General Carroll continued to oversee the development of the Alaska National Guard. The Department of Defense developed a series of winter war games for Alaska to test military equipment and soldiers in the harsh Arctic environment. The concept of cold weather warfare brought vivid pictures to mind of Napoleon's withdrawal from Moscow and the German disaster on the Russian Front during the Second World War. Winter had historically been an ally of Mother Russia. Americans became more aware of an over the Pole attack during the early 1960s and the Nation's possession at the top of the world became more important than ever before.

The Eskimo Scouts were invited to take part in exercise Willow Freeze in 1961. The Scouts were so effective on their home ground, the army asked the National Guard to take part in exercise Great Bear in 1962. Henceforth, the Alaska National Guard became a regular feature in the winter exercises. The army was often embarrassed when the Eskimo Scouts came out of the snow fronts, struck and disappeared while green regular troops were having enough trouble just surviving the bitter weather. The National Guardsmen gained new respect and the regulars realized they were valuable friends in the Arctic. By 1962, more modern equipment was being turned over to the Alaska National Guard and joint training became a way of life in the Far North.

President Kennedy inherited a Berlin Crisis and the Cold War intensified all over the globe. A new emphasis was put on the ready reserve program and more money began to be directed towards the Nation's National Guard. By the time the Cuban Crisis evolved in October of 1962, the National Guard's role as a backup force had become a matter of policy.

In Alaska, the Scouts along the Bering Sea became extremely important. They had gained some national recognition a few years earlier as a result of their rescuing a U.S. Navy patrol plane crew which had crash-landed on St. Lawrence Island after being attacked by a Russian MIG fighter plane from the Siberian side. Soviet activity became more widespread in the Far North. There had been stray aircraft incidents, over the border crossing incidents, stories about Alaskan Natives being detained in Siberia, stories about mysterious lights off the coast of Alaska and reports of raft landings on isolated

Alaskan beaches. The Scouts were the experts in the Arctic and they kept the army informed of any sightings or unusual happenings along America's lonely coast.

The death of President John F. Kennedy in November of 1963 left the nation stunned. The Cold War did not lessen and the war in Vietnam intensified. The massive buildup in that distant war included a call up for some National Guard units. Some individual Alaska Guardsmen volunteered for and fought in Vietnam.

On the domestic front, Alaskans became more aware of the direct benefits of having a well-trained National Guard. During the Carroll years, the National Guard performed search and rescue missions, was there for flood and fire relief and even provided avalanche control along the highways of South Central Alaska. The Air Guard supported the Rampart Dam Engineering Team studies, landed scientific study teams on Taku Glacier, flew wildlife transplant stock to remote sites and landed on a floating ice island in the Arctic Ocean to rescue a stranded scientific team. The Air Guard began flying its annual Operation Santa Claus trips to bring Christmas gifts to remote native villages. The Army Guard created good will in numerous towns and villages by being there whenever the citizens needed help. This was never more true than in March of 1964.

Good Friday—March 27, 1964, dawned as a bright early spring Alaskan day. The temperature was warmer than normal and Alaskans had survived another long dark winter. The daylight was lengthening and a sense of optimism stirred in the minds of the inhabitants. A millennium ritual which promised the resurrection of the north and the greening of the land was in the air. To the south, the ducks and geese had started the annual trek to mark the season and would soon be arriving by the thousands. Over a thousand National Guardsmen were finishing up their annual training at Camp Denali near Anchorage. The Scouts were anxious to return home to the villages for the spring hunt.

The words devastating, catastrophic, colossal and gigantic magnitude had little meaning for most Alaskans until 5:27 P.M., March 27, 1964. It was at this moment animals seemed to sense some impending disaster and a jarring alerted many to a far-off roar like a distant freight train approaching. The underground thunder raced and built up power and volume as it spread out in a huge arc-like pattern nearly 500 miles towards Anchorage, Valdez, Seward and west to Kodiak from the point deep below Prince William Sound near College Glacier where the continental plates had shifted.

The earthquake was the most powerful ever recorded in North America. It unleashed a force equal to 12,000 Hiroshima-sized atomic bombs. The twisting, wave-like motion travelled at more than one hundred miles-per-hour to bring death and destruction to Alaska's Southcentral district. There had been more destructive earthquakes. The great San Francisco earthquake and the fires that followed had taken many more lives as had earthquakes in Portugal, India and Japan. The Alaska earthquake took place in an area of a relatively small spread out population at the close of the business day when school was not in session and many people were headed home after work. The unseasonably warm weather averted additional suffering.

The earthquake affected communities differently. Portions of Anchorage were hit hard while other sections escaped major damage. A section of downtown Fourth Avenue dropped 30 feet and whole blocks of commercial buildings were nearly destroyed. Portions of the exclusive Turnigan Arm subdivision slid off towards Cook Inlet and expensive homes were destroyed. More than 150 commercial buildings were damaged, including the almost new J.C. Penney store where some people were killed. The control tower at Anchorage International Airport fell and the airport was closed to traffic for a time. An Air National Guard C-123 became an air traffic control center and broadcast to the world news of the disaster.

A National Guard party from Minnesota and Colonel Charles Casper were en route to Fort Richardson when the earthquake struck. Cars danced crazily on the road, streets dropped, wide fissures appeared and closed. Rail lines were torn apart, buildings toppled and power lines lay everywhere. At Camp Denali on Fort Richardson, a final parade and review was being held on the parade ground. A group of officers observing the review linked hands when the force hit to keep together in case the earth parted. The circle waved with the quake and Lieutenant Roger Schnell (later Colonel) would see the knees of the men across the circle, then their faces, then they would disappear and reappear as the earth danced. He observed the marching soldiers in formation—a moment later rifles sailed into the air and the marchers were knocked off their feet. The trees of Camp Denali bowed nearly to the ground in one direction then swayed the opposite way while the Chugach Mountains seemed to move up and down. It was as if God and Mother Nature had combined forces to remind man he was insignificant in the order of events.

Parts of Anchorage were left in shambles. When the ground ceased moving, it left mass destruction and personal tragedy. The roar was followed by a strange silence as people stood in disbelief and fear.

Guardsmen provided help to the community during the days and weeks following the earthquake in 1964.
U.S. ARMY

The earthquake left the U.S. Property and Finance Office in shambles. It took many days of work to restore the office to its normal routine.
ALASKA NATIONAL GUARD

Guardsmen remained on duty in Anchorage to discourage looters from entering homes and businesses. BG CHARLES CASPER

Mother Nature had prevailed and had tossed the Great Land around during unending minutes of tragedy. Other towns fared worse than Anchorage.

Kodiak felt the jolt well before the seismic wave. There was a smaller silent wave first, then a 30-foot wall of water lifted crab boats and tossed them like toys into the town. Fishing boats were scattered inland and people disappeared.

Valdez was hit by the jolt and wave almost simultaneously. Twenty-eight stevedores and onlookers watched the Alaska Steamship Company's SS *Chena* hit the bottom of the bay then frantically try to get underway to safety. The seismic wave took many lives and nearly all the residents were evacuated.

The National Guard Transportation Company from Seward was in Anchorage for training. They had heard that Seward had been devastated by the huge wall of water which destroyed the railway yards. Roger Schnell, the young officer in the circle at Camp Denali, had no way of knowing the wall of water had taken his grandfather's life and had nearly killed his parents. Seward was hit by the burning oil from the ruptured fuel storage tanks. The fire was carried by the wave that swept in and out of the harbor. The Seward truck company tried to get home but found out the bridges near Portage had been destroyed. They were flown home by the Air National Guard to help the stricken citizens of Seward.

Throughout the State, the National Guard and the Regulars gave no thought to long hours. The Eskimo Scouts did not go home. They were put on guard duty in downtown Anchorage to help survivors and to discourage potential looters. The Air National Guard flew mercy missions and delivered supplies wherever they were needed. The Army Guard Engineers were in demand wherever damage was found.

The cleanup and the after shocks would go on through April. A Federal Disaster Team was sent to Alaska after President Lyndon Johnson made relief funds available. Tons of supplies donated by fellow Americans poured into the stricken state and were distributed by relief agencies and the National Guard. The Governor and his advisors flew on Air Guard planes with federal officials to complete damage surveys. Everywhere, the Alaskans let the officials know that they would build a new and better Alaska. They were, after all, frontiersmen and pioneers.

On April 25, 1964, the State of Alaska suffered a second blow. A C-123 Air Guard plane piloted by Lt. Colonel Tom Norris flew Governor Egan and his party of 12 officials and newsmen into Valdez. The plane had come in under low clouds only a few hundred feet over the water. Upon arrival, one engine was kept running while the Governor's party and his vehicle was unloaded. The weather was squally and the Governor advised General Carroll he should consider remaining in Valdez until Sunday because of bad flying weather. Governor Egan was visiting his hometown to evaluate earthquake damage. A charity steak dinner had been scheduled to raise money for earthquake victims. The General was invited but felt he had to get back to Anchorage and joked he had not brought a fork for the steak feed.

As the Governor's party was taken into town, Colonel Norris taxied the C-123 Provider onto the runway for takeoff. The Governor said he did not hear, "the slightest bark or cough, to indicate there was any engine trouble." A Fort Wainwright soldier was standing at the remnants of the Valdez dock on guard duty. He watched the plane lift off and fly low over the water. Then it suddenly glided with fully running engines at an angle into the water.

The Governor's party turned into the dock about the time the plane hit the water and sped to the boat landing where a couple of skiffs and a large fishing boat were getting underway. The Governor saw the plane was still floating and remarked, "Thank goodness, they'll have a chance to get into a raft." But there was no time. The plane floated for 3 or 4 minutes, then disappeared into about 600 feet of water.

The pilot, Lt. Colonel Tom Norris, was a highly decorated World War Two flyer. He had often been picked to fly the Governor around the State. The Governor's other personal pilot, Colonel Dean Stringer, was not scheduled for the Valdez mission. Colonel William Elmore, back in Anchorage, stated the crew had called in and expressed fear that if they stayed overnight in Valdez, the plane would become covered with frost and would be unable to return to Anchorage with the Governor and his party.

General Carroll, Lt. Colonel Tom Norris, Major James Rowe, co-pilot and Technical Sergeant Ken Ayers went down with the plane. Only a flight book, an Air Force parka, a briefcase, a wing tank, a packaged life raft and part of the plane's hydraulic system were recovered.

The Governor returned on another C-123 the following day in clear and beautiful weather. As he flew over the Valdez Arm he could see the U.S. Coast Guard and Geodetic ship *Survey* anchored near the oil slick that marked the final resting place of four National Guardsmen. A nine-man Air Force investigating team came to the conclusion the pilot may have lost the horizon momentarily because of low visibility. The smooth glassy water plus the low ceiling added to a darkening sky and falling snow, all made for a situation of extremely poor visibility.

The Eskimo Scouts came to Anchorage for annual training and often marched in the Fur Rendezvous Parade during the 1960s. ALASKA NATIONAL GUARD

General Thomas Carroll had been a major figure in the history of the Alaska National Guard. The National Guard training site at Fort Richardson would be named Camp Carroll in his honor. Some 25 years later, the young officers he influenced would themselves become leaders in the Army National Guard and they would remember that their careers had been touched by General Carroll. Almost without exception, the old-time Guardsmen to this day claim that General Carroll was the greatest Adjutant General to ever hold the position.

Colonel Fred O. Reger, General Carroll's assistant, was appointed acting Adjutant General. He would hold that position through July, 1964. The reconstruction of earthquake damaged National Guard facilities continued under Colonel Reger and bids were let on three more scout armories. Colonel Charles Casper recommended that the Office of the Adjutant General be moved to Anchorage, but the suggestion was rejected by the Governor. Colonel Casper had been a major figure in the Alaska National Guard and had been a strong and efficient U.S. Property and Fiscal Officer. He was a strong candidate for the Adjutant General's position.

Lieutenant Colonel William S. Elmore became the first blue suit Adjutant General on August 1, 1964. The Air Guardsman had been a B-24 pilot during World War Two. He would serve until January, 1967 and again from January, 1971 to April, 1973. The Alaska National Guard continued to expand under the guidance of "Pappy" Elmore. The popular flyer was well-known throughout the state, especially in the remote villages he had flown into for many years. Pappy loved flying and when he made inspection trips, more often than not, he was at the controls of the aircraft. He was not one who went along for the ride. He had to be the Aircraft Commander as well as the National Guard Commander.

In 1965, the Army and Air National Guard took part in Exercise Polar Strike near Fairbanks and did exceptionally well. By 1966, some of the new equipment destined for the Alaska Army National Guard began to be directed to the ever-increasing war in Southeast Asia. At home, Governor Egan lost a close election and in January, 1967, Governor Walter J. Hickel took office. General Elmore was replaced by Conrad F. Necrason, a retired Air Force Major General. General Necrason, a West Point Class of 1936 graduate, would serve the State of Alaska longer than any other Adjutant General.

The force had increased tremendously by 1967 and Alaskans had created a new State. Alaska's Minutemen had served the Territory and state well during the National Guard's brief eighteen-year life. Alaska was on the threshold of greatness and the Soldiers of the Mists, like their predecessors of a thousand years, would be there to aid, protect and guide the Great Land through the final quarter of the 20th Century.

Sgt. Joseph Moongwook takes his men on patrol near Savoonga on St. Lawrence Island. The Eskimo Scouts have been vital for American defense since World War Two. ALASKA NATIONAL GUARD

William S. Elmore was one of the early jet pilots at Kulis Air Guard Base. Pappy loved flying. He would become a two star General and serve as Adjutant General of Alaska two different times.
ALASKA AIR NATIONAL GUARD

Eskimo Scouts M/Sgt. Peter Kummerfeldt, Sgt. Major Jim Aveoganna, center, show Major Jack Fuller, standing, and SFC Elroy Kulukhon, right, how to lay up the wall of a survival shelter.
ALASKA NATIONAL GUARD PHOTO BY BILL MACK

A completed survival hut with caribou skin door. The Eskimo Scouts were used by regular military forces to teach arctic survival courses.
ALASKA NATIONAL GUARD PHOTO BY BILL MACK

Eskimo Scouts report in after a routine patrol. The versatile soldiers know the land well and can survive the extreme weather conditions.
ALASKA NATIONAL GUARD

Eskimo Scouts on Little Diomede Island, Alaska, reported any unusual activity on the Soviet side of the border during the Cold War era. U.S. ARMY

Men of the Second Scout Battalion move swiftly and silently through difficult terrain to carry out a surprise attack on the enemy during the 1967 annual training at Camp Denali near Anchorage.
ALASKA NATIONAL GUARD

THE RENAISSANCE

IN THE FAR NORTHWEST reaches of the continent, a frontier sort of saga began with the discovery of oil on the Kenai Peninsula by the Atlantic Richfield Corporation in 1957. Before then, Alaska had not progressed far from its historic status as a distant colony of little political significance. As the Swanson River oil field began to create jobs and pump paychecks into the economy, Alaskans began to envision an economic means of developing the new 49th State.

The discovery of vast oil reserves in 1968 at Prudhoe Bay on the north slope of the Arctic coast would bring more wealth to the young state. Within twenty years, Alaska would surpass Texas as the leading oil producing state in the nation. There was a renaissance of interest in the Nation's northern treasure house by Corporate America, the Federal Government and energy hungry Americans.

Tales of northern wealth and high wages attracted a new wave of the same get-rich-quick-type crowd that the land had witnessed many times before and the boom-and-bust thread that had always woven through the fabric of Alaska's written history became a factor of fortune once more. The exploiters would come, take and leave with Alaska's bounty just as in the days of old. That phase of Alaskan history never seemed to change. There was, however, a slight difference this time around. Some of the wealth would stay in the North Country—thanks to a few true Alaskan visionaries. The man who would direct the fortunes of the Alaska National Guard during much of this time of turbulent growth had come from a far distant shore.

Snuggled in a valley along the shores of a beautiful lake—not far from the final resting place of Alaska's first New York general—lay the boyhood home of Alaska's second New York born general, Conrad F. Necrason.

The words quaint and picturesque are foreign to the American scene and are normally used by tourists to fill in the backside of postcards mailed from Rothenburg, Germany, tiny Dutch towns, or from thatched roof villages in Suffolk, England, to envious friends and relatives back home. Although the words are rarely used to describe American towns, Cooperstown, New York, could be an exception during the brilliance of the colorful hardwoods show of a New York Autumn.

In those idyllic days of simplicity, long before the Baseball Hall of Fame would come to dominate the tourist industry of the area, Cooperstown was a quiet village and the summer home of the wealthy. The elder Necrason had come from the old country to become an electrician and caretaker at the Anheuser-Busch estate. Young Conrad and his friends and relatives had the run of the estate when the Busch family returned to the brewery in St. Louis after the heat and humidity left the river city at summer's end. Old man Busch was popular with the townsmen and often brought a menagerie of animals to the village with him for the enjoyment of the local children. Cooperstown was an ideal place for a boyhood, but young Necrason's dreams went beyond the village and focused on the United States Military Academy on the Hudson River where the brightest and the best were transformed into warriors to serve throughout the world.

High above the historic river at West Point, where chains across the water had stopped British ships during the Revolutionary War, the gray castle-like walls housed the class of 1936. The air was heavy with history and tradition and the cadets who drilled on the plain, labored on the athletic fields or strolled along flirtation walk below the somber cannons overlooking the river, could see far away landscapes. It was a place of dreams where images of greatness, of becoming one of the chosen few who created legends and history for a grateful nation, did not escape even the lowest ranked classmen. They walked the sacred grounds of Lee, Grant, MacArthur, Patton, Bradley and Eisenhower and could not escape the experience untouched. The atmosphere reached within the soul and would mark them for life.

The Long Gray Line on the plains of West Point sometimes consisted of a single cadet walking off demerits, head and body ram-rod strait, but with an eye towards the blue heavens, where his career would mostly be spent. Within the walls of the living area was an interesting group of cadets who would serve the nation well during the Second World War. Some of Necrason's classmates would wield power and influence in future years and could be called upon by the Adjutant General of Alaska to benefit his adopted state. Down the hall was his good friend "Westy"—Cadet William Childs Westmoreland. Further along the hallway was Cadet Creighton Abrams and then Cadet B.O. Davis, who

Major General Conrad F. Necrason. The New York born West Pointer commanded the 7th Bombardment Group in the Far East during World War Two and would serve Alaska longer than any other Adjutant General. ALASKA NATIONAL GUARD

reorganizations of the Alaska National Guard in 1961, and again in 1964, in which service-type detachments had been added to increase mobilization readiness. Two ordnance detachments and a signal detachment had been added in 1961 to support the repair of vehicles, small arms and communications equipment. In 1964, the Third Battle Group, 297th Infantry was reorganized as the Third Battalion, 297th Infantry with Companies in Anchorage, Ketchikan, Petersburg, Sitka, Kodiak and in Kenai-Soldotna. Several new units were added in 1964. The 910th Engineering Company replaced a rifle platoon stationed in Juneau and the Alaska National Guard became one of the very few organizations nation-wide to have Green Berets when the 38th Special Forces Detachment was formed in Anchorage in January, 1964. It was soon joined by a Special Forces Detachment in Gambell, on St. Lawrence Island, and another Special Forces Detachment in Kotzebue. The name 38th had come from Major Nelson's old outfit, the 38th Infantry. The 38th Special Forces was a high-morale unit with a hot mission. They trained constantly and were directly under 7th Special Forces in the continental U.S. The cost of training to keep current eventually caused the Alaska National Guard to drop the Special Forces program.

The Adjutant General made an inspection trip to nearly every unit in the state to become familiar with his new command and began a long period of unprecedented growth and change in the Alaska National Guard to match the rapidly changing state and world situation. Anchorage had become the business hub of the young state and in July 1967, Governor Hickel made the decision to move the Office of the Adjutant General closer to the center of his widely scattered National Guard troops.

General Necrason and Walter Cronkite aboard a C-130 bound for Kotzebue. ALASKA NATIONAL GUARD

would become the first black Air Force general and a dozen more future military leaders. They all knew the big, good-natured football player from Cooperstown. General Necrason had commanded the famed 7th Bombardment Group in the China-Burma-India Theater during World War Two. The Group's motto, MORS AB ALTO—Death from Above, became familiar to Japanese commanders who suffered from its effective missions throughout the war. The young West Pointer returned from the war with a Silver Star for gallantry over Burma, the Distinguished Flying Cross with oak leaf cluster, a Legion of Merit, several Air Medals and shrapnel scars in his right shoulder. He served in Germany during the Berlin Airlift and was Chief of Staff of the Far East Bomber Command during the Korean War. After serving as Commander of the Alaska Air Command and 28th Air Division Commander, he came home to Alaska to stay.

Before Necrason's arrival, there had been major

General Westmoreland, commander of troops in Vietnam, meets the children of Elim, Alaska in 1971. U.S. ARMY PHOTO

General Westmoreland learns about gold panning from old-timer Herb Engstrom during a visit to Nome in 1971.
U.S. ARMY PHOTO

General Necrason completed the organization of a Naval Militia. His predecessor, General Elmore, had become interested in the project before leaving office and had initiated the program. Sailors of the Mists would join the brotherhood of arms and Alaska would have a sea-faring force of Minutemen for a while during the Necrason years.

Mother Nature never waits long in Alaska to instigate mischief. The new Adjutant had been in command only a short time when the Fairbanks Floods in August 1967, tested the Army and Air National Guard once more. Governor Hickel put Guardsmen on active duty and sent them to the Golden Heart City to help citizens fight the Chena River. The Air Guard flew men, women and children to Anchorage where they were put up at Camp Carroll and at Kulis Air Guard Base until the flood waters receded. The humanitarian effort by the

Army and Air Guardsmen won new support for the organization throughout the state. The Alaska National Guard had always been called upon to carry out unusual missions. At one time, the 216th Medium Truck Cargo Company in Seward had been a Transportation Sled Company. It had inherited the huge tractor-land-train units with oversized tires that had been used to haul material across the endless tundra during the Distant Early Warning Radar (Dew Line) construction days at the top of the world. It was thought the Army Guard could use the huge vehicles to haul supplies across the frozen tundra and rivers, but the idea proved to be impractical.

The Eskimo Scouts were used to teach Arctic survival skills to regular army soldiers and sled dog teams gave way to snow machines (iron dogs) as the Alaska Guard experimented with new applications in the ancient art of war. The small scout teams criss-crossed the Arctic and ran circles around the regular troops in joint maneuvers. The Alaska Army Guard tested cold weather gear and equipment for the U.S. Army. They knew what would work and what would not work in the Arctic.

In Southeastern Alaska, members of the National Guard became part-time sailors and manned their own navy landing-craft type ships. They learned to land and fight on beaches and became familiar with the hundreds of bays and islands that make up that land of deep forests, fogs and mountains. Other Southeastern Guardsmen became mountain soldiers and glacier experts or learned to fly army fixed wing aircraft and helicopters in this area of dangerous skies where there was no room for error.

Up in Anchorage, Guardsmen tested hovercraft on the Knik River for use by the military and drove Sheridan tanks for the 5th Squadron of the 297th Cavalry. In an area as vast as Alaska with its climatic zones and a terrain unmatched anywhere in the world, the Alaskans had to be adaptive, mobile and unique among the National Guard units of the United States. If the land was to be defended, the Alaskans would have to be the experts on their homeland. They could be the teachers of regular forces who could be moved north within a matter of hours to fight an enemy to a standstill at the Northern Fringe before it could strike inland towards the heart of America. This is what the Soldiers of the Mists were trained to do.

The major event during the decade of the '70s was the building of the Trans-Alaska Oil Pipeline to bring the Alaska crude from the vast reservoir at Prudhoe Bay to tidewater for transport to world markets. There was a wait after the discovery of oil

This strange machine is a Corsair air-cushioned vehicle. It was built by Air Cushion Technologies International, Inc., in Anchorage, Alaska, and was tested out by the Army National Guard. The craft could cruise over water at 30 knots and reach a top speed of 45 knots on land. It exceeded 60 knots on wind-packed snow and had a range of 280 miles. It consumed 12 gallons of gas per hour and cost nearly $123,000. There are none in use today by the National Guard. ALASKA NATIONAL GUARD

The Alaska Army Guard Hovercraft gets under way kicking up a cloud of snow on the Knik River flats near Palmer. ALASKA NATIONAL GUARD

The 216th Transportation Sled Company of the Alaska Army National Guard at Seward had control of the huge Overland Train once used by the U.S. Army during the Dew Line construction days. The strange machines were not practical for the National Guard. PHOTO BY GRANT SALISBURY

The cars pulled by the land train across the tundra were massive in size but did not carry a large load. PHOTO BY GRANT SALISBURY

LCM-8 unloads Southeastern Alaska Guardsmen on a beach for training. The craft have a speed of 9.2 knots when loaded and a range of 150 nautical miles. They can carry 200 combat-equipped soldiers and a crew of three. ALASKA NATIONAL GUARD

to decide on a route for the pipeline, then after the decision had been made in favor of an All-Alaska Route, another wait while environmentalists, the oil industry and the government presented arguments for and against the project. Congress approved the 48-inch diameter, 789-mile-long pipeline in 1974. It would be built under contracts by the Alyeska Pipeline Service Company at a cost of nearly $8 billion. The pipeline project would be judged a world-class engineering feat and big wages would be earned by thousands of workers who flocked North. It was the Gold Rush of '98 all over again and like the Rush of '98, much of the money left Alaska in the pockets of outsiders. The airport at Anchorage was filled with workers in jeans, Stetson hats and cowboy boots waiting for flights back to Houston or Tulsa. The oil began to flow in 1977 and the State budget was built around oil revenues. The pipeline itself became an object of military defense planning.

In 1975, the Alaska Command began a new series of cold-weather exercises. They were designed to test men and equipment for the defense of Alaska and to accumulate knowledge on Arctic warfare should the military be called upon to conduct operations in similar climatic zones outside the United States. The first four exercises were called JACK FROST and the Alaska National Guard participation began on a small scale but increased each year. The name was changed to BRIM FROST by the Readiness Command in 1981 and expanded to include several branches of the military and more elements from the Canadian Armed Forces.

The effectiveness of the Eskimo Scouts and other Alaska National Guard units grew with each succeeding exercise. BRIM FROST 83 became a turning point in the regular military's awareness of the National Guard's value in the defense of Alaska. The exercise that year gave the Army National Guard more responsibility than ever before. A new factor was figured into the scenario—the defense of the Alaska Pipeline.

5th Squadron, 297th Cavalry medium tanks on the firing line during annual training. The Alaska National Guard furnished the armor during BRIM FROST 83.
ALASKA NATIONAL GUARD

Besides the 152mm gun, which fired conventional rounds as well as Shillelagh missiles, the tank could be equipped with a variety of machine guns and had a grenade launching system. The vehicle could swim lakes and be air dropped.
ALASKA NATIONAL GUARD

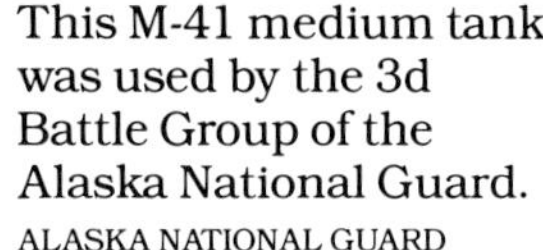

This M-41 medium tank was used by the 3d Battle Group of the Alaska National Guard.
ALASKA NATIONAL GUARD

BRIM FROST 83 had several objectives. It would be a joint/combined operation for air and ground forces to test the ground and air defenses of Alaska against both conventional and nonconventional forces. The Commander, Brigadier General Nathan Vail, U.S. Army, would use elements of the Alaska National Guard for his combined forces defense of Alaska. The Guardsmen of the 207th Infantry Group, the 5th Squadron, 297th Cavalry, the Eskimo Scouts, the 1898th Aviation Detachment with 14 UH-l helicopters and the Alaska Air Guard's 144th Airlift Squadron would play a prominent role in the successful winter exercise. The area of operations would be Interior Alaska in the Tanana River/ Delta River area near Forts Wainwright and Greely. The 207th Group Commander, Colonel John V. Hoyt would direct the Guardsmen and some regular army units.

The Eskimo Scouts of the Third Battalion, 297th Infantry were primarily subsistence hunters and fishermen. An Air Guard C-130 aircraft flew from village to village to collect the Scouts. From their staging area in Kotzebue, they deployed to the Blair Lakes area and began their mission of intelligence gathering and surveillance. They had not been in the field long before they discovered the enemy's headquarters and several of its units and relayed the valuable information to the U.S. Forces Headquarters.

The National Guard furnished the only armored troops used in the exercise. For his attack on enemy forces, General Vail relied on the Alaska Army Guard's 207th Infantry Group as an important element of his plan. The Alaska National Guard Commander planned a classic hammer and anvil envelopment maneuver to accomplish his mission. The tactic was completely successful and ensured a victory by friendly forces.

The Guard Commander, Colonel John V. Hoyt, was a true Alaskan product. Born and raised in historic Skagway, he had spent summers working for the White Pass and Yukon Railroad between college years. He had served in the regular army and was commissioned in the Alaska National Guard in 1961. By 1971, he had become a Commander of the Third Battalion, 297th Infantry and later the 5th Squadron, 297th Cavalry. In 1983, he was promoted to Brigadier General and became Assistant Adjutant General. An admirer of this son of Alaska said of him: "John Hoyt was decisive, to the point, a great tactician and if war broke out tomorrow, I would want him as my Commander." The Last Frontier was capable of turning out good soldiers at all levels of rank.

General Necrason began to explore the possibility of another major mission for the Alaska National Guard. Search and Rescue in the state had always been handled effectively by the U.S. Air Force and the U.S. Coast Guard. This had been augmented by the Civil Air Patrol, the State Troopers and ordinary Alaskan citizens helping the distressed. The mission seemed a natural for Alaska Guardsmen.

The concept was not new. Major Geist of the World War Two Territorial Guard had used his Eskimo Scouts on numerous occasions to look for downed Air Force pilots and civilians lost in the Arctic. He had even contacted 10th Rescue—the Air Force Search and Rescue Squadron, often called the Sourdough Savers—and had proposed a merging of efforts between that organization and the ATG. The National Guard, which was organized a few years later, carried on the assignment unofficially and Army Guard pilots and Eskimo Scouts were credited with many "saves" throughout the state. With the expansion of the Air National Guard, cooperation with the Coast Guard, the State Police and other rescue agencies became almost routine.

The General laid the groundwork for an Air National Guard Search and Rescue Squadron which

The Eskimo Scouts are the "eyes and ears of the Arctic" for the U.S. Army. Early photo shows scouts in training with M-1 rifles.

The vastness of the Arctic can be seen in this photo of an Eskimo Scout Patrol on duty for the Alaska National Guard. ALASKA NATIONAL GUARD

The "Iron Dog" snow machines replaced dog teams many years ago in the Alaska National Guard. ALASKA ARMY GUARD

Soldiers of the Alaska Army National Guard's 2nd Scout Battalion move into the field on an organizational snow machine towing a locally built Eskimo sled. From left are: Sp4 Wassillie Nicholai, Sgt. Moses Ayojiak, Pfc. Saul Lockuk, Sp4 William Kohuk, and Sgt. Posen Aelexie. All of the men are from Togiak, Alaska. STATE OF ALASKA, DMVA

Eskimo Scouts on patrol. They come and go with the blowing snow and are highly effective defenders of America's vast northern frontier.
ALASKA NATIONAL GUARD

Small groups of Eskimo Scouts often run circles around regular army troops during winter war games. They know the land and are excellent soldiers.
ALASKA NATIONAL GUARD

would not come about until the 1990s, long after he had left office. The first step in this long range project came about in the 1970s when the Air Guard received a world wide mission and eight C-130E Hercules airplanes. The C-123J aircraft had served the Territory and State well but the over-aged aircraft needed replacing. Manpower in the Alaska National Guard was at a low point as many Alaskans reaped huge wages during the pipeline construction years. The National Guard found it hard to recruit weekend personnel for the meager pay offered.

General Necrason "guaranteed" the bodies if the National Guard Bureau would furnish the equipment. He made a trip from Anchorage to Washington D.C. with his classmate, General William Westmoreland. They talked all night during the long flight. Necrason pointed out the importance of Alaska's strategic position and what it would take to modernize America's farthest north National Guard unit. By the time he arrived back home, General Nick pretty well had the equipment and planes committed that he needed to expand the Alaska Army and Air National Guard.

With the coming of the C-130's, came worldwide missions and deployments that would prove the Alaskans could handle nearly anything assigned to them. Down the road, the search and rescue issue would be worked and other far-reaching missions began to be visualized. Alaskans once more came forth and General Nick made good his promise to fill the ranks with soldiers and airmen.

During the 1970s, the National Guard had its

The face of a scout. Muktuk Marston thinks of his World War Two Eskimo Scouts as he observes a new generation of Guardsmen at Camp Carroll, Alaska. He founded the Scouts of the Territorial Guard during the darkest days of the war. U.S. ARMY

eye on the future but remembered its past. An old figure came back for one last effort to assure a bright future for the Alaska Guard. Major "Muktuk" Marston was called upon to help in a new recruiting drive for the Guard. He travelled and spoke to young Alaskans. He talked about the great adventure he had lived in helping to form the Alaska Territorial Guard and about the dedication of those historic Eskimo Scouts and white ATG soldiers of the Second World War. Marston had become a legend, a part of Alaska's story and new Minutemen could pause and reflect upon the Herculean efforts of those who had founded the Alaska Guard. Others who had served during the early days of Guard history also supported the recruiting effort.

Muktuk Marston, now a wealthy man through his real estate business, never forgot those loyal soldiers of the Arctic who had served him so well during the dark days of World War Two when Alaska was at peril. He invested in their education and pushed his Marston Garden Project which taught Natives to raise vegetables to supplement their hunt-

ing and fishing lifestyle. He maintained contact with Native leaders and talked up the National Guard. He had been a pusher for statehood and native rights. Late in life he wrote a book—*Men of the Tundra: Alaska Eskimos at War.* Although the book was one man's view of World War Two in Alaska, it was much more than just a military history of an unusual army. It was also an appeal for equality and understanding and a plea to Alaskans to include natives as equal partners in building a great state. In 1973, the State of Alaska gave Marston the rank the regular military had refused to grant him while he was Commander of the 4,000-member Tundra Army. He was designated a Brigadier General in the Alaska State Militia in special recognition of his ices to the State. He was now in his eighties and had outlasted those who had tried to destroy him.

In 1976, Marston made another appearance to a new force in the new National Guard. The Eskimo Scouts of World War Two had counted (unofficially) within their ranks, native women who wanted to serve the Nation. As of October 1, 1971, women had been able to officially join the Army National Guard. The Old Scout went out to Camp Carroll, the Army Guard Training Center on Fort Richardson to watch the first Women Scouts graduate before returning to their village units.

Marston watched the women march and walked the rifle ranges with them while they qualified with the same weapons the men used. He shared his experiences with the women and observed their misty eyes as they received their diplomas of accomplish-

General Nick and the founder of the ATG Scouts, Muktuk Marston, look on with pride at the women scouts during a training session. The women meet the same high standards of the National Guard as the men and are good soldiers. U.S. ARMY

The first woman to enlist in the Alaska Army National Guard, Specialist 5 Mary L. Cunningham, was given the oath of enlistment by Major General William S. Elmore, the Adjutant General, on October 14, 1971. She missed by two days being the first WAC enlisted into the Guard anywhere in the nation.
STATE OF ALASKA DMVA

Lt. Col. Hank Compton swears in newly enlisted Eskimo women scouts.
U.S. ARMY PHOTO

ment with visible pride. The Old Scout, too, became misty-eyed as he realized this was a new Alaska National Guard and that these new Women Eskimo Scouts were willing daughters of an earlier generation of truly great soldiers. The women, too, realized they were about to become a part of that tradition of service and were just the beginning of a growing force of young women who would swell the ranks of Alaska's Army.

In January of 1979, the National Guard came to Muktuk in Palm Springs, California, to present the 90-year-old Brigadier General with the National Guard Association's Distinguished Service Medal. There had been only six other persons who were not National Guard officers who had ever received the prestigious award, among them General Douglas MacArthur and Senator J. Strom Thurmond. The Governor of Alaska, Jay S. Hammond, honored the old General as well. It was a proud moment for the man who had accomplished much for the 49th State.

The death of Marvin Muktuk Marston on July 21, 1980, caused Alaskans to reflect on the changes this controversial soldier had seen and caused in the country he had come to love. Even those who looked upon Muktuk as something less than a legend had to admit the man had been a colorful character, a doer, a builder and a true Alaskan. Governor Bill Egan said of Muktuk, "To most of us he was just plain Muktuk. For as long as Alaskan men and women speak, they will remember his efforts to bring the native people into the mainstream. He was a human dynamo who dared to disturb the status quo."

Perhaps Dr. Fred McGinnis, one-time President of Alaska Methodist University said it best: "There was nobility in his naturalness and grandeur in his generosity. He walked confidently and directly into the future with all its problems and possibilities. . . . His energy mattered, his ideas mattered, his imagination mattered, his actions mattered." Alaskans would probably not see his likes again—there was only one Muktuk Marston cut from the fabric of that scarce cloth called adventure.

Far across the endless stretches of eternity, there may be an area reserved for a featureless never ending land of snow and cold. There may even be a figure behind a team of husky dogs mushing towards a dim far shoreline upon which stands in formation a group of white-clad soldiers awaiting orders. If the tall athletic figure is wearing 1942-military garb with the rank of Major and an Air Corps patch and is followed by a lone husky named Panda, it might be much more than a snowy mirage. Muktuk just might go on forever in that land of forever youth.

Native women are enthusiastic soldiers in the Alaska National Guard. They go through many of the same hardships of training that men scouts go through. U.S. ARMY

Women soldiers on the firing line. They uphold the tradition established by their grandfathers during World War Two and have been a welcome addition to the Alaska Guard since 1971. U.S. ARMY

Army Guard Aviation

The rugged grandeur which is Alaska covers an area of over a half-million square miles. Above the tundra, the river valleys, the uncountable no name lakes and over the jagged high rise mountains with their ancient moving glaciers is painted the clear blue background of the arctic sky. Its privacy is invaded here and there by aircraft flown by those who dare to try the sudden storms and the challenge of death that are the defense mechanisms of the unknown domain. The land below was created for the airplane. The Alaska Army Guard aviators know this world and have traversed its dangerous limits from the beginning of Alaska's Guard history.

The first aviators were from the Army Advisor Detachment. They were regular army men who were sent to organize and teach soldiering to the newly organized Alaska National Guard during the early 1950s. They flew army planes, mostly Cessna's and Beavers as an additional duty assignment. Terry Lennon, an Alaska Guardsman, attended the first National Guard Officer Candidate School at Fort Benning, Georgia. He became Commander of Company C, 208th Infantry Battalion (Separate) in Juneau. In August, 1955, he became one of Alaska's first two graduates from flight school. He and Richard Rountree, a maintenance specialist, brought the first Beaver aircraft north to Juneau.

In 1966, the aviation fleet consisted of three Beavers which were maintained by the 568th Transportation Aircraft Shop at Fort Wainwright under an inter-service maintenance agreement. The aircraft were assigned to Bethel, Nome and Juneau. In May of 1966, David Mock, a National Guardsman, was assigned as Organizational Maintenance Officer. He continued the work on the DA 1352 forms—Aircraft Inventory and Status Reports. In 1968, the first Otter aircraft arrived and the Bethel based airplane was fitted with floats. By 1969, Lt. Col. William Caldwell was serving as the State Aviation Officer.

Sometime in 1968, General Necrason received a report from his G-3, John V. Hoyt, which pointed out the critical need for aviators for the Alaska National Guard. There were no full-time Guard pilots at the time. General Nick got four flight school positions from the Guard Bureau. David Mock was among the first of the Alaska Guard's full-time technicians to become a qualified aviator. Lt. Col. David Mock would devote his long career as a Guardsman to the growth of the aviation unit.

Colonel John Spaulding, now the State Aviation Officer, expanded the role of Army Guard aviation. The years brought a variety of aircraft to the state and what had started out as one Beaver for each of the two Scout Battalions located in Nome and Bethel and another for Company C 3/297th Infantry in Juneau was expanded when Army Aviation Flight Activities were established in the 1970s.

The UH-1D helicopters came in 1971, the twin engine U8-D a short time later and then the U8-F in '76. The line continued with the Twin Otters in '76, the U-21F Beechcraft in '78 and the awkward looking CH-54B Heavy Lift Sky Crane helicopters in 1979. The hard-working arctic equipped Sky Cranes were especially useful for moving heavy equipment in Alaska. The CH-54's were named Isabelle, Penelope, Rochester and Ichabod Crane.

Penelope holds the world's record for heavy lift by a helicopter. The first Beechcraft twin engine C-12D arrived in 1982, and the newer C-12F came aboard during the summer of 1986. The state-of-the-art UH-60A Blackhawk helicopters became a reality in 1985. The 1898th Aviation Company (Assault) with its helicopters, was absorbed by the new aviation battalion in 1988. Today, Army Guard aviation is big business. Pilots are trained at Fort Rucker, Alabama, and special training is given for those who fly the UH-1 float helicopters in Southeastern Alaska. They are the only helicopters of that type on floats in the army's world-wide inventory.

Despite Alaska's claim of being the "Flyingest State," the people of the Aviation Battalion are often over-shadowed or forgotten and seem little-known within the Guard Community or by the general public. The laurels often go to the more glamorous big aircraft worldwide mission crews of the Alaska National Guard. The Army Guard aviators fly their missions in their olive-drab aircraft day after day, hauling people and supplies and occasionally pick up a save in the rescue business.

High overhead, an airplane or helicopter will appear and the friendly sound of an aircraft engine becomes reassuring to the isolated Alaskans below. The tiny speck in the bright blue Alaskan sky casts a long shadow across the land as it always has, and Alaskans can continue to say with growing confidence—the Guard is flying today.

This photo shows an early National Guard plane at a float plane hangar in Southeast Alaska. COURTESY LTC DAVID MOCK

Rare photo of a Cessna 195 on skis surrounded by Arctic Eskimos. The Army Guard aircraft were a welcome sight in the remote villages of Alaska. COURTESY LTC DAVID MOCK

The Army Guard Twin Otter is a familiar sight to villagers throughout the state. The aircraft hauls people and supplies to remote communities in the bush. PHOTO BY VAUGHN SALISBURY

A CH-54B delivers a personnel carrier from out of the mists of the Chugach Mountains near Anchorage. ALASKA NATIONAL GUARD

The skycrane can move mighty loads over Alaska's rugged landscape. ALASKA NATIONAL GUARD

This Alaska Army Guard CH-54B
is a world record holder.
PHOTO BY VAUGHN SALISBURY

Time is running out on the heavy lift CH-54B skycranes of the Alaska
Army Guard. Parts are difficult to obtain and the skycranes will soon
be gone. Two skycranes, minus main rotors, sit in front of the
Chugach range at Fort Richardson.
PHOTO BY VAUGHN SALISBURY

Older helicopters are being replaced by UH-60 Blackhawk aircraft. The Alaska Army Guard was one
of the first in the nation to receive the state-of-the-art helicopters. PHOTO BY VAUGHN SALISBURY

Now Forever and Then

BY DECEMBER 1982, General Necrason was coming to the end of his second tour as Adjutant General of Alaska. He had served the state nearly 12 years—longer than any general officer in Alaska's history. He had already completed a full Air Force career and had retired a Major General before his long tenure as Adjutant General of Alaska began. The National Guard had expanded and modernized under his leadership. He made one more trip around the state to inspect his troops and to bid a fond farewell to the men and women who had served under him. He said, "I commanded many organizations during my long military career, but none were more dedicated or more eager to serve than my Alaska National Guard. I came to value my association with the native people of Alaska and especially the Eskimo Scouts. The Scouts were great soldiers, and although I was their Commander, they were not overwhelmed by my position. It was a simple relationship—I was their General and they were my soldiers and friends."

The man who dealt most often with the troops in the field when the Adjutant General was unavailable was General Nick's Assistant Adjutant, Brigadier General William J. Sharrow. State Command Sergeant Major Dennis Metrokin remembers a flight by Twin Otter to isolated units with General Sharrow. The plane landed at Wainwright, a small coastal village north of the Arctic Circle, southwest of Barrow. The airstrip was located some distance from the village and there was not a soul in sight to greet the General and his party. The men remained in the Twin Otter to escape the bitter cold.

In the distance, tiny black dots appeared and could be seen moving across the snowy flatland. Soon, the visitors could see the local Eskimo Scout unit marching towards the plane in formation. They wore a mixture of military and civilian clothing in an effort to keep warm in the Arctic wind. As the visitors came off the plane, the soldiers drew up in formation and the Sergeant of the unit presented them to the General for inspection. They had marched all the way from the village for this event. General Sharrow dutifully went from man to man with military precision. The little fellow at the end of the formation stood proudly at attention fighting a runny nose. His uniquely un-military cap caught the General's eye. Across the front it bore the message: Don't eat the yellow snow! This was one inspection the General would never forget.

That evening, the whole village population turned out to honor the visiting Guardsmen. They had never seen a General before and this warranted a full blown celebration—a potluck dinner and Eskimo dancing. The General joined in and learned how to do some of the native dances. In their own

Governor Jay Hammond and General Conrad Necrason inspect Army Guardsmen at Bethel. General Nick served longer than any Adjutant General in Alaska's history. Governor Hammond, a bush pilot himself, enjoyed his position as Commander of the Guard.

ALASKA NATIONAL GUARD

way, the local citizens were celebrating much more than a visit, they were reliving a tradition that went back to the Marston years of World War Two. They were also honoring a way of life and a passage of manhood in which one generation followed another to become members of the Eskimo Scouts of the Alaska National Guard.

Down where the great backbone of the Continent has curled southwest from Mount McKinley to form the Alaska Peninsula and the mountains sink into the sea to leave emerald tips that appear again and again as the Aleutian Islands, a special way of life exists. The islands arc halfway to Japan for two thousand miles to divide the Pacific Ocean from the Bering Sea.

Here is the birthplace of northern Pacific storms. The Williwaw Winds blow the fog and mists in dizzy patterns and churn up the seas. It is a wild and beautiful place of great strength, dotted here and there by the orthodox crosses and onion-domed churches of old Russian America. It was here the white exploiters from Siberia first encountered the warrior spirit. In another time, it would be the site of the only foreign invasion of American soil during the Second World War. Young Americans and young Japanese would die in this remote corner of the world.

Alaska's first native general was born in the tiny village of Unga on one of the Shumagin Islands of the Aleutian chain. Edward G. Pagano would be educated in Kodiak and at the Eklutna Vocational School near Anchorage before being drafted into the U.S. Army in October of 1944. He would be sent to the Western Pacific with the 383d Infantry Regiment of the 96th Division which was preparing for the invasion of Okinawa. The young Alaskan found himself on a troop ship off the coast of the island taking in the bombardment of Okinawa. Then it was his turn to go over the side of the ship on the cargo nets, down to the bobbing landing craft far below.

The Aleutian Islander was in a foxhole on Okinawa when some VIP's lead by a big white-headed General went forward towards the Japanese lines. "What kind of fool General would be this far forward," said the young infantry Private to a GI buddy. Later that day, he heard that the Commander of the invasion of Okinawa—Lieutenant General Simon Buckner—had been killed by the Japanese.

After the war, Edward Pagano attended a university in San Francisco where he earned his degree in business administration. He returned to Kodiak and joined the Alaska National Guard. He served a number of years as an assistant to General Carroll, the Adjutant General of Alaska. In 1966, he returned to Federal duty and worked in the Selective Service System becoming a Regional Director in Philadelphia and in Chicago, where he worked with General Hershey. He retired from the U.S. Army in 1982. In December of that year, he was appointed Adjutant General of Alaska by Governor Sheffield.

The Alaska National Guard made many significant gains under the leadership of General Pagano. In July 1983, the 176th Tactical Airlift Group at Kulis Air Guard Base became one of the few Air Guard units nationally to receive factory-new C-130H Hercules aircraft. The first new plane was flown back to Alaska by the Group Commander, Colonel Paul Lindemuth. "They smell just like a new car," commented the veteran pilot who had flown nearly every type of airplane the Air Force possessed. With the new long-range aircraft came an increase of world-wide missions and more frequent VOLANT OAK missions in Panama. Aircraft with Alaska Guard markings would show up in Europe, Korea, Japan, the Philippines and lesser-known corners of the world in coming years.

In 1985, the National Guard began looking into the possibility of bringing a second flying unit to Alaska. Senator Ted Stevens had backed the idea of a refueling squadron of KC-135E aircraft to be positioned at Eielson Air Force Base near Fairbanks to supplement the Air Force Tanker Task Force sta-

Alaska's first native Adjutant General, MG Edward Pagano was born in the Aleutian Islands. He took part in the invasion of Okinawa as a young infantryman in 1945. ALASKA NATIONAL GUARD

Governor Bill Sheffield, a former enlisted man in the U.S. Army Air Corps, was a strong supporter of the National Guard during the mid-1980s.

tioned there. Studies were made with the backing of the Adjutant General, and on February 7, 1986, Senator Steven's office announced that four of the huge tanker aircraft would come to Eielson AFB from Little Rock, Arkansas, along with a $5 million annual payroll for the Fairbanks-North Pole region.

On October 25, 1986, General Pagano led an Activation Ceremony at Eielson Air Force Base and the 168th Air Refueling Squadron of the Strategic Air Command officially became a part of the Alaska Air National Guard. The man who had worked hard with General Pagano to make this day a reality was honored by having the unit named the Senator Ted Stevens Squadron.

General Pagano became interested in resurrecting the Naval Militia. The organization had existed for a time during the Necrason years, but interest in the Naval Reserve concept had waned in Alaska and the organization faded away. With the backing and interest of the Adjutant General, the Naval Militia once again became a functioning part of Alaska's military picture.

The General began work on another historic Alaska organization. The local militia idea had pretty well died with the disbanded World War Two Alaska Territorial Guard. A new State Militia would soon be organized and General Pagano would become its commander after leaving the Alaska National Guard. The Militia's shoulder patch would have a familiar look to older Alaskans. The cobalt blue patch with the white ATG letters and the Big Dipper with the North Star would once again be seen in the Great Land. Muktuk Marston would have been proud.

Two more missions were investigated during General Pagano's term of office. Preliminary studies were made on the Search and Rescue mission for the Alaska Air National Guard and plans went forward for a new modern armory for Anchorage. The Guard was growing and reaching out for goals thought impossible just a few short years before.

In December of 1986, Governor Steve Cowper announced that the Alaska National Guard would be commanded by another native son. John W. Schaeffer was born and raised in Kotzebue, north of the Arctic Circle. As the oldest son in a large family, he learned leadership and responsibility at an early age. He often had to be the man of the house in the absence of his father who struggled to make a living from the harsh land for his large family. The father had served in the Territorial Guard during World War Two and the reorganized National Guard following the war. He had mushed dogs with Muktuk Marston and was one of the better-known hunters and guides in the Kotzebue area. Young John Schaeffer had practically grown up with the ATG and the National Guard. It was only natural he would enlist in the Eskimo Scouts in 1957. He would be commissioned the following year and spend most of his career with the Scouts. He would become America's first Eskimo two-star general.

General Schaeffer would bring an extensive administrative background to the Office of the Adjutant General. He had served as Mayor of the Northwest Arctic Borough and had been President of the Native Regional Corporation for 14 years, an organization with over $50 million in assets. Perhaps his greatest gift was his personality, which helped him become a role model for thousands of young Alaskan natives who saw in him a possibility to rise to a high position in life.

John Schaeffer had been a civic leader for many years which gave him valuable contacts for the good of the National Guard. His contributions to the State of Alaska were recognized when he received an honorary Doctor of Public Service degree from Alaska Pacific University shortly after becoming the Adjutant General. Yet, he felt at home with the common soldier in the field and enjoyed jumping with the airborne troops. He never forgot his roots and despite his busy schedule, it was not uncommon for

John W. Schaeffer helps with a reindeer roundup near Kotzebue. He became the leader of a multi-million dollar native corporation and Adjutant General of Alaska. COURTESY OF THE SCHAEFFER FAMILY

Maj. John W. Schaeffer listens to Gen. William C. Westmoreland, the American commander in Vietnam. Schaeffer later became a two star general. ALASKA NATIONAL GUARD

The general and his lady. Mary and John Schaeffer are much admired throughout the state. The National Guard went through a period of rapid and expanded growth during the Schaeffer years. ALASKA NATIONAL GUARD

the General to spend long hours after duty on dark winter nights in his Anchorage office listening patiently to the problems of old friends in Kotzebue. His counsel and advice was always available for those who needed help. He was a people man as well as a soldier.

General Schaeffer served the state during an interesting period of history. A thaw in the Cold War presented the Governor and his National Guard with an opportunity to meet neighbors west of the Ice Curtain. For many years, native Alaskans had been unable to meet friends and relatives on the Siberian side of the Bering Sea. Indeed, records of crossings and contacts between natives on both sides of the international border had been maintained by the U.S. Government and the Eskimo Scouts' prime mission had been surveillance and intelligence gathering. They had watched across the frozen frontier for anything unusual from the beginning of the Cold War and had been the eyes and ears of the Arctic for the U.S. Army.

The first visible thaw along the Arctic border occurred as a result of heavy fog near the village of Gambell on St. Lawrence Island in June 1988. The island communities had sent out a fleet of boats to hunt for walrus. Six members of the Slwooko family and a local white teacher were in two open boats which did not return from the hunt. The heavy fog had separated them from the rest of the hunting party. They lashed their two boats together and drifted and prayed in the heavy seas and fog. Occasionally, they would pull the boats up on floating ice and hunt to survive.

They would spend three weeks navigating between floating ice islands before they would be rescued. The searchers thought that they may have

Junior (Vernon) Slwooko, leader of the lost walrus hunters, shows the strain of a three-week ordeal at sea. The Soviets for the first time cooperated with the Alaska National Guard in a search and rescue mission.
PHOTO BY SGT. GREG SUHAY

Grateful citizens of Savoonga, St. Lawrence Island, Alaska, welcome the lost hunters upon their arrival back home.
PHOTO BY SGT. GREG SUHAY

Alaska National Guard Twin Otters were the first American military planes to fly in Soviet airspace since World War Two. The Soviets granted permission during the joint effort to find the American walrus hunters. PHOTO BY SGT. GREG SUHAY

drifted across the 40-mile sea to the Soviet Union.

The massive search by the Army and Air National Guard pioneered a cooperative effort with the Soviet Union's MAR FLOT search and rescue organization. The Soviets used several ships and a helicopter to search for the walrus hunters. Although the Soviets eventually gave up the search, they did give Governor Cowper permission to order three Alaska Army National Guard Twin Otter airplanes to fly along the Siberian coast for a final six-hour search for the missing Alaskans. No American military planes had flown over Soviet air space since World War Two.

The Air Guard flew a C-130 to the village of Wales to refuel the UV-18 Twin Otters from its tanks. Messages flowed between Washington and Vladivostok. The Super Powers were talking to each other and it would be the beginning of understandings by both sides which would grow during future joint ventures in Alaska during the Schaeffer years. In its own way, the Last Frontier State was pulling the rest of the nation towards the dawn of a new age in world history.

The drama of the trapped whales attracted a world audience. Here, citizens of Barrow, Alaska, lend a hand to free the whales. ALASKA AIR GUARD PHOTO BY MICHAEL ECHOLA

The hunters eventually found their way back to Southeast Cape on their home Island of St. Lawrence and they were reunited with their families. Their ordeal had focused attention on the Arctic and a new relationship between an American State and an old enemy. They had cooperated to search for lost Americans. The thaw had started along a cold frontier—of all places.

In October 1988, the world once more focused its attention on the northern extreme of America. A native of Barrow, Alaska—America's most northern town—by the name of Roy Ahmaogak, discovered three California Gray Whales trapped in the ice near the top of the world. Men and nations struggled with the problem of saving the whales, which took cooperation and innovative ideas to solve. The small town of Barrow became a bedlam of activity as media people from all over the world zeroed in on the whales. The whales won the hearts of the world and millions watched the drama of the freeing of the creatures play itself out on world television.

One possible solution for Operation Breakout, as the adventure was termed, was towing an ice-breaking hover barge operated by the Atlantic Richfield Company and the VECO organization from Prudhoe Bay by helicopter. The National Guard's heavy lift CH-54B Skycrane helicopters were the obvious craft to do the job. However, even two Skycranes towing the craft could not overcome the ice and weather conditions and the barge project was abandoned.

Next, plans were developed to break breathing holes through the ice to keep the whales alive by using a basher fitted to the Alaska Army Guard Skycrane. The idea was to create a path through the ice to the open sea. The problem was to get the whales to follow the path to freedom. Ideas continued to flow north to Barrow from all over the world as time began to run out on the whales. Even President Reagan and the first lady became intrigued by the attempt to free the whales.

Eventually, the Soviets became interested in the drama. A Russian heavy-duty ice breaker broke through the ice pack and the whales headed south for the winter. In their own way, they had become ambassadors for international cooperation. One wag noted, "We could have used those whales during the Stalin years," while another commented, "They should have never gotten lost in the first place—They must not have had their Berings Strait."

During 1989, relations between the Soviet Union and the United States continued to improve. Governor Cowper pushed for trade missions and a Pacific Rim philosophy for the state. Many schools throughout the state began to offer Russian and

The Veco Archimedes Screw was one of many methods tried to gain freedom for the trapped whales. The Soviet ice breakers in the background were successful in breaking a path to the sea. The joint Soviet-U.S. effort drew world-wide attention.
ALASKA AIR GUARD PHOTO BY MICHAEL ECHOLA

The Arco Basher and an Army Guard CH-54B was used in the attempt to free the whales. The ice barrier in the background was formed by pressure forcing up ice ridges.
ALASKA AIR GUARD PHOTO BY MICHAEL ECHOLA

Japanese courses and scientific and cultural exchanges between Alaska and Siberia became more common. The cooperative effort by the two political entities during the Walrus hunters episode and the whale drama began to bear fruit. Talk of business ventures grew and the trickle of Soviet visitors to Alaska expanded as the 45-year barrier began to crumble.

Spring is a much-sought-after state of mind as well as a physical change for Alaskans each year. Cabin fever has run its course by March as the days lengthen and the land gets ready to awake after the great white sleep. Energy levels rise as the sap in the trees begins to stir and eyes begin to search the skies for migratory birds who bring the good news north on the wing. The process begins some time halfway through March—long before the ice prepares to leave the rivers in a rush to seek death in the salt seas. As an Alaskan ages, the search for spring begins a little earlier each year. The Spring of 1989 would be a little different.

Good Friday is a misnomer for many Alaskans. On this day in 1964, the state suffered the greatest earthquake ever recorded in North America. As Good Friday began on March 24, 1989, the U.S. Coast Guard received a call from the super tanker EXXON VALDEZ at 12:28 A.M. The vessel had gone hard aground on Bligh Reef in Prince William Sound near the oil pipeline terminal city of Valdez, Alaska.

At 12:30 A.M., the Port of Valdez was closed to all marine traffic and personnel at the Alyeska Oil Terminal began to gather equipment for deployment. By 3:23 A.M., Coast Guard personnel had boarded the EXXON VALDEZ and reported that approximately 5.7 million gallons of crude oil had already been lost. By 5:30 A.M., it was evident that a world-class disaster was in the making and the nation awoke to the unfolding drama of the world's worst oil spill.

Within 24 hours, the oil spill estimate jumped from 5.7 million gallons to 10.5 million gallons. No one agency seemed prepared to handle a situation of such magnitude and as the precious hours slipped away the massive oil slick started its journey towards the open sea. Birds and sea life could not escape the man-made disaster and what had been pristine wilderness became a black sticky reminder that man had historically destroyed the beauty the Creator had given him. The Alaska National Guard became involved almost from the beginning to support the cleanup of Prince William Sound.

The Adjutant General made an initial study and assessment of the situation on March 25. He designated the Operations and Plans Officer, Lt. Colonel Willard Masker, as the officer in charge of controlling and coordinating the support effort. Operations were centralized at the Valdez National Guard Armory and the communications and logistical base was run from that facility. A Command Post was set up at State Headquarters and all reporting requirements and coordination was accomplished through the Office of the Adjutant General in Anchorage to the appropriate agency. At the height of the crisis, approximately 125 Guard personnel supported the oil spill cleanup effort. As operations progressed from initial response to actual cleanup, the Alaska Guard handed off their responsibilities to the Alaska Division of Emergency Services and other civilian agencies.

One of the first Guardsmen on the scene at Valdez was Master Sergeant Tom Henery from the 176th Aerial Port Flight at Kulis Air National Guard Base in Anchorage. He spent the first few days in Valdez almost by himself. From the airport in Valdez he loaded cargo, rigged slings for helicopters and helped to direct air traffic, which grew by the hour. The local airport was overwhelmed and airport workers sought direction and guidance from the Guardsman.

It soon became apparent the tiny airport could not handle the air traffic bringing people into the disaster area. An Air Coordination and Control Center was set up on March 28, to overcome the shortfalls at the Valdez Airport. The local airport was not equipped or manned to support the large volume of air traffic. The various types of aircraft arriving or departing could not be loaded or off-loaded with the resources available. There were no plans for parking excess aircraft at Valdez. The Air National Guard provided an Aerial Port Team with equipment to take care of the problem. Guardsmen assisted the airport manager in laying out aircraft parking and helped designate taxiways for fixed wing and rotary wing aircraft.

The shortage of civilian fire-fighting equipment and personnel also became a problem at the Valdez Airport, so the Air Guard deployed a fire truck and four firefighters to Valdez during the crisis. The Army and Air Guard provided air resources during the initial phases of the oil spill. Air Guard C-130's flew support missions, deploying badly needed equipment and boom material while the Army Guard provided lift support with its CH-54B Skycrane and UH-60 Blackhawk helicopters. The National Guard also furnished a 5,000-gallon tanker and a 1,200-gallon tanker for fueling aircraft and established a second refueling point at the airport to cut down on the confusion during refueling operations.

The National Guard coordinated the use of tactical satellite radios and the Air Guard provided

The ship that will forever be linked to Alaska history—the EXXON VALDEZ—being escorted by a fleet of tugs in Prince William Sound.
ALASKA NATIONAL GUARD

The Air Guard furnished fire crash protection at the Valdez airport during the oil spill crisis. The overcrowded small airport at Valdez became a beehive of activity during the oil spill.
ALASKA NATIONAL GUARD

Two National Guard CH-54Bs prepare for a flight at the Valdez airport. The awkward-looking aircraft performed admirably during the EXXON VALDEZ oil spill.
ALASKA NATIONAL GUARD

operators for the vital communications net needed in such an operation. To support the horde of media people who came to Valdez from all over the world to write the story, a National Guard public affairs team, led by Lt. Mike Haller, established a centralized public affairs office in Valdez. A special "Oil Spill News" report was put out to keep the public informed.

The Federal Aviation Administration had to establish a temporary air traffic control tower at Valdez in an old tower building and used Coast Guard, Army and Air Guard air traffic controllers. Normally, the small airport handled a mere 10 to 20 takeoffs and landings a day, but within a few days of the oil spill, Valdez became the third busiest airport in Alaska. On March 28, the temporary tower handled 687 takeoffs or landings and averaged nearly 500 a day for the next few weeks. There was a reason why the National Guard was welcomed in Valdez.

On the other hand, as with any major happening involving human beings, there was a dark side to the oil spill. Although hundreds of volunteers poured in to help save the seabirds and mammals, there were thousands of job seekers who turned Valdez into a wild, restless town like Alaska had seen during the great gold rushes at the turn of the century. Opportunists and criminals were also attracted to Valdez and helped to create an unprecedented crime wave in the small town. Prices skyrocketed as everyone seemed bent on making money. The media people pushed and shoved to get stories and guards even had to be hired to protect the animal victims being brought into the cleaning station set up in Valdez. Tempers flared with the lengthening work hours and unemployed workers threw rocks at Exxon and Alyeska Pipeline vehicles. A story broke out that the U.S. Army was being sent into Valdez to clean the beaches, thus eliminating the need for Exxon to hire cleanup workers. Guardsmen asked for special baseball hats to be sent to Valdez to identify them so angry workers could determine they were Guard and not regular troops.

The population grew from 3,000 to 11,000 people during the cleanup and the Valdez Police Department needed help to control crime. During the 5-month cleanup, police calls jumped to 3,848 with 543 arrests. The previous summer had recorded one car stolen. During the cleanup, there was one stolen every three days. The Guard flew in State Troopers from six other towns to help in an August 24th drug raid. Even the drug pushers had shown up for their pound of flesh. To help cut crime, Exxon paid $60,000 per month for police overtime pay and gave Valdez an open check to buy a police paddy wagon, prisoner cages, radar units, handcuffs, etc. It was

a rerun of the wild, wild west. Many people in Alaska for the first time began to understand the need for a well-trained National Guard.

Another world-class event took place in Alaska during the Spring of 1989. A 50-day journey by dog sled and ski from Anadyr, Siberia to Kotzebue, Alaska, started in early March. It was to be completed with a ceremony at the International Date Line, the border between Little Diomede Island (Alaska) and Big Diomede Island (USSR). The two leaders of the journey were Paul Schurke of Ely, Minnesota, and Dmitry Shparo of Moscow. The trip was made to promote good will and would be the first official crossing since the start of the Cold War in 1945. The team included three Eskimos from each country. Robert Soolook of Little Diomede was a member of the Alaska National Guard's famous Eskimo Scouts and a member of the expedition.

The expedition drew international coverage and was sponsored by the DuPont Corporation and the Science Diet dog food people. The Soviet Ministry of Foreign Affairs granted approval for the cooperative venture on the Siberian side of the border.

The face of a scout. Elia Abruska of St. Michael takes part in summer training at Fort Richardson in 1983. Alaska's natives have been outstanding soldiers for many generations. THE *TUNDRA TIMES*

A heavy lift CH-54B skycrane brings home a
World War Two PBY. AIR GUARD PHOTO BY RUSS WESTON

Even in the remote Arctic the realities of chemical warfare have to be dealt with. An Eskimo Scout team trains near their home village.
ALASKA NATIONAL GUARD

Alaska's sea-going soldiers. Landing craft are used in Southeastern Alaska to transport supplies and troops to isolated areas where roads are a rarity.
NATIONAL GUARD PHOTO

A violent windstorm made a shambles of this village in Southeastern Alaska, but the Guard was there to help.
NATIONAL GUARD PHOTO

The 144th Tactical Airlift Squadron of the Alaska Air National Guard supported the Bering Bridge Crossing when the long trip came to the international border. At first, it was planned that the C-130 carrying the Governor of Alaska, the Adjutant General and other dignitaries might land on the ice of the Bering Sea; but the expedition was delayed as the result of bad weather. As the continuing bad weather added days, then weeks to the rendezvous, concern grew about the thickness of the ice and the weight of the aircraft. By the time the event took place, it was decided to haul the passengers to Tin City, then to use Army Guard helicopters to shuttle the passengers on to Little Diomede Island.

On the day of the ceremony where two ways of life were to meet, high winds and blowing snow grounded the American delegation and Governor Cowper had to watch the proceedings on a television screen in Nome and talk through the signing of a proclamation designed to ease travel across the border. A satellite earth dish had been anchored out on the ice earlier in the week so the event could be seen by people in both countries. Surveyors figured out exactly where the border was located and blue paint marked the dividing point between the world of Democracy and the world of Communism. Everything was set up, but the snow and fog came and the official act had to be done long distance. The Russians did make it to the site because they had a tracked vehicle, but the Governor of Alaska had to conduct the business at hand via a telephone.

While the expedition had been designed to ease tensions between two very different worlds there was a dramatic turn of events. Two of the young Soviet journalists accompanying the Soviet team defected and asked for political asylum. The Soviets were getting ready to leave Little Diomede Island following the ceremonial exchange between Governor Cowper and his counterpart from Siberia. The two journalists approached one of the Alaska Guard Eskimo Scouts and told him they wanted to remain in the United States. The Russian journalists spent two days in the National Guard Armory before the weather allowed the Guard to fly them to Anchorage where they applied for asylum. It was somewhat of an embarrassing situation because a friendly accord had just been signed by both parties.

There seemed no end to the State missions of the National Guard. An extreme cold wave during the winter of 1990 brought discomfort and emergencies throughout the state and the Guard was there to help. Forest fires would come in the summers and floods could come at anytime, anywhere in the state. Villages would run out of heating fuel, lose power plants or medical emergencies would occur and the people of Alaska would call on their National Guard for assistance.

Beyond service to the state was always the primary mission of training to defend the nation. The new Air Guard refueling squadron at Eielson Air Force Base took on greater responsibilities and its long range KC-135E tankers refueled a variety of aircraft over North America, in Europe and across the Pacific to as far away as Midway Island. Guardsmen performed a variety of military duties within the state and at many sites throughout the world.

The 6th Light Infantry Division moved into Alaska and the Army National Guard found itself needing to furnish a round out battalion for the regular army. A 6th battalion was added to the National Guard for a role with the regular army division and members of the National Guard took part in exercises in the Aleutian Islands with regular forces. The Americans had not really looked at the Aleutians through military eyes to any great extent since the 7th Division had been there during World War Two. It had been a Navy world and now the Navy and others began to show interest on a much larger scale. The term "Home Porting"—the stationing of Naval vessels—began to be discussed in Alaska. The planners did not want this area of the world to become a "Forgotten War" as it was during World War Two should harms way come to the Aleutians.

An old goal that had started with the Territorial Guard during World War Two became a reality during General Schaeffer's time. The Air Force announced that it would not be able to furnish the search-and-rescue capability the state required due to cutbacks in defense appropriations. Senator Stevens saw an opportunity for an Air National Guard search and rescue mission. The Senator and the Alaska National Guard set to work to acquire a new flying squadron for the people of Alaska. On March 16, 1989, the National Guard Bureau announced the new 210th Search and Rescue Squadron of the Alaska Air National Guard would be located at Kulis Air National Guard Base in Anchorage.

When the Persian Gulf Crisis came in August of 1990, it was anticipated that reserve forces might be called up to help deal with the problem on the other side of the world. How well those forces performed would, to a great extent, depend on their training and their dedication. Alaska Guardsmen, too, would be called upon to boost American Forces in the Arab world. As troops began to pour into that distant hot land and the January deadline changed Desert Shield to Desert Storm, Alaska Guard soldiers and airmen volunteers found themselves in a strange new world, but yet an ancient world. The clean cold beauty of Alaska took on a new mean-

Long-range search and rescue utilizes the latest equipment and technology available. The Air Guard 210th Search and Rescue unit took over the Air Force mission in 1991. ALASKA AIR NATIONAL GUARD

ing to those who found themselves in a hot, not so clean or beautiful environment. Alaska Army Guardsmen serving with army units in the Gulf and 168th Tankers of the Air Guard flying out of Jidda, Saudia Arabia, gave a good account of themselves during the intense, decisive victory over Iraq.

The Spring of 1990 marked the beginning of the construction of the new Anchorage Armory at Camp Denali on Fort Richardson. The long-range project had started some twenty years before. The Armory would cost over $27 million and provide over 200,000 square feet of area to house over 1,300 troops from 14 units. The Office of the Adjutant General, Headquarters of the Air National Guard, the Veterans Division and the State Emergency Services would also be housed in the huge armory. The project also provided an 18,000-square-foot Organizational Maintenance Shop for military vehicles.

On August 3, 1991, Major General Hugh Cox, the new Adjutant General of Alaska, hosted the grand opening ceremony. Senator Stevens and Governor Hickel headed a distinguished company of visitors who had come far distances to open up the facility. As the Governor looked across the gathering in front of the new armory, he appeared to be thinking of the past. He commented that he could not help but think about Muktuk Marston and all the other defenders over the years who had led to this building and this day. They had all been a part of building the National Guard in Alaska.

The end of the 20th Century was marked by the dawn of potential peace and a finish to the gradual death of Communism came with dramatic suddenness. Scholars from two distinct worlds could look anew at the long history of the great Northland and its impact upon world history. How a migrating people came to cross over to Alaska to populate an entire hemisphere created interest once more. Answers needed to be found for the story of one of America's newest states which was also its oldest historical state in terms of mankind's occupation of the land.

And what of the Soldiers of the Mists who had been a part of that history from the very beginning? There is no easy ending to the story of Alaska's Minutemen; it shall continue as the years stretch out towards eternity. It will continue to play a part in

Alaska's Senator Ted Stevens has given strong support for National Guard growth in the state. The Aerial Refueling Squadron of the Alaska Air Guard at Eielson AFB is called the Ted Stevens Squadron. U.S. GOVERNMENT PHOTO

that great adventure called Alaska.

Along the stormy shores of Southeastern Alaska, a lonely National Guard landing craft wends its way towards home. It is dwarfed by the mountains that rise straight up on both sides of the decks. Whimsical fogs drift up and down the forested slopes to occasionally reveal the jagged mountain ranges—the home of glaciers and mountain goats—and then again, the isolated beaches where the Sitka deer play.

It is an eerie place where the eyes and ears can play tricks on an insecure mind. The wind whispers through the mists and distant voices can be heard coming from the land. Can that be the sound of ancient native warriors gearing up for conflict against the Russian intruders? There now, come the sounds of a barroom piano and the shouts of Soapy Smith's Militia near a shrouded Skagway. A cadence from youthful voices penetrates the fog from hidden Chilkoot Barracks as the boat heads south towards its home port. As the boat nears the city of Juneau, ghostly figures stand in formation on the city dock. A First World War Home Guardsman without a jacket stands proudly with his wooden rifle along side his fellow Militia soldiers awaiting the order to defend and protect.

In the high Arctic, the Eskimo Scouts still patrol the lonely shores of America's farthest reach. The past is never far from the present. Near Point Hope, trapped in the sands of an empty beach, is Muktuk Marston's supply boat, the *Ada*, a victim

The new Anchorage Armory became headquarters of the Alaska National Guard in 1991. The ultra-modern building is located at Camp Denali on Fort Richardson, Alaska.
ALASKA NATIONAL GUARD

of storms and vandalism. There was a time, not so long ago, that it was a part of an unbroken tradition that went back, back in an unbroken history of a thousand years of time. The *Ada* becomes a pivotal point of history where the past remains, but the Soldiers of the Mists march forward towards unknown fields of adventure.

The mists across Alaska reveal only what they wish to reveal, but the giant land remains as it was created—a thing of indescribable beauty and it still has need of these soldiers. It always has and it will now and forever more.

The Eskimo Scouts represent the State of Alaska in the inauguration parade for President George Bush. The scouts' last march down Pennsylvania Avenue was in 1961 for President John F. Kennedy. In the background is the U.S. Capitol Building. ALASKA NATIONAL GUARD

The Alaska Veterans Memorial is located on the Parks highway, near Denali National Park. Each star represents a branch of the U.S. military. The figures represent the Scouts of the Territorial Guard.
ALASKA NATIONAL GUARD

Gov. Wally Hickel passes the command to the new Adjutant General, Maj. Gen. Hugh Cox. Gen. John Schaeffer stands behind Governor Hickel while Chief James Herrick accompanies General Cox.
ALASKA NATIONAL GUARD

BIBLIOGRAPHY

Berton, Pierre. *The Klondike Fever—The Life and Death of the Last Great Gold Rush.* New York: Alfred A. Knopf, 1958.

Chevigny, Hector. *Lord of Alaska—Baranov and the Russian Adventure.* New York: Viking Press, 1944.

Chevigny, Hector. *Russian America—The Great Alaskan Venture, 1741—1867.* New York: Viking Press, 1965.

Collier, William R. and Edwin V. Westrate. *The Reign of Soapy Smith—Monarch of Misrule in the Last Days of the Old West and the Klondike Gold Rush.* Garden City: The Sun Dial Press, 1937.

Engle, Eloise. *Earthquake!* New York: The John Day Company, 1966.

Garfield, Brian. *The Thousand Mile War, World War Two in Alaska and the Aleutians.* New York: Ballantine Books, 1969.

Greenhous, Brereton. *Guarding the Goldfields—The Story of the Yukon Field Force.* Toronto: Dundurn Press, 1987.

Gruening, Ernest (Ed.). *An Alaskan Reader, 1867–1967.* New York: Meredith Press, 1966.

Gruening, Ernest. *Many Battles.* New York: Best Books, Liveright, 1973.

Henckley, Ted C. *The Americanization of Alaska.* Palo Alto: Pacific Books, 1972.

Hunt, William R. *Arctic Passage—The Turbulent History of the Land and People of the Bering Sea, 1697–1975.* New York: Charles Scribner's Sons, 1975.

Keim, Charles J. *Aghvook, White Eskimo.* College: The University of Alaska Press, 1969.

Miller, Leon and Polly. *Last Heritage of Alaska—The Adventure and Art of the Alaskan Coastal Indians.* Cleveland: The World Press, 1962.

Oswalt, Wendell H. *Alaskan Eskimos.* New York: Chandler Publishing Company, 1967.

Poor, Henry Varnum. *The Cruise of the Ada.* Private Printing, no date.

Robertson, Frank C. and Beth Kay Harris. *Soapy Smith—King of the Frontier Con Men.* New York: Hastings House Publishers, 1961

Ross, Sherwood. *Gruening of Alaska.* New York: Best Books, Inc., 1968.

Sherwood, Morgan B. (Ed.). *Alaska and its History.* Seattle: The University of Washington Press, 1965.

Thorson, Robert M., Jean S. Aigner, R. Dale & Mary L. Guthrie, William E. Schneider and Richard K. Nelson. *Interior Alaska—A Journey Through Time.* Anchorage: The Alaska Geographical Society, 1986.

Wren, Melvin C. *The Course of Russian History.* New York: The MacMillan Company, 1958.

ABOUT THE AUTHOR

C.A. Salisbury completed a 28-year teaching career in Alaska, New Zealand, England, France, Germany and Canada. He received his Graduate Degree from Washington State University in 1968. He is a graduate of the U.S. Air Force Historian's School at Maxwell Air Force Base, Alabama and the Command and General Staff College, U.S. Army History Instructors School at Fort Leavenworth, Kansas. Senior Master Sergeant Salisbury has been an Air National Guardsman for the past 15 years and is Command Historian for the Alaska Army and Air National Guard.

ABOUT THE COVER ARTIST

The son of a commercial fisherman, Steve Hillyer grew up on boats and the sea from Baja, California, to Alaska. Military combat flying in the Korean Conflict followed and later, a world ranging career in aviation. A native Oregonian, Steve has lived and traveled in more than 20 countries, making Alaska his home base for the past 30 years. He studied art in California and worked previously as a successful illustrator before shifting to fine art.

Following military service, Steve went to Alaska and a career in aviation as a commercial and "bush" pilot. He flew winter supply runs on the oil-rich North Slope throughout the 1970s and flew four-engined L-100 Hercules cargo planes world-wide.

Steve began painting as a hobby in the late 1950s, portraying the colorful aircraft, rich history and spectacular landscape of Alaska. By 1982, demand for his aviation and railroad art was such that he became a full-time professional artist, researching and painting private and corporate commissions and doing freelance illustrations.